THE CONDUCTOR'S ART

THE CONDUCTOR'S ART

Edited and with an Introduction by

CARL BAMBERGER

Illustrated by B. F. Dolbin

McGRAW-HILL BOOK COMPANY

New York   Toronto   London

The Conductor's Art

Library of Congress Catalog Card Number: 65–15926

FIRST EDITION
03597

Acknowledgments

CARL MARIA VON WEBER: "About the Interpretation of *Euryanthe.*" From a letter to the Music Director Praeger of Leipzig.

HECTOR BERLIOZ: "On Conducting: Theory of the Art of Conducting." Translated by Theodore Front. Copyright 1948, Edwin F. Kalmus, New York. Reprinted by permission.

ROBERT SCHUMANN: "About Conducting, and Especially about the Mania of Conducting." From *Neue Zeitschrift für Musik,* April 15, 1836.

FRANZ LISZT: "Letter on Conducting to Richard Pohl in Dresden."

RICHARD WAGNER: "About Conducting." Selections from the essay of 1869. English version based on the translation by Edward Dannreuther, adapted by Luna Wolf.

FELIX WEINGARTNER: "About Conducting." Selections from the essay of 1905, translated by Ernest Newman. Reprinted by permission of Edwin F. Kalmus, New York.

RICHARD STRAUSS: "Ten Golden Rules" and "On Conducting Classical Masterpieces," from *Recollections and Reflections.* Edited by Willi Schuh; translated by L. J. Lawrence. Copyright 1949, by Atlantis-Verlag, Zurich. Copyright of English text 1953, by Boosey and Hawkes, Ltd., London. Reprinted by permission of the publisher.

HANS PFITZNER: "On Conducting: Judgment about the Conductor." From *Werk und Wiedergabe,* Volume 3, Chapter V.

SERGE KOUSSEVITZKY: "On Creative Conducting." Originally published as "Vom Schöpferischen Dirigieren" in *Osterreichisheö Musikzeitschrift,* Vienna, in 1957. Reprinted by permission.

PABLO CASALS: "Casals as a Conductor." From the book *Conversations with Casals,* by J. Ma. Corredor; translated by André Mangeot. Copyright © 1957, by E. P. Dutton and Company, Inc., New York, and by Hutchinson and Company (Publishers), Ltd., for the British Empire. Reprinted by permission.

BRUNO WALTER: "The Conductor." From *On Music and Music-Making,* Chapter III; translated by Paul Hamburger. Originally published by S. Fischer Verlag, Frankfurt, in 1957. Copyright © 1957 by Bruno Walter. English translation copyright © 1961 by Faber and Faber, Ltd. First American edition, W. W. Norton & Company, Inc., 1961. Reprinted by permission.

BRUNO WALTER: From *Gustav Mahler,* Chapter 11. Copyright © 1957 by Alfred A. Knopf, Inc., New York. Published in Great Britain by Hamish Hamilton, Ltd., London. Reprinted by permission.

LEOPOLD STOKOWSKI: "Conducting." From *Music for All of Us,* Chapter 27, published by Simon and Schuster, Inc. Copyright 1943 by Leopold Stokowski. Reprinted by permission of the author.

WILHELM FURTWÄNGLER: "About the Handicraft of the Conductor." From *Vermächtnis.* Copyright © 1956 by F. A. Brockhaus, Wiesbaden. Reprinted by permission.

SIR ADRIAN C. BOULT: "Arthur Nikisch." Originally published in *Music and Letters* in April, 1922. Reprinted by permission of the author.

HERMANN SCHERCHEN: "On Conducting." From *Handbook of Conducting,* pp. 1–3, 59–60, and 186–189. Translated by M. D. Calvocoressi. Oxford University Press, London. Reprinted by permission.

PAUL HINDEMITH: From *A Composer's World,* Chapter 7: "Performers," Section IV. Harvard University Press, Cambridge. Copyright 1952 by the President and Fellows of Harvard College. Reprinted by permission of the publishers.

SIR JOHN BARBIROLLI: "The Art of Conducting." Reprinted by permission from *The Penguin Music Magazine,* Issue No. 12, 1947.

EUGENE ORMANDY: "Art of Conducting"—reprinted from *Encyclopedia International,* by permission of the publisher, Grolier Incorporated, New York.

LEONARD BERNSTEIN: Selections from chapter entitled "The Art of Conducting," from *The Joy of Music.* Copyright © 1954, 1955, 1956, 1957, 1958, 1959 by Leonard Bernstein. Reprinted by permission of Simon and Schuster, Inc.

ARTURO TOSCANINI: Quotes from *This Was Toscanini,* by Samuel Antek. Copyright © 1963 by Alice Antek. Published by the Vanguard Press, Inc. Reprinted by permission.

GIUSEPPE VERDI: Remarks about conductors from letters to Giulio Ricordi, one dated April 11, 1871, and the other probably written in 1872. From Verdi: *The Man in His Letters,* by Werfel and Stefan, copyright 1942 by A. A. Wyn Incorporated (formerly the L. B. Fischer Publishing Corporation), New York. Reprinted by permission of the publisher.

FRITZ BUSCH: Quotes from his book, *Der Dirigent*—Copyright © 1961, Atlantis-Verlag, Zürich. English translation printed by permission of the publisher.

GUSTAV MAHLER: From *Erinnerungen an Gustav Mahler,* by Natalie Bauer-Lechner. Copyright 1923 by E. P. Tal Verlag, Leipzig.

ARNOLD SCHOENBERG: From *Ausgewählte Briefe,* selected and edited by Erwin Stein. Copyright © 1958 by B. Schott's Söhne, Mainz. English translation copyright © 1964 by Faber and Faber, Ltd., London. Published in the United States by St. Martin's Press, Inc. Reprinted by permission.

Translations from the German, unless otherwise indicated, are by Luna Wolf.

Preface

This collection of essays on conducting, while naturally dealing with aspects of the craft, is primarily intended to present the thoughts that conductors themselves have had about their art—this art which has fascinated and puzzled musician and listener alike. I doubt whether the mystery will be solved, but I think that these articles will at least give the reader an insight into the workings of the conductor's mind, his evaluation of his function, his tools, his problems. It is my hope that they will place the activity of the conductor in proper perspective, giving him his rightful place while avoiding the extremes of thoughtless adulation and equally thoughtless dismissal.

In the material gathered here the Germans are heavily

represented; this is so because they have expressed themselves far more frequently on the subject than their colleagues in other lands.

In my Introduction I have tried to show, in a necessarily brief and sketchy manner, how the development of music brought about the need for the conductor. This introduction in no way pretends to be a complete outline of the history of music nor a lesson in basic music appreciation. I have tried to keep technical terms at a minimum, and when I did use them to do so in a way which would not interfere with the general comprehension of the layman. It is merely intended to show the major happenings which led first to the leader, then to the interpreter.

It is with gratitude that I take this opportunity to thank Mr. Edgar Trauer of the Süddeutsche Rundfunk, Stuttgart, Germany; Dean Carl Schachter of the Mannes College of Music; Dr. Josef Braunstein of the Juilliard School of Music, Manhattan School, and Mannes College of Music; and my editors at McGraw-Hill for their invaluable comments and suggestions.

Contents

Introduction

The memory which we carry of a painting or sculpture —its line, color, proportion, perspective—reflects the reality of the work of art. When we return to it we find it unchanged in harmony and structure. The organic work, once created, retains its molded unity independent of any interpreter. As it was fashioned so it remains.

By and large, this is true of all the arts but music. Even the play, which essentially also needs to be performed, can be read, understood, and savored by the literate person without an intermediary. But the notes scattered on staves are meaningless to all but the expert few until they become sound. The listener, in whose receptiveness music finds its fullfillment, has no direct access to it, but must get it through the interpreter.

The time element, too, sets music apart. In visual art the completed work shows one instant of time; the observer himself creates the before and the after as he contemplates the work. But this becoming-being-becoming actually happens in music. The same is true of literature, but, like the other descriptive arts, it deals with impressions from and associations with actual life. Music in its essence has no such associations, and that is what makes it unique. Neither the sounds of nature nor the supposed factual content of program music are the basis of our response to music. Our aesthetic perception of it is conditioned only by our memory of purely musical elements. Music is the only art which develops abstract material in time. And the re-creator's main task lies in the proper understanding of the time element and its logical rendition.

In the interpretation of songs, operatic or other vocal works, the singer must capture his audience with the quality and technique of his voice; the instrumentalist performing sonatas or chamber works reaches the listener through the instrument over which he has gained mastery. But if the interpreter is a conductor the direct technical command and expressive skill are taken away from him. He is dependent on the craft of others and must draw from these human beings the sounds which his inner ear requires. The orchestra is his intermediary in the projection of his concept of the technical, intellectual, and emotional demands of the music to the audience. He must therefore be able to communicate this concept to his players, influence them, lead them in such a manner that they will render it as he wishes.

But how is it done? What makes one conductor great, another merely adequate, a third not even that, although all three may be trained musicians and beat time generally in the same way? Why is one performance electric, memorable, another just dull, although both consist of the same notes played without striking differences? There are many theories. Indeed, few people, whether musicians or audience, seem to be without one. The methods, techniques, and approaches expounded by the experts, the conductors themselves, probably have as many variations as there are practitioners of this most intangible of interpretative functions. They do, however, seem to agree on one thing: the skill of conducting can be learned, but not the *art*.

This art, the conductor's art, is a relatively recent development in the history of Western music. From modest and purely functional beginnings, it grew into a complex, mysterious, often misunderstood, underrated or overglamorized endeavor which seems to hold a special fascination for musician and listener alike.

In the mighty creative span that preceded the Classical period the interpretative conductor as we know him today was not necessary. Music consisted principally of the interaction of contrapuntal voices in which steady motion was dominant. Whether simple or highly florid, this style was marked by a uniform rhythmical foundation which enabled the participating players to pursue the melodic line by themselves; the meter or pulse which coincided with the flow of the melody furnished the constant support of a rhythmical center of gravity. This was underlined in the Baroque period by the percussive style of the harpsichord and the emphatic bowing of the strings. Nor was orchestration a concern in itself; its function was to serve the horizontal line of the music, and thus it was conceived and used. Although there were solos and alternations between solo and tutti, it was in the black-and-white manner of an etching rather than as instrumental coloration. Structural drama, which implies interaction, counteraction, and development of all musical elements, did not exist, and in that sense, a composition was timeless, as if coming out of infinity and returning to it. The theme, molded by variation, imitation, change of voice, did not yet develop in a dramatic manner: it did not struggle with a contrasting theme or contrasting note values.[1]

Music was scored for small ensemble. The transparency and simplicity of the orchestration allowed the players to hear one another without difficulty. The structure of the music was such that the necessary freedom existed within the frame of the expected, but without counteracting the natural pulse of the music. In addition, the works performed were of the period, usually under the direction of the composer, and in the accepted contemporary style. This combination of factors—small ensemble, uniformity of and familiarity with style, a rhythmically even physiognomy, a melodic structure without dramatic aim—created an art with which a group of artists could cope out of their natural musical sense. With few exceptions the music's inner momentum could carry it from beginning to end.

When a leader was necessary—as, for instance, in opera or enlarged ensembles—it was more for organizational reasons than for interpretative ones. Opera in particular, with its continuous action on stage, required someone to keep the various elements together, and this was usually done from the cembalo or by the concertmaster. Although undoubtedly creation was far ahead of re-creation or presentation, there were some exacting taskmasters who tried to raise the level of performance. Among the first was Jean Baptiste Lully (1632–1687), a Florentine who became the leading French composer of his time at the court of Louis XIV. He imposed a meticulous bowing technique on his orchestra, and his controversial use of a stick to pound out the beat on the floor soon gained general acceptance in France and Italy. It is difficult for us today to reconcile his fastidiousness with the extramusical noise such pounding implies, but in fact performances of the time and later were usually presented amid tumultuous pounding, stamping, singing, and shouting on the part of the leader inconceivable to modern audiences.

In 1722, the French composer Jean Philippe Rameau (1683–1764) published his scientific-philosophical treatment of harmony, the *Traité de l'Harmonie*. The effects of this work spread slowly but eventually did much to finish the reign of the thorough bass,[2] which meant the end of the predominantly polyphonic style and the coming to the fore of homophonic music. From Italy came the concerto grosso which in time formed the basis for the symphony; the trio and solo sonatas out of which grew the modern sonata form; and the new, free, melodic style of Italian *opera buffa*. These manifold influences eventually brought to an end the period of Baroque music: melody supported by a harmonic structure replaced polyphony, or, to put it differently, the filling and accompanying voices which formed a contrast to the leading melody were born. The balancing of main themes against sustaining voices gave an entirely new aspect to the musical physiognomy. The sonata-symphony form, with its contrasts in themes and note values, its completely different tensions and suspenses as compared to the suite, required a new dramatic sense of proportion.

In addition, steady, regular motion made way for an ebb and flow of movement. Thus perspective, the third dimension, slowly came into being, with a foreground, middle ground, and background in the pictorial sense. These developments brought with them the need for balance and counterbalance, weight and counterweight, stress and restraint. As music began to tend away from its former chamber-music give and take the necessity for a watchful ear outside the performing group grew. The operatic reforms of Christof Willibald Gluck (1714–1787) were aimed at creating works which had dramatic as well as musical coherence. They made Gluck more demanding in performance, foreshadowing the modern interpreter. Often called tyrannical at rehearsals, he laid great stress on the proper dynamics, insisting on real pianos, pianissimos, fortes, and fortissimos, and denouncing the "lazy" mezzoforte.

Melody also underwent a transformation. The style based on the regularity of repeated note values found its climax in the work of Johann Sebastian Bach (1685–1750). Then melody started developing dramatic suspense. The mixture of note values, supported by changing harmonies in a three-dimensional world, gave melody an entirely new aspect. It had to face a destiny; the life of a melody became comparable to a human life. If we can say that pre-Romantic music is objective—as opposed to the subjectivity of Romanticism—in that it does not mirror the material existence of its creator, we might further state that the symphonic development form allowed the creator to intrude into his creation. The work of Josef Haydn (1732–1809) and Wolfgang Amadeus Mozart (1756–1791) carries the germ of this, although its introverted spirituality and understatement still produce a crystalline interplay of tones beyond the human. But the germ was there, and led in direct line to Ludwig van Beethoven (1770–1827).

Orchestration of necessity reflected these changes, but generally it can still be said that the instrument served the musical intent without a built-in coloring aim. It only gradually drew away from the purity of pre-Classical instrumentation, and the architectural edifice was still united to an objective form.

Haydn, in middle age, worked out in its final shape the principle of developing the main theme in the sonata. This step accomplished the change from the suite, which was not an organic unity but a chain of quasi-independent sections, to the modern sonata form, with its deliberate development pattern and consequent wholeness. The symphony as a coherent drama was born.

Side by side with the intellectual development of the form of the symphony, the sound body evolved in striking fashion, and sound for its own sake became important. In 1742 the Bohemian composer Johann Stamitz (1717–1757) came to Mannheim and there laid the groundwork for an orchestral manner (soon to be called "mannerism" by Leopold Mozart [1719–1787]) in which dynamics were the main feature; the Mannheim orchestra developed nuances never before attempted, and became especially famous for its spectacular crescendo. Later on Beethoven's particular genius adopted it and turned it into a forceful and moving means of expression.

It was also Beethoven who decisively introduced the "I" into music, with all of its attendant subjective emotions. He brought an entirely new musical language into being and molded the orchestra to fit this new language. But his conception far transcended the standards of his time, and his inner ear evolved a larger sound body than the small, inadequate ones usually at his disposal. Although his scoring by and large uses the Classical orchestra as it had been established by Mozart and Haydn, the cast of his thematic material was such that it clearly had to rest on a more powerful sound foundation.

Added to this was the introduction of daring rhythmical innovations, and a totally new declamatory style. The prophetic eloquence of this style imposed on each player a much more intense participation in the symphonic web, and vastly increased the virtuoso demands on performers, whether as soloists or in groups.

The pause as a creative substance became increasingly important, and silence, the major element of suspense for the listener, required a control, a judgment of proportion hitherto virtually unknown. Nor could the eruptive beginnings breaking out of nowhere (the *Fifth Symphony* or the final movement of the *Ninth*), the improvisandos (last movement of the *First*, or the revolutionary *recitativo* passage for celli and double basses in the last movement of the *Ninth*) be played without the ruling baton, putting the conductor into a completely new position of central control. Although these complex passages were not performed adequately in Beethoven's time[3] they nevertheless created the need for the conductor in modern terms.

Although Haydn, Mozart, and Beethoven are usually considered the triumvirate of Classical music, Beethoven actually speaks to us from an entirely new sphere: Romanticism. Where heretofore music was marked by firmness of form, a veiled spirituality, a purity of color close to the black and white of preceding times, tempo changes mostly limited to different movements, and a disciplined freedom into which the creator's subjective emotions did not intrude, with Beethoven the drama of the ego and of a personalized humanity was admitted. During the nineteenth century there was an ever-growing intensity of subjective utterance—Romanticism in full flower. The Romantic composer wanted his work to reflect the fate of the world as well as his own fate; the form he used, dealing with human tensions, joys, and pains, became fluid, with freer execution, rubatos, ritards. It tried to amalgamate abstract music and concrete ideas, to explain transcendental concepts with the thinking mind. But one of the most striking characteristics of Romanticism is consciousness; in contrast with Romantic trends in earlier music, the nineteenth-century composer brought Romanticism into the musical concept by willful planning, in the sense of Schiller's statement: "Purposeful Romanticism is different from inadvertent Romanticism."

In inadvertent Romanticism the individual remained outside his work; in the nineteenth century, the creator, with his joys, sorrows, desires, problems, with his fate, was an intrinsic part of his creation. To express the personal thoughts, emotions, and reactions with which the Romantic idiom is infused, the composer again adapted and expanded his material. The parts written for orchestral instruments made full use of each instrument's individual potential. Layers of sound were created enforcing the impression of perspective. With his handling of sound and sound combinations (for instance, pianissimo trumpets) Mendelssohn introduced an aura of instrumental mystery into the orchestra. Melodic elements acquired prominence, a personal expressive value, a longer or a shorter life. By now music, with its subtleties, its treatment of personal and philosophical matter, had become far removed from the objective chamber-music style of earlier periods. Conducting became an increasingly important and independent activity. From then on the orchestra leader assumed more and more stature and power.

At first, the conductor's new and provocative position of importance aroused some hostility, and his activity was often condemned as a foreign, distracting element. Nevertheless, the multiplying difficulties of musical speech made him increasingly the center of authority and attention.

Although the nineteenth century was still an age in which most musicians performed multiple functions and virtuosi in all fields composed as well as performed, men appeared who are important in the history of conducting.

The Italian opera composer and conductor Gasparo Spontini (1774–1851), after success in France, made Berlin the main and most effective center of his thoroughly autocratic regime. His orchestra consisted of nearly one hundred members, seated in the modern manner, that is, in front of the conductor. He achieved the dramatic impact and unity he desired through countless section and tutti rehearsals and personal stage direction. Refusing to conduct from the cembalo he made his baton the center of command, and the respect he generated among his players was enormous. He obtained his results by authority and unrelenting severity, thus becoming a precursor of the tyrannical conductor of later times.

Carl Maria von Weber (1786–1826), had similar ideals of opera as an artistic whole. During his activity as *Kapellmeister* of the German Opera at Dresden and elsewhere, he reached this goal by inspiring his co-workers rather than intimidating them as Spontini did. A further difference between the two was that Weber continued to cling to the old seating arrangement, the conductor standing close to the stage with the orchestra at his back.

In orchestral music Louis Spohr (1784–1859), primarily a violinist, brought the instrumentalist's imagination to the orchestra and indulged in a lush *cantabile*. He is responsible for an important milestone in rehearsal organization and procedure, the introduction of reference numbers in scores. This shows that Spohr worked on specific passages instead of merely playing a work through.

Felix Mendelssohn-Bartholdy (1809–1847), the educated,

intellectual man of the world, transferred to his conducting the subtle, almost impressionistic dynamics of his compositions. Under his direction the Leipzig Gewandhaus Orchestra achieved international stature. Mendelssohn was, in addition, responsible for reviving general interest in the music of Johann Sebastian Bach, with his all-important performance of the *Passion according to St. Matthew* in 1829. In contrast, the French composer Hector Berlioz (1803–1869) was the image of intense, exuberant egocentricity. Primarily because no one else would do so Berlioz usually conducted his own works. Visualizing enormous masses of sound, he used the orchestra in a massive, colorful way; his treatise on orchestration is still respected and studied today. He was also the first to write theoretically on the subject of conducting—and this work too has retained its validity and usefulness.

With the expansion of the orchestra sound color came into being. An endless variety of novel combinations gave the instrumental body a new dimension. It now had to represent a realm of unexplored tonal fantasy and extramusical matter; the world was brought in and was reflected and transfigured in the orchestra. Score markings had now gone far beyond the relatively simple indications of Haydn, Mozart, and Beethoven and acquired a poetry of their own. The conductor, more than ever the re-creator, had to grasp with his own imagination the fantasy of orchestration and transmit it to his players and his audience.

With the composition of Weber's *Euryanthe* and *Freischütz* German Romantic opera was born. The *Gesammtkunstwerk* of Richard Wagner (1813–1883), the music drama, is its direct descendant, and, as Alfred Einstein put it, "the culmination of romanticism. . . ." Einstein goes on to say that Wagner "does not belong exclusively to the history of music.

Wagner the artist is the incarnation of his age."[4] In addition to Weber many influences went into the making of Wagnerian art: the late Beethoven, the innovations of Berlioz and Liszt, even the "grand opera" works of Meyerbeer and Halévy, as well as the literary and philosophical utterances of his time. But Wagner created an entirely new cosmos. From Weber, the orchestra precipitously rose to the entirely new Wagnerian idiom. The demands of the libretto, now far removed from the aria-carrying vehicle fashioned to serve the singer, played a dominant part in shaping musical expression. The operatic orchestra became a symphonic one. The constant interaction between singers and instruments, the symbolism of the thematic developments in the orchestra, the modifications of tempo so strongly emphasized by Wagner—all these striking innovations required a controlling spirit. Where until recently the need had been for a rehearser with discipline, precision, and a sense of style, the newly conceived dramatic cosmos demanded a master of that cosmos. Beating time, until then a relatively simple activity, had to become an independent technique capable of balancing the masses of sound and bringing out at the proper moment a theme in the orchestra, a vocal phrase on stage, an interjection by the chorus, or a trumpet signal offstage. Physically the conductor's gestures had to encompass an increasing variety of sound combinations, and constant control was necessary because of the incessant flow and flexibility of rhythm and color. Spiritually the conductor had to project the new *atmosphere* which had been created, something which the best, most precise orchestra and soloists could not do alone. He had to reunite the audience and the work now separated by the sheer size of the Romantic's apparatus.

Wagner's creative mind was equally great in re-creation.

He formulated highly important theories on tempo and its modifications, as well as the concept of the melos[5] and its proper comprehension as the only way of bringing out the inner truth of a composition. As a conductor his interpretation of Beethoven, especially the *Ninth Symphony*, formed the basis for the modern idea of Beethoven's works.

Wagner's cosmos drew to it the major musicians of his time: Felix Mottl (1856–1911), Hermann Levi (1839–1900), Franz Wüllner (1832–1902), Hans Richter (1843–1916), and the most important of them, Hans von Bülow (1830–1894), an outstanding pianist as well as the first great conductor who was not primarily a composer. Bülow conducted the first performances of *Tristan und Isolde* and *Die Meistersinger.* Later he left the Wagnerian sphere, and became a strong supporter and interpreter of Johannes Brahms (1833–1897). Out of the small Meiningen court orchestra he welded together a great ensemble with which he eventually toured Europe with sensational success. Aside from countless section rehearsals for precision, he revealed a new awareness of style and characteristic phrasing. He was the first to conduct from memory and his performance had a plasticity and freedom which sometimes came close to being excessive. Qualities in the hands of a master, these traits were often abused and distorted by his less gifted followers.

Bülow was the first of the towering virtuoso conductors. The freedoms which he brought to tempi were extended to sound by another giant, Arthur Nikisch (1855–1922). Nikisch brought to life hitherto unnoticed middle voices, making them weave in shimmering threads around the leading melodies. A man of kindness and nobility, he obtained his results through a gentle power of conviction and the highly individual technique of his eloquent baton. He was more a musician of emotion and intuition than of analytical intellect, and was a matchless interpreter of all music of Romantic inclination.

In strongest contrast to the calm conviction of Arthur Nikisch stood his equally great contemporary, Gustav Mahler (1860–1911). Intense, demonic, Mahler struggled throughout his life for success as a composer and as an innovator of dramatic performances. The traditionally executed opera repertoire became, in his hands, a completely remolded presentation through the fusion of acting, scenery, costumes, and music. He created a tradition of performing Gluck, Mozart, and Wagner which lives to this day. The scores of Mahler's own works show his innovations in dynamic shadings and tempo freedoms; his directions for the realization of the stylistic subtleties of his music are not only detailed but written with poetic imagination.

The curve which started with the Wagnerian orchestra found its culmination in the aural effects and complexities of Richard Strauss (1864–1949). At first, Strauss based his technique entirely on the Wagnerian idiom, but with *Salome* came an entirely different, declamatory style, along with a highly original, rhapsodic instrumental speech which carried the symphonic independence of the orchestra much further than Wagner's compositions. There was an increased elaboration of detail in which unexpected potentialities of various instruments were realized, such as the exploiting of their highest and lowest registers. Strauss, unlike many other composers, was famous for his masterful renditions of his extremely complex scores.

The sumptuous orchestra and emotional sensuality of the late Romantics found its counterbalance in the tone-color sensuousness of Impressionism, which appeared simultaneously in the visual arts. Reality was constantly negated in sound, texture, and form. The melos was woven into chord progressions that had an opalescent quality, and the impact of the large orchestra was diffused into floating subtleties, of which color, with infinitely delicate gradations, was the essential characteristic. Instead of being used vertically, the huge variety of instruments manifested itself in small units, each one painting another color cluster, all of which were a part of the melodic unit. Therefore, as one must look at an Impressionistic painting from a distance so, too, should one figuratively observe the music from afar, so that the clusters can fuse and form a whole.

As the twentieth century progressed, Arnold Schoenberg (1874–1951) and his school revolutionized the melos and tonality. Rhythmical structure was completely transformed by Igor Stravinsky (1882–   ) and Bela Bartók (1881–1945) with the introduction of scrambled rhythms (5/8, 7/8, 11/8, etc.) which worked against regular pulsation.

As a consequence of these momentous changes, music became amorphous, pointillistic; small clusters of tones in various combinations floated unsupported in space. The beat pattern, formerly fused with the drive of the melos, shrank to the point where it was no more than a center of orientation for the orchestra player, and the function of the conductor switched from the flexible improviser to the strict guide for converging and diverging sounds and rhythms.[6]

Paul Hindemith (1895–1963), in contrast, returned to mode, chant, the horizontal line, basic rhythmical regularity; voice leading once again conquered the fluctuation of sound colors, and vagueness gave way to the clear line.

The virtuoso conductor was produced, on the one hand, by the growing difficulties of musical language and, on the other, by the widening chronological distance between the interpreter and the composer of the past, bringing about the need for reconstructing a given style in a period unfamiliar with its basic and largely unwritten rules.

The conductor became a powerful force in a nineteenth century society quite differently constituted from our present-day one. The public, still unsated, could listen to a relatively small repertoire performed by a handful of conductors at (by our standards) infrequent concerts, which were always an event. The more those few masters of the baton had something to say, the more they were owned by the audience. After Bülow and Nikisch, Felix Weingartner (1863–1942) continued to interpret Beethoven with lucid simplicity. Bruno Walter (1876–1962) carried on the great Mahler tradition of operatic theater, and infused the big choral works with warm humanity. He can also rightly be credited with the Mozart renaissance, and interpreted the finely textured Mozart compositions with the same artistry as he did the large choral masses.

Wilhelm Furtwängler (1886–1954) was also of the great Germanic stream. Virtuosity, usually connected with brilliance, was, for him, solely of the spirit, a spirit which conquered technique. He produced interpretations of the highest organic coherence with an exceptionally beautiful sound that had a weightless quality. Sound in itself, though, did not exist for him; it had to be part of the symphonic entity, a tool rather than an aim itself.

The Italian maestro Arturo Toscanini (1869–1957) might be called the high priest of the written text, following the composer's instructions to the greatest possible degree.

Meticulous, with intensity, drive, and strict discipline toward himself and others, he hypnotized his musicians and his audiences alike. In addition to his dramatic flair for Italian opera, he was one of the authentic interpreters of great European music, with far-reaching influence on the interpretative approach of generations of conductors.

Great men often link past and future. It was Toscanini who made radio concerts an important element in cultural life, thus emphasizing the growing significance of the communications industry in the field of music. In the decades that have since passed, the methods of preserving and projecting sound have achieved such a high level of technical proficiency that for a time they presented serious competition to concert attendance. But even the most perfect reproduction cannot render the unexplainable currents which flow between audience and artists. Nor can the relentless, undeviating sameness of the recorded performance take the place of the stimulus which the interpreter receives as the music comes to life around him, and to which the listener reacts. But no one will deny that the era of recorded music has brought with it significant advantages, preserving the interpretations of masters and making easily available much which otherwise would have been beyond the reach of most individuals.

However, this wealth has caused many changes. The repertoire of standard works which had sufficed for the relatively small series of concerts of former times has become insufficient. The audience is history-minded, and listens with the same calm enjoyment to music of the far-distant past, minor works of Classical and Romantic composers, and *avant-gardist* experiments. To the musician, the steadily growing versatility of the listener has meant a steadily decreasing versatility for him, and the specialist has appeared; the scholar-conductor has carved a place for his activity, arousing nearly as much interest for his researches as for his renditions. And at the other end are the bold experiments with every conceivable means of producing sounds, including the use of purely mechanical elements (*musique concrete* or electronic music) in which the conductor sometimes becomes a moderator.

While the day of the virtuoso conductor is by no means over, the demand for variety may in part be a healthy reaction against the adulation of the star interpreter, who sometimes even overshadowed the composition, and against the abuses and excesses which resulted. The great technical proficiency of instrumentalists and groups alike has also tended to change the function of the conductor. The appetite for variety, for anything from ancient to *avant-garde* works, for the smallest and the largest ensembles, has produced countless conductors of varying gifts and inclinations, many of whom serve music in a much more anonymous way than the virtuosi of the past.

CARL MARIA VON WEBER

About the Interpretation of Euryanthe

I take the liberty of adding a few general remarks which have occurred to me in connection with this work. The singer's individuality is the actual involuntary dispenser of color to each part. The singer with an easily moving, flexible throat will do the same role in an entirely different way from the artist with a magnificent tone. The one will certainly be quite a bit livelier than the other, and yet both can equally satisfy the composer if each, by his own yardstick, correctly understands and renders the gradations of emotion as the composer

CARL MARIA VON WEBER: Born in Eutin, Germany, 1786; died in London, 1826. Called "the father of German opera," he composed ten operas, the three best known being *Der Freischütz* (1820), *Euryanthe* (1823), and *Oberon* (1826), and many other works. As a conductor his most important position was at the German Opera at Dresden.

indicated them. But preventing the singer from letting himself go too much, or performing what merely appears comfortable at first glance—that is the conductor's task. In certain passages it is necessary to see to it that the inner motion of the composition is not made to suffer because of one vocal flourish or another. Whoever, for instance, cannot render the last passages in the aria of Eglantine with searing fire, had better simplify this part rather than allow the passion of the whole piece to cool. Whoever cannot sing the vengeful aria of Elvira during the sacrificial ceremony with the necessary rage will harm the work less by omitting it than by presenting it to the listener as a quiet solfeggio exercise. It will always remain the most difficult task to link voice and instrument in the rhythmical motion of a composition so that they are fused together and the latter lifts and carries the former, furthering its emotional expression. Singing and instruments are, by their very nature, in contradiction. Singing, because of breathing and articulation, brings a certain undulation to the meter comparable to the even breaking of waves. The instrument (especially any of the strings) divides times into sharp grooves like the swing of a pendulum. Truthfulness of expression demands the fusing of these opposing characteristics. The meter (tempo) must not be tyrannically inhibiting or a driving hammer, but should be to music what the pulse is to human life. There is no slow tempo without passages which demand a quicker motion to avoid any impression of dragging. And there is no presto which does not demand, in contrast, a quieter delivery of certain parts, so as not to impede the means of expression with too much zeal. But the foregoing should not, in heaven's name, be taken by any singer as justification for the type of eccentric interpretation which arbitrarily distorts certain bars, and arouses in the listener a painful reaction as unbearable as watching a juggler deliberately put his limbs out of joint. The acceleration of tempo, as well as the retarding, must never give rise to a feeling of abruptness, jolting, or violence. Thus changes can only be made, in the musical-poetic context, through periods and phrases, according to the demands of emotional expression; in a duet, for instance, two contrasting characters can have different interpretations. The duet between Licinius and the High Priest in *Vestale*[7] can serve as example. The quieter the phrases of the High Priest, and, in contrast, the more violently the speeches of Lucinius are poured forth the more vividly the characters will stand out and the greater will be the effect. In music we have no symbols to express this interpretation. They exist only in the responsive human heart. If they are not there then nothing can help: neither the metronome, capable of preventing only the gross mistakes, nor the highly inadequate indications, which I had been tempted to elaborate much further. But I was warned by experiences from which I formed the inescapable conclusion that these indications are superfluous and useless, as well as in danger of being misinterpreted. Nevertheless, they may appear here; they were solely a response to friendly urging.

HECTOR BERLIOZ

On Conducting

Music is probably the most exacting of all arts and certainly one of the most difficult to cultivate. Its works are rarely presented to us under conditions which allow their true value to be recognized and their character and meaning to be completely discerned.

Among creative artists the composer is almost the only one depending upon a host of intermediaries between him and the public—intermediaries who may be intelligent or stupid, friendly or hostile, diligent or negligent. It is in their power

HECTOR BERLIOZ: Born in France in 1803; died there in 1869. He wrote large choral and orchestral works, including *Romeo and Juliet* and *Symphonie Fantastique.* He was a master of orchestration and his treatise on the subject is still used.

either to carry his work on to brilliant success or to disfigure, debase and even destroy it.

Singers are often considered the most dangerous of these intermediaries; I believe that this is not true. In my opinion, the conductor is the one whom the composer has most to fear. A bad singer can spoil only his own part, but the incapable or malevolent conductor can ruin everything. A composer must consider himself happy if his work has not fallen into the hands of a conductor who is both incapable and hostile; for nothing can resist the pernicious influence of such a person. The most excellent orchestra becomes paralyzed, the best singers feel cramped and fettered, all energy and unity are lost. Under such direction the noblest and boldest inspirations can appear ridiculous, enthusiasm can be violently brought down to earth; the angel is robbed of his wings, the genius is transformed into an eccentric or a simpleton, the divine statue is plunged from its pedestal and dragged in the mud. Worst of all, when new works are performed for the first time, the public and even listeners endowed with the highest musical intelligence are unable to recognize the ravages perpetrated by the stupidities, blunders and other offenses of the conductor.

For all the obvious shortcomings of a performance the conductor is not blamed; his victims shoulder the burden. If he misses the entry of the chorus in a finale, if he causes a wavering between the chorus and orchestra or between distant groups in the orchestra, if he drags or rushes the tempo, if he interrupts a singer before the end of a phrase, people say: "The chorus is terrible, the orchestra lacks assurance, the violins have spoiled the melodic line; nobody has vigor and fire, the tenor has made mistakes, he does not know his part; the harmonies are confused; the composer does not know how to write accompaniments for singers, etc., etc."

Only when he is listening to familiar and recognized masterworks can the intelligent listener distinguish the real culprit and do justice to the other partners in the performance. However, the number of such listeners is still so small that their opinion carries but little weight. Thus, the incapable conductor maintains himself with all the calm of a bad conscience in the presence of a public that would hiss an excellent singer pitilessly at the slightest vocal mishap.

Fortunately I am now speaking only of exceptions: capable or incapable conductors who are at the same time malevolent are very rare.

The conductor who is willing but incapable, on the other hand, is very common. There may be some doubt regarding the good faith of the many mediocre conductors who frequently have to conduct artists far superior to themselves. But nobody will accuse an author of conspiring against the success of his own work, and yet there are many composers who unknowingly ruin their best scores because they fancy themselves to be great conductors.

Beethoven, it is said, more than once spoiled performances of his symphonies, which he liked to conduct even at the time when his deafness had become almost complete. In order to keep together, the musicians finally agreed to follow the slight signs of the concertmaster and to ignore Beethoven's baton. Moreover, it should be remembered that conducting a symphony, an overture or any other composition with extended movements which contain few changes and contrasts is child's play in comparison with conducting opera and other works containing recitatives, arias, and numerous orchestral passages interspersed with irregular pauses. The example of

Beethoven just cited shows that the direction of an orchestra, very difficult for a blind man, is entirely impossible for a deaf one, whatever may have been his technical skill before he lost his hearing.

The conductor must *see* and *hear,* he must be resourceful and energetic, he must know the nature and the range of the instruments and be able to read a score. Besides the specific talent whose component qualities we are going to discuss he must have other, almost indefinable gifts, without which the invisible contact between him and the performers cannot be established. Lacking these, he cannot transmit his feelings to the players and has no dominating power or guiding influence. He is no longer a director and leader, but simply a time-beater, provided he is able to beat and divide time regularly.

The players must feel that he feels, understands and is moved; then his emotion communicates itself to those whom he conducts. His inner fire warms them, his enthusiasm carries them away, he radiates musical energy. But if he is indifferent and cold, he paralyzes everything around him, like the icebergs floating in the polar sea, whose approach is announced by the sudden cooling of the atmosphere.

The conductor's task is very complex. He must not only be able to conduct a work with which the performers are familiar, according to the intentions of the composer, but also, in the case of a new work, to make them acquainted with it. During the rehearsals he has to point out to each of the performers his mistakes and errors. He must be able to employ the resources at his disposal so as to secure the greatest result from them in the shortest time possible; for, in most cities of Europe, musical art is in a sad plight. Musicians are poorly paid and the necessity of thorough study is so little understood that the economical utilization of time is one of the most imperative requisites of the conductor's skill.—Let us now see what constitutes the mechanical aspects of his art.

While not requiring particularly outstanding musical qualities, the art of beating time is nevertheless rather difficult to learn; very few people really possess it. The signs which the conductor makes are generally very simple, but they may occasionally become quite complicated by the divisions and subdivisions of the meter. The conductor must above all have a clear idea of the main features and the character of the work to be performed so that he can determine without hesitation and error the tempi planned by the composer. Unless he had the opportunity of receiving instructions directly from the composer or is familiar with the traditional tempi, he must consult the metronomic indications and study them thoroughly. Most modern composers mark compositions at the beginning and whenever there is a change of tempo. I do not mean to say by this that it is necessary to imitate the mathematical regularity of the metronome, which would give the music thus executed an icy frigidity; I even doubt whether it would be possible to maintain this rigid uniformity for more than a few bars. The metronome is nevertheless an excellent medium for determining the initial tempo of a piece and its main alterations.

If the conductor has neither the instructions of the composer nor traditional or metronomic tempo indications—as is frequently the case with works written before the invention of the metronome—he has no other guide than the customary, very vague tempo markings; for the rest he must rely on his own instinct and his feeling for the composer's style. To be sure, it cannot be denied that these guides are frequently insufficient or misleading. This is proved by the manner in which older operas are given in towns where the tradition for these works has been lost. Out of ten different tempi at least four will be wrong. I once heard a chorus from *Iphigénie en Tauride* performed in a German theater; instead of Allegro non troppo in 4-4 time it was played Allegro assai in 2-2 time, i.e. twice as fast. I could quote an immense number of similar mistakes caused either by the ignorance and negligence of the conductor, or by the fact that sometimes it is really very difficult even for the most talented and careful man to discover the exact meaning of the Italian tempo marks. Of course, nobody will fail to distinguish a Largo from a Presto. If the Presto has two beats to a bar, an intelligent conductor, by examining the passages and melodic designs contained in the piece, will soon find the degree of speed intended by the author. But with a Largo in 4-4 time and of simple melodic design, what means has the unfortunate conductor of discovering the correct tempo? The different degrees of slow movement that may be used for such a Largo are very numerous; only the individual feeling of the conductor can be the guide in such a case, although what matters most is the composer's rather than the conductor's feelings. Therefore, composers ought not to neglect furnishing their works with metronomic indications, and it is the conductor's duty to study them closely. To neglect this study is equal to an act of dishonesty toward the composer.

We now assume that the conductor is thoroughly familiar with the tempi of the work to be performed or rehearsed. His next task is to impart the rhythmic feeling within him to the orchestral players, to determine the duration of each bar and to make all participants observe this duration uniformly. This precise and uniform collaboration of a more or less large orchestral or choral body can be attained only by means of certain signs given by the conductor.

These signs indicate the main divisions—the *beats* of each bar, and frequently also the subdivisions—the *half beats.* It is not necessary to explain the difference between the strong and weak beats; I assume that I am writing for musicians.

The orchestral conductor generally uses a small light stick, about 20 inches long (better white than of dark color, for the sake of visibility). He holds it in his right hand and distinctly marks with it the beginning, the divisions and the close of each bar. Some concertmasters use the violin bow for conducting, but it is less suitable than the baton. The bow is somewhat flexible; this lack of rigidity and the greater resistance it offers to the air because of the hair make its movements less precise.

The simplest of all meters—*two* in a bar—is indicated very simply. After raising the baton so that the hand is on a level with his head, the conductor marks the first beat by dropping the point of the baton perpendicularly (as far as possible by bending the wrist and not by moving the entire arm) and the second beat, in the opposite way, by raising it again:

The meter with *one* beat in a bar is, especially from the conductor's point of view, the same as a meter with two beats in a very rapid tempo; therefore, it is indicated like the preceding. The necessity of raising the point again after lowering it divides the movement in two anyway.

With *four* beats in the bar, it is customary to mark the first strong beat (the beginning of the bar) by a downward movement. The second movement of the baton diagonally upward from right to left marks the second (the first weak) beat. The third, horizontally from left to right, marks the third (the second strong) beat and a fourth movement diagonally upward marks the fourth (the second weak) beat. These four movements result in this figure:

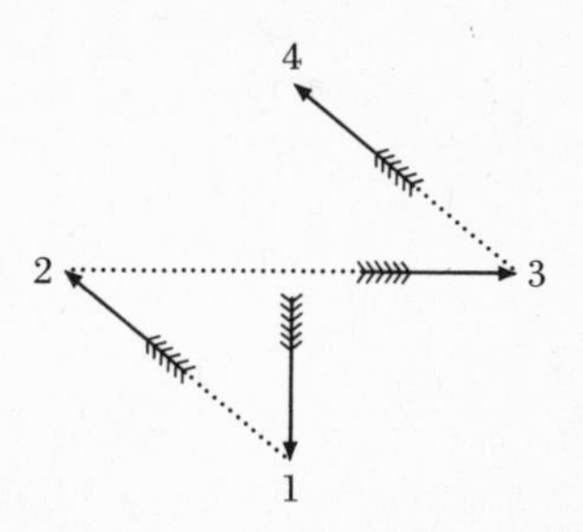

It is important that the conductor use his arm as little as possible for these movements and consequently does not let the baton cover too much space; for each movement must be almost instantaneous or, at least, should occupy a moment so short as to be practically incommensurable. If the time interval becomes appreciable, it causes—since it is repeated many times—a retardation of the intended tempo and a very unpleasant heaviness in the orchestral performance. Moreover, this mistake has the result of needlessly tiring the conductor and of producing exaggerated, almost ridiculous movements of the body, which distract the attention of the listeners.

In a bar with *three* beats, the first downward movement is customary for marking the first beat; but there are two ways of marking the second. Most conductors beat from left to right:

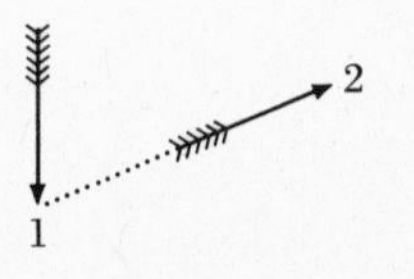

some German conductors, however, do the contrary and carry the baton from right to left:

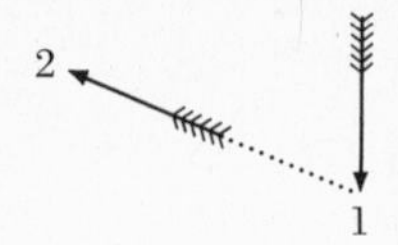

If the conductor has his back turned to the orchestra, as is customary in theaters, the latter method has a disadvantage in that only few players can see this very important marking of the second beat since the body of the conductor hides the movement of his arm. The other method is better because the second movement is outwards and the baton therefore remains perfectly visible to everybody, especially if the conductor raises it slightly above the level of his shoulders. If the conductor faces the orchestra, it is immaterial whether he makes the second movement to the right or to the left. The third beat is indicated in all cases by a diagonal, upward movement, like the last beat in 4-4 time:

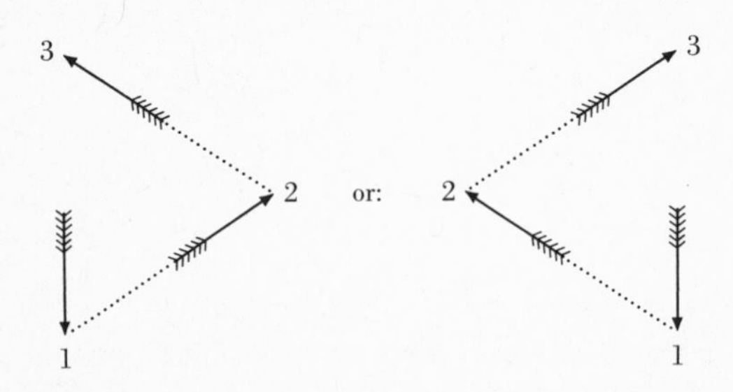

The meters with *five* and *seven* beats in a bar are not indicated by special series of gestures, but are treated as combinations of simple meters: the five beats as consisting of three and two beats, and the seven as four and three. They are therefore marked as follows:

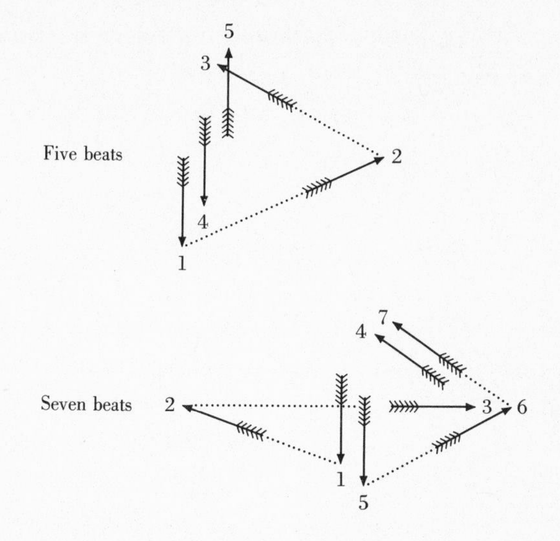

These divisions of the various meters are suited for moderate tempi. However, if the tempo is very fast or very slow, this method would be inadequate. As we have already seen, two beats in a bar can be marked only as shown above, however fast the tempo. On the other hand, if the tempo is exceptionally slow, the conductor has to subdivide each beat. A very rapid four in a bar should be marked by only two movements, since the four movements as used in moderate tempo would follow each other so rapidly that the eye could not follow them clearly; the players would be irritated rather than made secure. Moreover, and this is even more important, the conductor checks the rhythmic flow by the unnecessary four motions and loses all freedom of movement which he would retain with the simple division of the bar into two halves.

In such cases it is usually wrong for composers to indicate a 4-4 meter. When the tempo is very fast, they should always use the time signature ¢ and not C, which is misleading.

Triple time, i.e., rapid 3/4 and 3/8 meter, is treated similarly. The conductor does not mark the second beat, holding the first gesture for two periods and raising his baton only on the third beat:

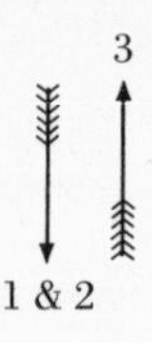

It would be ridiculous to mark all three beats in a Beethoven Scherzo.

If the tempo is very slow, each beat must be subdivided; consequently, quadruple time is marked by eight movements, triple time by six movements, by repeating each of the previously indicated main movements in abbreviated form:

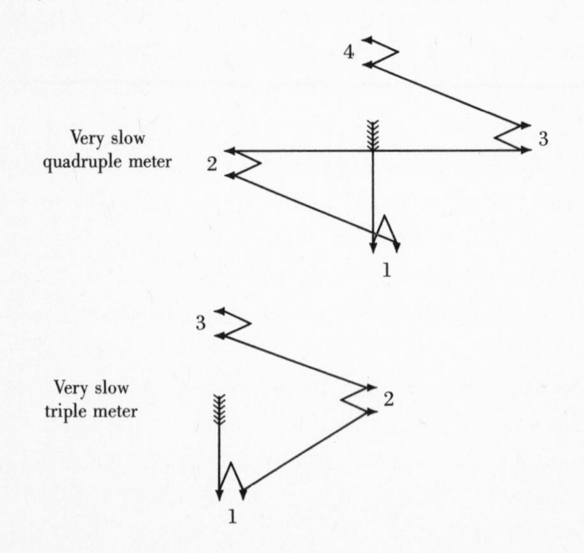

The arm should not take part in the short supplementary gestures marking the subdivisions of the bar; these are carried out by the wrist alone.

The purpose of this subdivision of the beats is to prevent rhythmic divergences which could easily arise in the orchestra during the intervals between two beats. If the conductor gives no sign at all during this long interval (which is unusually extended because of the slow tempo), the orchestra is left to itself for too long a time. Since not all players have the same rhythmic feeling, some will rush while others drag behind, and the ensemble will soon be destroyed. The only exception from this rule is a first-rate orchestra composed of virtuosos knowing each other very well and accustomed to play together, and who know the work to be performed almost by heart. Even then the carelessness of a single player may cause a mishap; why incur such a risk? I know that it hurts the vanity of some artists to be thus kept in leading-strings (like children, as they say); but with a conductor whose main aim is the excellence of the performance such considerations should have no weight. Even in a quartet the individual feeling of the players can rarely be allowed to follow its own paths. In a symphony the conductor's conception alone must rule. The quality of the performance depends on his conception and on the art of realizing it; the feelings of the individual players must never make themselves manifest.

Once this is clearly understood it becomes obvious that in very slow compound meters (such as 6/4, 6/8, 9/8, 12/8, etc.) the subdivision is even more important. These meters with triple time can be divided in various ways. If the tempo is rapid or moderate, only the simple beats are indicated according to the procedure adopted for the analogous simple meters. Hence, a 6/8 Allegretto or 6/4 Allegro requires a beat similar to duple meters (₵ or 2 or 2/4); 9/8 Allegro—like 3/4 Moderato or 3/8 Andantino; 12/8 Moderato or Allegro—like 4/4. But if the tempo is Adagio, Largo assai or Andante maestoso, all eighth-notes (or a quarter followed by an eighth-note) require beats, according to the form of the melody or the predominant figuration.

In this triple meter it is unnecessary to mark all eighth-notes; the rhythm of a quarter plus an eighth-note to a beat is sufficient. One uses the little supplementary gestures indicated for subdivisions of simple meters, dividing each beat, however, into two unequal parts because it is necessary to mark the value of the quarter as well as of the eighth-note.

If the tempo is still slower, all eighth-notes require beats regardless of the meter; only thus can uncertainty be avoided and complete mastery assured.

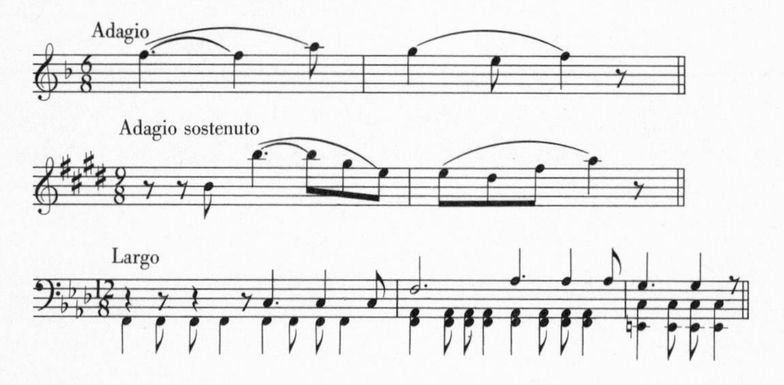

With the indicated tempi, the conductor will beat in the 6/8 meter three eighths to each time unit, i.e., three beats down and three beats up:

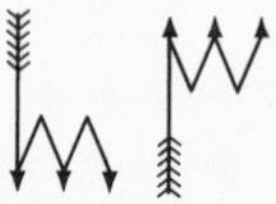

in the 9/8: three down, three to the right, three up:

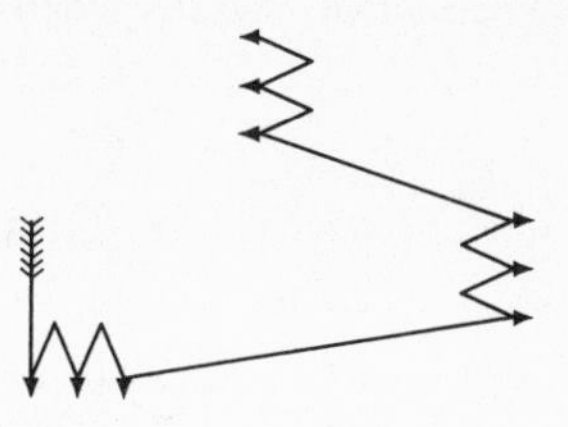

in the 12/8: three down, three to the left, three to the right, three up:

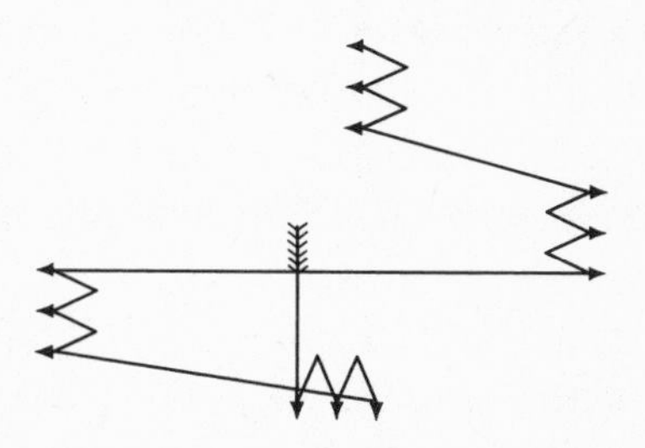

Sometimes a difficulty arises if certain voices in a score are given a triple rhythm for the sake of contrast, while the others continue in duple rhythm:

If the players of the wind instruments are very musical, there will be no need to change the manner of marking the bar and the conductor can continue to beat six or simply two. The majority of players, however, usually become uncertain when the syncopation begins and the triple rhythm clashes with the duple; they need assistance, which can be given to them in the following manner. The uncertainty in a group of performers caused by the sudden entry of this unexpected rhythm conflicting with that of the rest of the orchestra always makes them look instinctively at the conductor, as if seeking his assistance. He should also look at them, turning a little toward them and marking the triple rhythm by small movements of his hand (as if this were the real meter); but this must be done in such a fashion that the violins and other instruments continuing the duple rhythm cannot see the altered beat, which would otherwise confound them completely. Thus, the new triple rhythm, being marked furtively by the conductor, is executed with assurance, while the duple rhythm, already firmly established, continues without difficulty although no longer indicated by the conductor.

On the other hand, in my opinion nothing is more objectionable and contrary to good musical sense than the application of this method where not two different and contrasting rhythms clash, but where simple syncopation is introduced. If the conductor divides the bar according to the number of accents in it, he destroys the effect of the syncopation for all listeners who see him, substituting an ordinary change of time for a rhythm of stimulating charm. Such is the case in the following passage from Beethoven's *Pastoral Symphony* if the conductor marks the accents instead of the beats:

by making six movements to a bar, as indicated above the

notes, instead of the four previously maintained; only the latter enable the listener to recognize and feel the syncopation clearly:

This voluntary submission to a rhythmical form which the composer actually intended to be resisted is one of the gravest stylistic mistakes a conductor can make.

Another difficulty, extremely troublesome to the conductor and requiring all his presence of mind, is caused by the combination of different meters. It is easy to conduct a duple meter, each of whose beats is subdivided in two, together with a superimposed duple meter whose beats are divided in three, if both have the same tempo. Their bars have the same duration and it is only necessary to divide them in half and to mark the two principal accents:

However, if a new, fast figure is introduced into a slow movement and if the composer has adopted for this new tempo the corresponding, short bar (either to facilitate the execution of the fast tempo or because it could not be written otherwise), two or even three of these short bars may then coincide with one bar of the slow movement:

It is the conductor's task to hold these unequal bars together. He will attain this in the quoted example by beginning to subdivide the beats from bar No. 1 of the Andante, which precedes the entrance of the Allegro 6/8, and then by continuing this division, perhaps even more markedly. The players of the Allegro 6/8 will understand that the two gestures represent the two beats of their short bar, while the players of the Andante take these same gestures merely for a divided beat of their long bar.

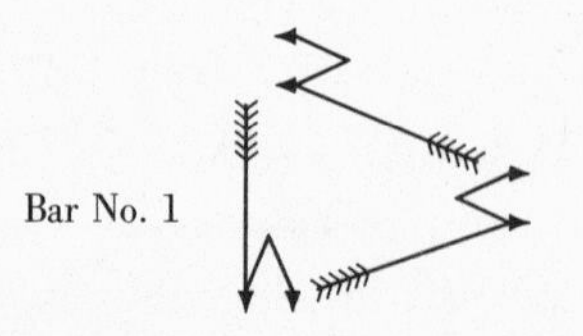

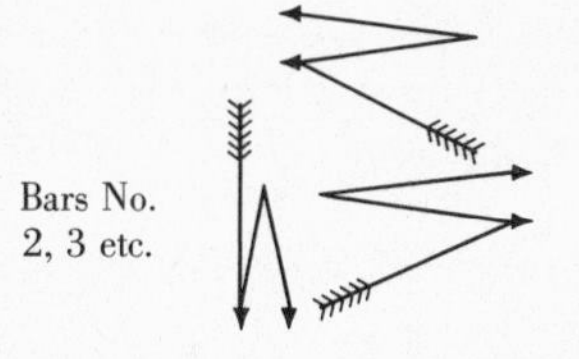

One sees, this is really quite simple because the divisions of the short bar coincide with the subdivisions of the long bar. The following example, however, in which a slow bar is superimposed over two short ones, but without this coincidence, offers greater difficulties:

Here the three bars of the Allegro assai preceding the Allegretto are conducted as usual, two to a bar. When the Allegretto begins, the conductor marks two *divided* beats for the long bar with two (unequal) movements down and two up:

The two large movements of the conductor divide the long bar in half and indicate its value to the oboes without confusing the violas, who maintain their fast movement supported by the shorter, subsidiary gestures dividing the short bar in half. From bar 3 on, the conductor ceases to divide the long bar in four because of the triple rhythm of the 6/8 melody entering here, with which this gesture would interfere. He confines himself to marking the two beats of the long bar. The violas, already accustomed to their fast rhythm, continue it without difficulty knowing that each movement of the baton marks the beginning of their short bar.

The preceding shows that subdividing a beat must be avoided if a part of the instruments or voices execute triplets on this beat. Such a division cutting through the second note of the triplet would make its execution insecure or actually impossible. The division should be avoided even a short time before the start of a triple rhythm or of a melody in triplets in order not to give the performers the feeling of a rhythm contrary to the one they are to execute.

In this example it is advisable to divide the entire bar No. 1 in six, i.e. to subdivide each beat in two carrying out the following movements:

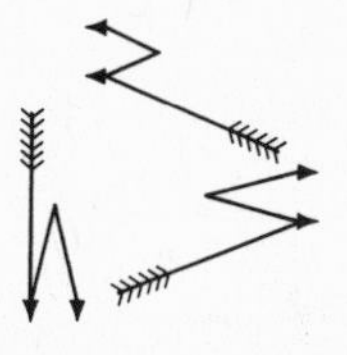

With the beginning of bar No. 2 it is necessary to omit the subdivision and to carry out only the simple movements:

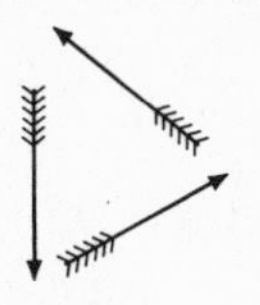

because of the triplets entering on the third beat, which would be impeded by the double movement. In the famous ball scene in Mozart's *Don Giovanni,* where three orchestras in three different meters are combined, the difficulty of holding them together is not as great as might be assumed. It is sufficient to mark each beat of the Tempo di menuetto by a downward movement:

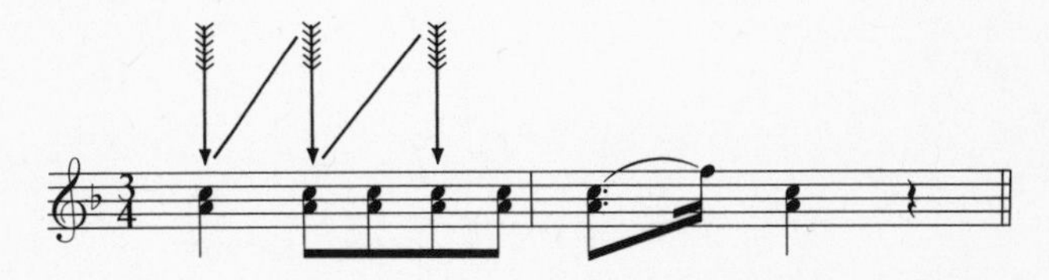

Once brought together, the two Allegros—the small one in 3/8 whose whole bar is a third (i.e., one beat) of the minuet bar, and the other in 2/4, whose bar is two thirds (i.e., two beats) of the minuet bar—fit together as well as with the main theme and proceed together without the slightest difficulty. The main thing is to make them enter correctly.

A gross fault that I have seen committed consists in slowing up the tempo of a piece in duple meter when triplets in half-notes occur:

The third note adds nothing to the duration of the bar, as some conductors seem to imagine. They may mark such passages with three beats if the tempo is slow or moderate, but the duration of the whole bar must remain exactly the same. If triplets occur in a very short bar in duple meter (Allegro assai), three beats would cause confusion. Only two should be marked—one down on the first note, the other up on the third. Owing to the quickness of the movement the two beats differ little from those of the bar with two equal beats and do not affect the execution of the parts continuing in duple meter.

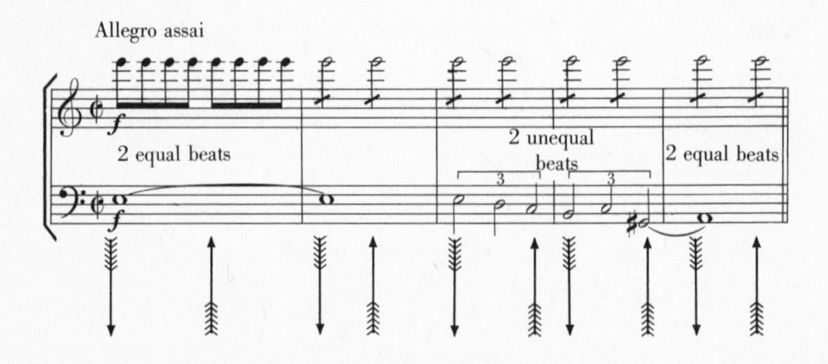

We shall now consider the method of conducting recitatives. Here the singer or instrumentalist is not confined to the regular divisions of the bar. The conductor must therefore follow their recitation attentively and must see to it that the chords and other instrumental passages inserted in the recitative are executed precisely and uniformly by the orchestra. If the recitative is accompanied by sustained notes or a tremolo in several voices and the harmony changes, he must indicate the change at the proper moment; sometimes the least conspicuous of the voices is the one whose progression changes the harmony and on which the conductor must therefore concentrate his attention.

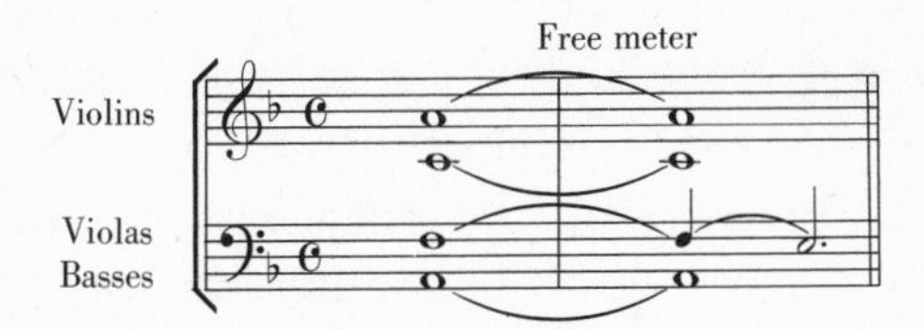

In this example the conductor, while following the reciting, metrically free part, must also watch above all the viola part and make it move from F to E at the correct moment at the beginning of the second bar. Since this part is executed by several players, some might hold the F longer than others and thereby cause a momentary dissonance.

Many conductors have the habit of completely disregarding the written divisions of the bar when conducting recitative; they mark an up-beat on a heavy beat if it precedes a short chord of the orchestra, even if this chord comes on a weak beat:

In a passage such as this they raise the baton on the quarter-rest at the beginning of the bar and lower it on the second beat to mark the entry of the chord. I cannot approve this absolutely unjustifiable method; it may frequently cause mishaps in the execution. I cannot see why in recitatives the bar should not be divided regularly and the real beats be marked in their proper place as in music played strictly according to meter. I therefore recommend marking the first beat in the preceding example with a downward motion, as usual, and to move the baton to the left with the entry of the chord on the second beat; and accordingly in other, similar cases, always dividing the bar regularly. It is also very important to divide it according to the tempo previously indicated by the composer; if it is an Allegro or Maestoso and the reciting voice has sung for some time without accompaniment, one must not forget when the orchestra re-enters to give each beat its proper value in an Allegro or Maestoso. If the orchestra plays by itself, it usually does so in strict time; it plays in irregular meter only when accompanying a reciting voice or instrument. In the exceptional case where the orchestra or chorus itself or part of them have to execute a recitative and where it is thus essential to keep a certain number of performers (in unison or in several parts) uniformly together although not in strict time, the conductor himself becomes the real reciter, giving to each bar the duration he considers to be correct. According to the form of the phrase, he sometimes marks the main beats, sometimes the subdivisions, sometimes the accents, sometimes the sixteenth-notes; in short, he designs with his baton the melodic form of the recitative. Of course the performers must know their music almost by heart and keep their eyes constantly on him; otherwise, no security or precision is possible.

Even with music in strict time, the conductor must generally insist that the players look at him as often as possible. *An orchestra which does not watch the conductor's baton has no conductor.* For instance, frequently after a pause the conductor is forced to wait before marking the re-entry of the orchestra until he sees the eyes of all performers fixed upon him. It is his task to accustom them during rehearsals to look at him simultaneously in all decisive moments.

Since in the preceding example the first note is indefinitely prolonged by the pause, the notes following it cannot be executed with the necessary verve and precision if this rule is disregarded; for without looking at the baton the performers cannot know when the conductor proceeds to the second beat and resumes the tempo momentarily suspended by the pause.

The obligation on the part of the performers to look at the conductor implies an equal obligation on his part to make himself visible to all of them. Whatever the arrangement of the orchestra may be, whether on steps or on a horizontal plane, the conductor must select his place so that he can be seen by everybody. The greater the number of performers and the larger the space occupied by them, the higher must be his place. His desk should not be too high lest the board carrying the score hide his face. For his facial expression has much to do with the influence he exercises. If a conductor practically does not exist for an orchestra unable or unwilling to look at him, he exists just as little for one unable to see him completely.

Noises caused by striking the desk with the stick or by

stamping feet are to be banned completely; they are not only inexpedient, they are crude. Only if the chorus is unable to see the baton because of some stage action, the conductor is forced—for the sake of a secure entry by the chorus—to mark the beat preceding the entry by a slight tap of his baton on the desk. This is the only exception warranting the employment of an audible signal in conducting; even then the necessity of using it is to be regretted.

While speaking of chorus singers and their operations on the stage we may mention that chorus masters often allow themselves to beat time backstage without being able to see the conductor's baton or even to hear the orchestra. Hence this arbitrary time, beaten more or less badly, cannot correspond with that of the conductor and causes a rhythmic discrepancy between the chorus and the orchestra; instead of aiding cooperation it impedes it.

There is another traditional barbarism which every intelligent and energetic conductor should abolish. For choral or instrumental pieces which are to be executed behind the scenes, sometimes without participation of the main orchestra, a second conductor is indispensable. If the main orchestra accompanies this group, the first conductor, who hears this music from the distance, is strictly bound to let himself be guided by the second conductor and to follow his lead by ear. But if—as frequently happens in modern music—the full sound of the large orchestra prevents him from hearing the backstage music, the application of a special mechanism transmitting the meter becomes necessary to establish an instantaneous communication between the conductor and the distant performers. For this purpose a number of more or less ingenious experiments have been carried out, whose results have not always met expectations. Only the electric metronome set up by Verbrugghen in the Brussels theater leaves nothing to be desired. It consists of copper wires attached to a voltaic pile placed beneath the stage; these wires connect the conductor's desk with a movable baton attached by a pivot in front of a board which is placed at any desired distance from the conductor. The desk is furnished with a copper key similar to a piano key, which has at its bottom a small protuberance of about a quarter of an inch. Immediately under this protuberance is a little copper cup filled with quicksilver. When the conductor wants to mark a beat, he presses the copper key with the forefinger of his left hand (his right hand holds the baton, as usual), whereby the protuberance makes contact with the quicksilver. The electrical connection thus effected makes the baton at the other end of the wires oscillate. The electrical contact and the movement of the baton take place simultaneously, regardless of the distance. The musicians behind the scenes watching the electric baton are thus practically under the immediate direction of the conductor, who might, if it were necessary, conduct from the middle of the Opéra orchestra in Paris a performance taking place in Versailles. It is only necessary to agree beforehand with the chorus singers or with their conductor (if there is one, as an additional precaution) on the manner of beating the time: whether the conductor is to mark all main beats or only the first beat in each bar. For the oscillations of the electric baton, taking place in only one direction, give no precise indication in this respect.

When I first used this valuable instrument in Brussels, its action disclosed one shortcoming. Every time the copper key was pressed down it touched another copper plate and, however soft the contact, there was a short noise which attracted the attention of the audience during the pauses of the orchestra, to the detriment of the musical effect. I pointed out the defect to M. Verbrugghen, who substituted for the copper plate the cup with quicksilver previously mentioned. The protuberance of the key enters into it without any disturbing noise. Only the electric spark emitted during the use of the instrument is still noticeable, but its crackling is so weak that the audience does not hear it. The installation of the metronome is not expensive. Large opera houses, churches and concert halls should have been provided with it long ago. Yet it is nowhere to be found except at the Brussels theater. This might appear unbelievable if the carelessness of many theater managers, to whom music is only a means toward an end, were not well known. We are only too well acquainted with their instinctive aversion to whatever is off the beaten track, with their indifference to the interests of art, their parsimony where an expenditure for the best of music is needed, and with the ignorance of the basic principles of our art among those in whose hands its fate rests.

Not all has been said as yet about those dangerous auxiliaries called chorus masters. Very few among them are really able to direct a musical performance so that the conductor can rely upon them. He must therefore supervise them closely when he needs their participation. Most to be dreaded are those whom high age has deprived of their energy and skill. The maintenance of any somewhat rapid tempo is impossible to them. However fast the initial tempo of a piece entrusted to their direction, little by little they slacken its pace until they have reached a certain degree of moderate slowness which corresponds with the blood circulation of their enfeebled organism. It must be added, however, that old men are not the only ones with whom composers run this risk. There are men in the prime of life, but with a sluggish temperament, whose blood seems to circulate *moderato*. If they have to conduct an Allegro assai, they gradually let it become a Moderato; if on the contrary, it is a Largo or Andante sostenuto of some length, they will have accelerated to a Moderato long before the end has been reached. Moderato is their natural pace, and they return to it as infallibly as a pendulum whose oscillations have been accelerated or retarded for a moment. These people are the born enemies of all characteristic music and the greatest destroyers of style. May orchestral conductors shun their cooperation at any price!

Once, in a large town which I will not name, a very simple chorus in 6/8 Allegretto was to be performed behind the scenes. The assistance of the chorus master was needed; and he was an old man. The tempo of the chorus was determined by that of the preceding orchestral introduction, and our Nestor followed it quite nicely during the first few bars; but soon he became so slow that it was impossible to continue without making a farce of the piece. It was started over again two, three, four times; half an hour was spent in increasingly irritating efforts, but always with the same result. The good man simply could not maintain an Allegretto. At last the orchestral conductor, out of all patience, asked him not to conduct any more, and made the chorus singers simulate a march movement by raising their feet alternatingly without moving from the place. This tempo corresponded exactly with the duple meter of the 6/8 Allegretto, and the singers, no longer hampered by their director, executed the piece correctly and without any slackening, as if they were singing on the march.

Nevertheless, I admit that some chorus masters or assistant conductors are really useful and even indispensable for the maintenance of unity among great masses of performers if it is absolutely necessary to place them so that a part of the instrumentalists or singers turn their backs on the conductor. He then needs a certain number of assistants placed in front of those performers who cannot see him to transmit his tempo indications to them. In order that this transmission is absolutely precise the assistant conductors must not take their eyes off the main conductor's baton for one moment. Should they cease to watch him for as little as three bars, to look at the score, there will immediately be a discrepancy between their tempo and his, and all will be lost.

At a music festival in Paris where 1200 performers were assembled under my direction, I employed five chorus conductors for the singers and two assistant conductors for the orchestra (one for the wind and one for the percussion instruments). I had urged them to look at me incessantly. They did not fail to do so, and our eight batons, rising and falling without the slightest rhythmic discrepancy, achieved a unity among the 1200 participants of a perfection never before experienced. With one or more electric metronomes this expedient will probably be no longer necessary. In fact, one can thus easily conduct a chorus placed with the back toward the conductor; but attentive and intelligent assistants are always preferable to a machine.

They must not only beat the time like a metronome, but they must also speak to the groups near them, drawing their attention to various shadings and giving them the cue for their re-entry after a rest. In a space arranged as a semicircular amphitheater the conductor alone can direct a considerable number of performers, since all participants can look toward him. I should nevertheless prefer to employ a number of assistant conductors, because of the great distance between the chief conductor and the performers placed at the extreme ends. The greater this distance, the smaller the conductor's influence upon the performers. It would be best to have several assistant conductors and several electric metronomes besides, marking the main beats of the bar before their eyes.

We now come to the question whether the conductor should stand or sit. In theaters, where works of tremendous length are performed, it is rather difficult for the conductor to endure the fatigue caused by standing the entire evening. On the other hand, it is obvious that the conductor loses part of his power by being seated, and that he cannot give free course to his temperament (if he has any).

Furthermore, should he conduct from the full score or from the first-violin part, as is customary in some theaters? He should doubtless use the full score. Conducting from a single part containing only the principal instrumental cues, the melody and the bass requires a needless effort of memory on the part of the conductor. Moreover, if he tells one of the performers whose part he does not have before him that he has made a mistake, he exposes himself to the risk of being answered: "What do you know about this?"

Placing and arranging the players and singers, especially for concerts, is also among the duties of the conductor. It is impossible to state categorically the best manner of grouping the performers in a theater or concert hall. Much depends on the size and shape of the particular place; the number of participants and sometimes the style of the composition to be performed must also be considered.

An amphitheater of eight or at least five different levels is generally indispensable for concerts. The semicircular form is best for the amphitheater. If the space is large enough to take in the entire orchestra, the instrumentalists will be arranged on the steps as follows: the first violins in front on the right, the second violins on the left, the violas in the middle between the two violin groups; the flutes, oboes, clarinets, horns, and bassoons behind the first violins; two rows of violoncellos and double-basses behind the wood-wind instruments; the harps in front, near the conductor; the kettle-drums and other percussion instruments behind the brass; the conductor, his back toward the public, at the base of the amphitheater, near the front desks of the violins.

There should be a plain, more or less wide space in front of the first step of the amphitheater. Here the chorus singers are arranged in the form of a fan, their faces turned three-quarters toward the public so that they can comfortably watch the conductor. The grouping of the singers by voices varies according to the number of voices employed in a given work. In any case, the sopranos and the altos should take the front rows, seated; the tenors stand behind the sopranos and the basses behind the altos.

The soloists (singers as well as instrumentalists) occupy the center of the front space and should place themselves so that they can always see the conductor's baton by slightly turning their heads.

These indications, I repeat, are only approximate; they may be modified in many different ways, for various reasons.

In the Paris Conservatoire, where the amphitheater has only four or five steps (not forming a semicircle), the violins and the violas are on the stage, and only the basses and wind instruments occupy the steps; the chorus is seated in the front of the stage, looking toward the audience. All the sopranos and altos are unable to see the movements of the conductor, since their backs are turned directly toward him. The arrangement is very inconvenient for this part of the chorus.

It is always of the greatest importance that the chorus singers placed in front of the stage shall be lower than the violins, since they would otherwise greatly impair their sonority. If there are no additional steps for the chorus in front of the orchestra, it is necessary for the same reason that the women be seated and the men remain standing, so that the tenor and bass voices, issuing from a higher point than the sopranos and altos, can spread freely and are neither stifled nor intercepted.

As soon as the presence of the chorus in front of the orchestra is no longer necessary, the conductor should send them away, since this large number of human bodies diminishes the sonority of the instruments. The performance of a symphony would lose much if the orchestra were thus muffled.

There are some additional precautions concerning the orchestra which the conductor must observe to avoid certain defects in performance. The percussion instruments, placed on one of the last and highest rows of the amphitheater, have a tendency to drag the tempo. A series of strokes on the bass drum at regular intervals in a fast tempo, such as these:

will sometimes lead to the complete destruction of a fine rhythmic climax by checking the flow of the orchestra and ruining its unity. The drummer almost always gives the first stroke a little too late because he does not observe the conductor's first beat. This delay increases with each succeeding stroke and must eventually lead to a rhythmic discrepancy of fatal effect. The conductor will vainly try to restore unity in such a case. All he can do is to require the drummer to memorize the number of strokes in the passage and, instead of looking at his part, to watch the conductor's baton closely.

A similar retardation, but from different causes, frequently occurs in the trumpet part when it contains rapid passages such as the following:

The trumpeter, instead of taking breath before the beginning of the first bar, does so only during the eighth-rest. Not counting the time required for breathing he gives the rest its full value, thereby prolonging the first bar by an eighth. The resulting effect:

is all the worse because the final accent, struck by the rest of the orchestra on the first beat of the third bar, comes too late in the trumpets, thus destroying the unity of execution in the final chord.

To prevent this, the conductor must point out in advance this inaccuracy to the players; for they are usually unaware of it. Then, while conducting, he must look at them at the decisive moment and give them, a little ahead of time, the first beat of the bar in which they have to enter. It is incredible how difficult it is to prevent the trumpeters from doubling such an eighth-rest.

Where the composer has indicated an extended *accelerando poco a poco* to pass from an Allegro moderato to a Presto, most conductors accelerate the tempo by jerks instead of enlivening it by a gradual and unnoticeable increase of speed. This mistake should be carefully avoided. This applies equally in the opposite instance; the smooth transition from a fast to a slow tempo is even more difficult.

Often a conductor demands from his musicians a certain exaggeration of the nuances indicated by the composer, either from a lack of delicate musical feeling or from a desire to give emphatic proof of his zeal. He does not understand the character and style of the work. The nuances become distortions, the accents turn into outcries. The intentions of the poor composer are completely disfigured; and those of the conductor, however honest they may be, are like the caresses of the ass in the fable, who killed his master by fondling him.

We now turn to some bad habits which can be found in almost all European orchestras—habits which reduce composers to despair, and whose early elimination is the duty of conductors.

Players of string instruments rarely take the trouble to produce a correct tremolo. They substitute for this very characteristic effect a mere repetition of notes, twice or even three times as slow as the real tremolo. Instead of sixty-fourth-notes they play thirty-second and even sixteenth-notes, i.e. instead of 64 notes to a bar (4-4, Adagio) they play only 32 or 16. The rapid motion of the arm necessary for the real tremolo is doubtless too great an effort for them. This laziness is intolerable.

Many double-bass players take the liberty of simplifying their part—either out of indolence or from fear of being unable to master certain difficulties. This system of simplification, generally accepted for the past forty years, can no longer be tolerated. The double-bass parts in older works are so simple that there is no reason for weakening them even more. Those in modern works are more difficult, it is true:

but, with very few exceptions, there is nothing impracticable in them. Composers who are masters of their art always write these parts with the greatest care and exactly as they should be performed. If the players simplify things out of laziness, the energetic conductor has sufficient authority to force them to do their duty; if they do it because of incompetence, he should dismiss them. It is in his own interest to rid himself of musicians who cannot play their instrument properly.

The flutists, accustomed to lead the other wind instruments and unwilling to play occasionally below the clarinets and oboes, frequently transpose entire passages to the higher octave. A conductor who does not read the score carefully and who does not know adequately the work to be performed, or one whose ear lacks acuteness, will not notice the strange liberty thus taken by the flutists. Many more examples of this kind could be cited; such abuses should no longer be tolerated.

It happens everywhere (I purposely do not say: in certain orchestras) that violinists, of whom usually ten, fifteen or twenty execute the same part, do not count the rests, but rely instead on the other players. The result is, of course, that scarcely half of them come in again at the right moment, while the others still hold their instrument under the left arm and stare in the air. The entry is thus weakened, if not entirely missed. I invoke the conductors' full attention and severity against this intolerable habit. However, it is so deep-rooted that the conductor will only succeed in eradicating it by making a large number of players liable for the fault of a single player, e.g., by fining a whole row if one of them misses coming in correctly. The amount of the fine may be small, but I warrant that each violinist will count his rests and see to it that his neighbor does the same, since the fine can be inflicted on the same player five or six times in the course of one performance.

An orchestra whose instruments are not in tune individually and in relation to each other is a tonal monstrosity. The conductor must therefore take great care that the musicians tune accurately. But this should not be done in the presence of the audience. Any kind of instrumental noise or of preluding during intermissions offends the ears of all refined listeners. One can immediately recognize the poor training and the musical mediocrity of an orchestra by this obnoxious noise made during the periods of quiet in an opera or concert.

It is also the conductor's duty to see to it that clarinetists do not always use the same instrument (usually the clarinet in B♭) without regard to the author's indications, as if the different clarinets, especially those in A and D, did not have their own individual character, whose special value is well known to the intelligent composer. Moreover, the clarinet in A reaches a semitone lower than the one in B♭, namely to C♯, which is of excellent effect. This C♯ represents the actual sound of the written note E, which on the clarinet in B♭ produces D.

Another habit, just as bad and even more dangerous, is found in many orchestras regarding the use of the valve horns. It consists in the execution as *open* tones (by means of the new mechanism) of those notes which are intended by the composer to be played as *stopped* tones (by introducing the right hand into the bell of the horn). Furthermore, horn players now use almost exclusively the horn in F (because of the facility of playing it in different keys by means of the valves), regardless of the key indicated by the composer. This habit causes a great many abuses, from which the conductor should preserve the works of composers *who know how to write.* As to the works of others, I must admit that there the damage is much less grave.

Furthermore, the conductor must resist the parsimonious custom, existing in certain theaters, of having the cymbals and the bass drum played by the same musician. The sound of these cymbals attached to the bass drum (the only way in which this economy is made possible) is only a vulgar noise fit for dance bands. Moreover, this custom leads mediocre composers into the habit of never using one of the two instruments alone and of considering it their sole purpose to stress the heavy beats very forcefully. This opinion caters to the predilection for vulgar noise and has brought upon us those ridiculous excesses which will sooner or later doom dramatic music unless a stop is put to them.

Finally, I must express my regret concerning the generally poor organization of rehearsals. Everywhere the system of mass rehearsals is retained for large vocal or orchestral works. All chorus singers as well as all instrumentalists are rehearsed together. Deplorable errors, innumerable mistakes, especially in inner voices, are the natural consequence—errors which neither the chorus master nor the orchestral conductor will notice. Once established, such errors grow into habits and become part and parcel of the performance.

The poor chorus singers receive the worst treatment of all with this type of rehearsal. They need an able *director,* who knows the correct tempi and is proficient in the art of singing, to beat the time and make critical observations; furthermore, they require a *good pianist,* playing from a *well-arranged* piano score on a *good* piano; and finally a good *violinist* to play in unison or in the octave with the voices as they study each part individually. Instead of these three indispensable artists they are given—at two-thirds of the European opera houses—a single instructor, a man who usually knows as little of conducting as of singing, who has scarcely any musical education and who is selected from among the worst pianists to be found, or who perhaps cannot play the piano at all; a pitiable invalid who, sitting before a battered and untuned instrument, tries to decipher a confused score which he does not know, plays false chords (minor instead of major and vice versa) and—under the pretext of conducting and accompanying at the same time—teaches the singers a wrong rhythm with his right hand and a wrong intonation with his left one.

One is carried back into the middle ages when he has to witness such an exhibition of barbarism for the sake of economy.

I firmly believe that a faithful, spirited and enthusiastic performance of a modern work, even by outstanding artists, can be achieved only by sectional rehearsals. Each choral part must be studied individually until the necessary security is reached; only then should it be rehearsed together with the other parts. One should proceed in the same fashion in rehearsing symphonies, if they are at all complicated. First the violins should be rehearsed alone, then the violas and basses, then the wood-winds (with a small group of strings to fill out the rests and to accustom the wind instruments to their cues); likewise the brass alone; sometimes it is even necessary to rehearse the percussion instruments by themselves; finally the harps—if they are numerous. The general rehearsals are then far more profitable and much faster, and one is assured of a fidelity of execution only too rare nowadays.

The performances obtained by the old method of rehearsing are never more than approximations of correct interpretations. Yet the conductor puts down his baton, after ruining another masterpiece, with a smile of satisfaction. Should he, nevertheless, feel some slight doubt whether he has fulfilled his task satisfactorily—and who can verify whether he has?—he murmurs to himself: "What of it? *Vae victis*!"

ROBERT SCHUMANN

About Conducting

AND ESPECIALLY ABOUT
THE MANIA OF CONDUCTING

One of the peculiarities of our age is the desire to do away with obsolete abuses which have become second nature through habit dating back to the dim past. But, conversely, there are indulgences and habits which in recent times have become abuses; among these I place overconducting at musical performances, and particularly the mania of conducting.

Conducting, leaving aside any effect of the conductor's personality, remains a distraction for the listener, and can

ROBERT SCHUMANN: Born in Germany in 1810; died there in 1856. He was equally active and highly regarded as a composer and a writer on music. Although he held positions as a conductor, he was not as successful in this as in his other activities.

only be condoned as a necessary evil. But should cases arise when this necessary evil is not necessary then one should not force such buffoonery upon the public. Nevertheless the evil occurs, as the author has repeatedly witnessed, now more than ever, even with many good orchestras, and often in a striking manner. The principal reason for this lies, I believe, in the vanity and self-importance of the conductors who do not want to relinquish the baton, partly to be constantly before the audience, partly to hide the fact that a competent orchestra can acquit itself well without their leadership.

A good orchestra—and only such a one is meant here—needs to be conducted in symphonies, overtures, and such only at the start and at changes in tempo. For the rest, the conductor can quietly stand on the podium, following the score and waiting until his direction is again required. In slow, drawn-out tempi, largo, adagio, etc., continued time-beating is no doubt helpful to keep the orchestra playing efficiently. But it must not become an affected, distorted conducting: striking loudly at forte, less loudly at piano, or scowling at the culprit when a mistake is made. All this belongs, at most, to rehearsals but not before the audience.

One must, in any event, differentiate between rehearsal and performance. At rehearsal each musician must matter-of-factly work toward technical perfection in order to free the work of art from its mechanics. But if it has survived this ordeal and stands ready, artistically realized and without flaws, then the conductor should stop playing the fool and let the listener enjoy the music quietly.

To the virtuoso conducting can only be a disturbance. Should it nevertheless impose itself in solo works with accompaniment, then either the soloist is not sure of his ground, or the orchestra is unable to accompany by itself. If both are good, the conductor becomes an iron hand clamped between them. In such a situation the orchestra pays little attention to the soloist and accompanies its conductor, thereby overlooking all fine nuances; it fails to adapt itself to the soloist and is an independent body, a state within a state.

Things are different with singing. The singer can never sufficiently dominate the orchestra. He cannot, like the instrumentalist, emphasize single notes to bring out the strong beats. Most compositions are quite free in their flow, and singers often disturb the strict tempo because of elocution or frequent cadenzas. In choral passages, and particularly in the recitatives, when everything should move with precision, a conductor is most necessary. Indeed, nowhere do greater errors occur than in recitatives; there one usually sees an exertion, a toiling, an effort without equal, and still it does not click. Many things might well be due to a misunderstanding of the director's signs, but the trouble is that signs are given which the orchestra cannot obey punctiliously; for instance, the gesture cutting off a changing tempo. A line in the air is not a single point, and thus cannot be obeyed instantly.

The job on the podium is a difficult one because the conductor of an orchestra is not a foreman who directs the machine or determines its movement, but is actually the embodiment of the composition. What the composer felt vitally and created out of his inner self must be recognized by the director, who can only achieve understanding through vast knowledge. The spiritual greatness of music cannot be apprehended solely by learning the figured bass, or by studying and serving an apprenticeship, but also by diligent study of every science connected with music.

Who would deny that the high esteem which orchestra

members have for the scholarly knowledge of its director does not mightily contribute to the electric effect of a performance. Is it not then as if the spirit of the composition projected from the podium upon the orchestra? And, conversely, an uninspired conductor can, in spite of the most military of methods, achieve at best a mechanical brilliance. The orchestra should not be a mechanism which plays its tones like a clock but the individual emotion of each participant should attach itself to the spirit of the composition. It is not the playing of forte and piano which renders the spirit of the composition but the conception and execution of it as a work of art.

The post on the podium is also delicate because every motion of the conductor is exposed to the public's eye. If the gestures are merely affected, distorted, or unnecessary then the individual occupying the conductor's stand is irksome. What is the audience to do with all the noise, foot stamping, head shaking, grimaces, angry looks at those who err, the violent motion of hands and feet, etc.? None of this belongs to the public. Not only does such nonsense distract the audience from giving due regard to the composition, it puts the orchestra in a particularly bad light, in line with a generally accepted principle: the less an orchestra is led the higher its standing; or, the more an orchestra has to be led the lower the level of its attainment.

FRANZ LISZT

Letter on Conducting

TO RICHARD POHL IN DRESDEN.[8]

In various accounts that I have read of the Festival at Carlsruhe, there is one point on which people seem pretty much agreed—namely, the *insufficiency* of my conducting. I will not examine here what degree of *foregone judgment* there may be in this opinion, or even seek to know how much it has been influenced by the simple fact of the choice of myself as conductor. It certainly would not be for me to raise pretensions quite contrary to the assertion which

FRANZ LISZT: Born in Hungary in 1811; died in Bayreuth in 1886. One of the great virtuoso pianists of all time, he was an innovator as a composer and much beloved as a person for his generosity and help to other musicians.

seeks to establish my insufficiency if this assertion were based on facts or on justice. But this is precisely what I cannot help contesting in a very positive manner.

As a *fact* one cannot deny that the *ensemble* of the Carlsruhe programme was very remarkably performed, that the proportion and sonority of the instruments, combined with a view to the *locale* chosen, were satisfactory and even excellent. This is rather naïvely acknowledged in the remark that it is really surprising that things should have gone so well "*in spite of*" the insufficiency of my conducting. I am far from wishing to deck myself in the peacock's feathers of the Carlsruhe, Mannheim, and Darmstadt orchestras, and am assuredly more disposed than anyone to render full justice to the talents—some of them very distinguished—of the members of these three orchestras; but, to come to the point, whatever may be said to the contrary, it is acknowledged, even by the testimony of my adversaries, that the execution was at times astonishing, and altogether better *than there had been reason to expect,* considering that I was conductor.

This *fact* placed beyond discussion, it remains to be seen whether I am so completely a stranger there as they try to make out, and what reasons there can be for thus crying down a conductor when the execution was satisfactory, especially if, as is just, one bears in mind the novelty of the works on the programme for almost the entire audience. For, as everyone knew at Carlsruhe, the *Ninth Symphony*, as well as the works of Wagner, Berlioz, Schumann, etc., were not well known by anyone but myself, seeing that they had never been given before in these parts (with the exception of the Berlioz piece, which a *portion* only of the Carlsruhe orchestra had played under the direction of the composer).

Now as regards the question of *right*—to know whether

in good conscience and with knowledge of the matter one can justly accuse me of being an insufficient conductor, inexperienced, uncertain, etc.: without endeavouring to exculpate myself (for which I do not think there is any need amongst those who understand me), may I be permitted to make an observation bearing on the basis of the question?

The works for which I openly confess my admiration and predilection are for the most part amongst those which conductors more or less renowned (especially the so-called "*tüchtigen* Capellmeister"*) have honoured but little, or not at all, with their personal sympathies, so much so that it has rarely happened that they have performed them. These works, reckoning from those which are commonly described nowadays as belonging to Beethoven's *last style* (and which were, not long ago, with lack of reverence, explained by Beethoven's deafness and mental derangement!)—these works, to my thinking, exact from executants and orchestras a *progress* which is being accomplished at this moment—but which is far from being realized in all places—in accentuation, in rhythm, in the manner of phrasing and declaiming certain passages, and of distributing light and shade—in a word, *progress* in the style of the execution itself. They establish, between the musicians of the desks and the *musician chief* who directs them, a link of a nature other than that which is cemented by an imperturbable beating of the time. In many cases even the rough, literal maintenance of the time and of each continuous bar | 1, 2, 3, 4, | 1, 2, 3, 4, | clashes with the sense and expression. There, as elsewhere, *the letter killeth the spirit,* a thing to which I will never subscribe, however specious in their hypocritical impartiality may be the attacks to which I am exposed.

*Qualified conductors.

For the works of Beethoven, Berlioz, Wagner, etc., I see less than elsewhere what advantage there could be (which by-the-bye I shall contest pretty knowingly elsewhere) in a conductor trying to go through his work like a sort of *wind-mill,* and to get into a great perspiration in order to give warmth to the others. Especially where it is a question of understanding and feeling, of impressing oneself with intelligence, of kindling hearts with a sort of communion of the beautiful, the grand, and the true in Art and Poetry, the *sufficiency* and the old routine of usual conductors no longer *suffice,* and are even contrary to the dignity and the sublime liberty of the art. Thus, with all due deference to my complaisant critics, I shall hold myself on every occasion ulterior to my "insufficiency" on principle and by conviction, for I will never accommodate myself to the rôle of a "*Profoss*"* of time, for which my twenty-five years of experience, study, and sincere passion for Art would not at all fit me.

Whatever esteem, therefore, I may profess for many of my colleagues, and however gladly I may recognize the good services they have rendered and continue to render to Art, I do not think myself on that account obliged to follow their example in every particular—neither in the choice of works to be performed, nor in the manner of conceiving and conducting them. I think I have already said to you that the real task of a conductor, according to my opinion, consists in making himself *ostensibly quasi*-useless. We are pilots, and not mechanics. Well, even if this idea should meet with still further opposition in detail, I could not change it, as I consider it just. For the Weymar orchestra its application has brought about excellent results, which have been commended

*Overseer or gaoler.

by some of my very critics of today. I will therefore continue, without discouragement or false modesty, to serve Art in the best way that I understand it—which, I hope, will be the best.

Let us then accept the challenge which is thrown to us in the form of an extinguisher, without trouble or anxiety, and let us persevere, conscious of right—and of our future.

RICHARD WAGNER

About Conducting

Looking back upon my earliest youth I remember having had unpleasant impressions from performances of classical orchestral music. At the piano, or while reading a score, certain things appeared animated and expressive, whereas they could hardly be recognized at a performance, and failed to attract attention. I was puzzled by the apparent flabbiness of Mozartian melody (*cantilena*) which I had been taught to regard as so delicately expressive. Later in life I discovered the reasons for this, and I have discussed them in my report on a "German music school to be established at Munich."[9]

RICHARD WAGNER: Born in Leipzig in 1813; died in Venice in 1883. One of the towering geniuses, his operas are among the most important and influential in music. He was also a great conductor, especially of Beethoven, and wrote innumerable articles and books.

Assuredly, the reasons lie in the lack of a proper Conservatory of German music in which the traditions of the classical masters' own style of execution are preserved in practice. Of course, this would imply that the masters should, at least once, have a chance to personally supervise performances of their works there. Unfortunately German culture has missed all such opportunities, and if we now wish to become acquainted with the spirit of a classical composer's music, we must rely on this or that conductor, and upon his notion of what may or may not be the proper tempo and style of execution.

In the days of my youth orchestral pieces at the celebrated Leipzig Gewandhaus Concerts were not conducted at all; they were simply played through under the leadership of Conzertmeister Mathai, like overtures and entr'actes at a theatre. At least there was no "disturbing individuality" in the shape of a conductor! The principal classical pieces which presented no particular technical difficulties were regularly given every winter; the execution was smooth and precise; and the members of the orchestra evidently enjoyed the annual return of their familiar favorites.

BEETHOVEN'S NINTH SYMPHONY

Only with Beethoven's *Ninth Symphony* could they not get on, though it was considered a point of honor to give that work every year. I had copied the score for myself, and made a pianoforte arrangement for two hands; but I was so much astonished at the utterly confused and bewildering effect of the Gewandhaus performance that I lost courage, and gave up the study of Beethoven for some time. Later, I found it instructive to note how I came to take true delight in performances of Mozart's instrumental works. It was when I had a chance to conduct them myself, and when I could indulge my feelings as to the expressive rendering of Mozart's *cantilena.*

I received a good lesson in Paris in 1839, when I heard the orchestra of the Conservatoire rehearse the enigmatic *Ninth Symphony.* The scales fell from my eyes; I came to understand the value of correct execution and the secret of good performance. The orchestra had learned to recognize Beethoven's melody in every bar—that melody which had escaped the worthy Leipzig musicians. And the orchestra sang that melody. This was the secret.

Habeneck, who solved the difficulty, and to whom the great credit for this performance is due, was not a conductor of special genius. While rehearsing the symphony, during an entire winter season, he had felt it to be incomprehensible and ineffective (would German conductors have confessed as much?), but he persisted throughout a second and a third season until Beethoven's new melos* was understood and correctly rendered by each member of the orchestra. Habeneck was a conductor of the old stamp; he was the master and everyone obeyed him. I cannot attempt to describe the beauty of this performance. However, to give an idea of it, I will select a passage by the aid of which I shall try to show the reason why Beethoven is so difficult to render, as well as the reason for the indifferent success of German orchestras when confronted by such difficulties. Even with first-class orchestras I have never been able to get the passage in the first movement performed with such perfection as I then (thirty years ago) heard it played by the musicians of the Paris Conservatoire Orchestra.[10] In later life I often recalled this passage, containing both motion and sustained tone, together with the principle of dynamics. It clarified for me the essentials of orchestral music. The masterly execution of this passage:

*Melody in all its aspects.

by the Paris orchestra consisted in their playing it exactly as it is written. Neither in Dresden, nor in London[11] when, in later years, I had occasion to prepare a performance of the symphony, did I succeed in making the changes of bow and strings unnoticeable. Still less could I suppress an involuntary accentuation as the passage ascends. Musicians, as a rule, are tempted to play an ascending passage with an increase of tone and a descending one with a decrease. With the fourth bar of the above passage we invariably got into a crescendo so that the sustained G flat of the fifth bar was given with an involuntary yet vehement accent, enough to spoil the peculiar tonal significance of that note. The composer's intention is clearly indicated, but it remains difficult to prove to a less refined listener that there is a great gap between the usual reading and the reading meant by the composer. No doubt both readings convey a sense of dissatisfaction, unrest, and longing, but the true sense of the passage cannot be conveyed unless it is played as the master imagined it, and as I have not hitherto heard it performed except by the Parisian musicians in 1839. I remember that the impression of dynamic monotony (if I may risk such an apparently senseless expression for a phenomenon difficult to describe) together with the unusually varied and ever irregular movement of intervals in the ascending figure entering on the prolonged G flat (to be sung with infinite delicacy, to which the G natural answers with equal delicacy) initiated me, as by magic, to the incomparable mystery of the spirit. Keeping my later practical experience in view, I can ask how the musicians of Paris arrived at so perfect a solution of the difficult problem. By the most conscientious diligence. They were not content with mutual admiration and congratulation, nor did they assume that difficulties must disappear before them as a matter of course. French musicians in the main belong to the Italian school; its influence upon them has been beneficial inasmuch as they have been taught to approach music mainly through the medium of the human voice. The French idea of playing an instrument well is to be able to sing well upon it. And that superb orchestra sang the symphony. The possibility of its being well sung implies that the true tempo had been found, and this is the second point which impressed me at the time. Old Habeneck was not the medium of any abstract aesthetical inspiration. He was devoid of "genius," but he found the right tempo while persistently fixing the attention of his orchestra upon the melos of the symphony.

The right comprehension of the melos is the sole guide to the right tempo; these two things are inseparable. The one implies and qualifies the other.

The conductor's choice of tempo will show whether he understands the piece or not. With good players the true tempo induces correct phrasing and expression, and, conversely, with a conductor an idea of appropriate phrasing and expression will induce the conception of the true tempo.

I am persistently returning to the question of tempo because this is the point at which it becomes evident whether a conductor understands his business or not.

Obviously the proper pace of a piece of music is determined by the particular character of the interpretation it requires. In order to determine the former, we must decide on the latter, and establish whether the sustained tone, the vocal element, the *cantilena,* or the rhythmical movement predominates. The conductor should lead accordingly.

The Adagio stands to the Allegro as the sustained tone stands to the figuration. The sustained tone regulates the Tempo Adagio; here the rhythm is, as it were, dissolved in self-sufficient, pure tone. In a certain delicate sense it may be said of the pure Adagio that it cannot be taken too slowly. A rapt confidence in the sufficiency of pure musical speech should reign here; the languor of feeling grows to ecstasy. That which in the Allegro was expressed by changes of figuration is now conveyed by means of variously inflected tone. Thus the least change of harmony may call forth a sense of surprise; and again, the most remote harmonic progressions prove acceptable to our expectant feelings.

None of our conductors is courageous enough to take an Adagio in this manner; they always begin by looking for some bit of figuration, and arrange their tempo to match. I am perhaps the only conductor who has ventured to take the Adagio section of the third movement of the *Ninth Symphony* at the pace proper to its peculiar character. This character is distinctly contrasted with that of the alternating Andante in three-quarter time, but our conductors invariably contrive to obliterate the difference, leaving only the rhythmical change between four-quarter and three-quarter time. In the section in twelve-eight time this movement (assuredly one of the most instructive in the present context) offers a conspicuous example of the breaking up of the pure Adagio by the more marked rhythms of an independent accompaniment, during which the *cantilena* is steadily and broadly continued. In this section we may recognize a fixed and consolidated reflection of the Adagio's tendency towards infinite expansion. There, limitless freedom in the expression of sound, with fluctuating yet delicately regulated movement; here, the firm rhythm of the figurated accompaniments imposing the new regulation of a steady and distinct pace. When the movement is fully developed we have arrived at the law that regulates the movement of the Allegro.

We have seen that sustained tone with its modifications is the basis of all musical execution. Similarly the Adagio, developed, as Beethoven has developed it in the third movement of his *Ninth Symphony,* may be taken as the basis of all regulations of musical time. In a certain delicate sense the Allegro may be regarded as the final result of a modification of the pure Adagio character by the more restless moving figuration. On careful examination of the principal motives of the Allegro, it will be found that the predominating melody derives from the Adagio. The most important Allegro movements of Beethoven are ruled by a predominant melody which exhibits some of the characteristics of the Adagio, and in this wise Beethoven's Allegros receive the emotional sentimental significance which distinguishes them from the earlier naive species of Allegro. However, Beethoven's:[12]

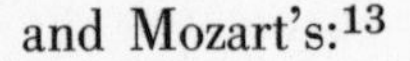
and Mozart's:[13]

or:

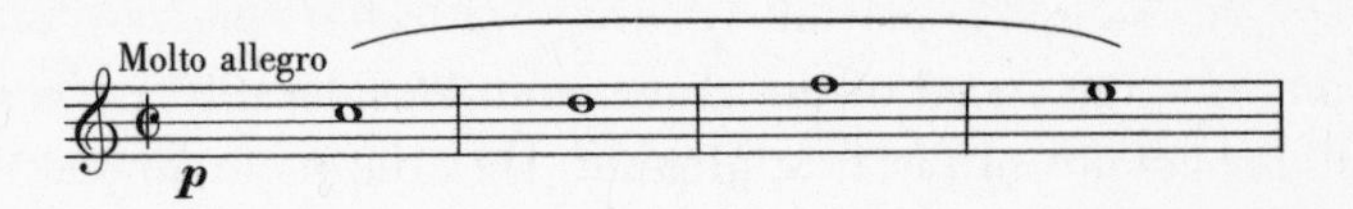

are not far apart. And with Mozart, as with Beethoven, the exclusive character of the Allegro is only felt when the figuration gets the upper hand of the melody; that is, when the reaction of the rhythmical movement against the sustained tone is entirely carried out. This is particularly the case in those final movements which have grown out of the Rondo form; the Finales to Mozart's *Symphony in E flat*, and to Beethoven's in A, are excellent examples. Here the purely rhythmical movement, so to speak, celebrates; it is consequently impossible to take these movements too quickly. But whatever lies between these two extremes is subject to the laws of mutual relationship and interdependence. Such laws cannot be too delicately and variously applied, for they are fundamentally identical with the laws which modify all conceivable nuances of the sustained tone.

BEETHOVEN'S EIGHTH SYMPHONY

The tendency to hurry is so characteristic of our entire musical life that I propose to enter into some details with regard to it. I have often been astonished at the singularly slight sense for tempo and execution evinced by leading musicians. I found it impossible, for instance, to communicate to Mendelssohn what I felt to be a perverse piece of negligence with regard to the tempo of the third movement in Beethoven's *Symphony in F Major, No. 8.* This is one of the instances I have chosen out of many to throw light upon certain dubious aspects of music.

We know that Haydn in his principal later symphonies

used the form of the Menuet as a refreshing transition between the Adagio and final Allegro, and that he thus was able to increase the speed of the movement considerably, contrary to the character of the true Menuet. He even incorporated the *Ländler** for this purpose, particularly in the Trio—so that, with regard to the tempo, the designation *Menuetto* is hardly appropriate, and was retained for conventional reasons only. Nevertheless, I believe Haydn's Menuets are generally taken too quickly; undoubtedly the Menuets of Mozart's symphonies are. This will be felt very distinctly if, for instance, the Menuetto in Mozart's *Symphony in G Minor,* and still more that of his *Symphony in C Major,* are played a little more slowly than is customary. It will be found that the latter Menuet, which is usually hurried and treated almost as a Presto, will now show a graceful, festive character. Otherwise the trio, with its delicately sustained motive:

will be reduced to a meaningless jumble. Now Beethoven, as is not uncommon with him, meant to write a true Menuet in his F major symphony; he places it between the two main Allegro movements as a sort of complementary antithesis to an Allegretto Scherzando which precedes it, and, to remove any doubt as to his intentions regarding the tempo, he designates it not as a *Menuetto,* but as a Tempo di Menuetto.

This novel and unconventional characterization of the two middle movements of a symphony was almost entirely overlooked. The Allegretto Scherzando was taken to represent the

*A South German country dance in 3/4 time from which the modern waltz is derived.

usual Andante, the Tempo di Menuetto the familiar "Scherzo," and, as the two movements thus interpreted seemed rather paltry, and none of the usual effects could be gotten with them, our musicians came to regard the entire symphony as a sort of accidental hors d'oeuvre of Beethoven's muse—who, after the exertions with the A major symphony, had chosen "to take things rather easily." Accordingly, after the Allegretto Scherzando, which is invariably somewhat dragged, the Tempo di Menuetto is universally served up as a refreshing Ländler, which passes the ear without leaving any distinct impression. Generally, however, one is glad when the tortures of the Trio are over. This loveliest of idylls is turned into a veritable monstrosity by the passage in triplets for the violoncello; which, if taken at the usual quick pace, is the despair of violoncellists, who are worried by the hasty staccato across the strings and back again, and find it impossible to produce anything but a painful series of scratches. Naturally, this difficulty disappears as soon as the delicate melody of the horns and clarinets is taken at the proper tempo; these instruments can thus cope with their special difficulties which at times render the clarinet likely to produce a "quack" even in the hands of a skillful player. I remember an occasion when all the musicians began to breathe easily on my taking this piece at the true moderate pace. Then the humorous *sforzato* of the basses and bassoons:

at once became intelligible, the short *crescendi* became clear, the delicate *pianissimo* close was effective, and the gentle gravity of the returning principal movement was properly felt.

We have now reached an important and decisive point, an appreciation of which is indispensable if we want to arrive at a satisfactory conclusion regarding the execution of classical music, now so often spoiled by bad habits and carelessly performed. A bad habit can be seemingly correct, since a style of execution has come into being which to an extent agrees with the wrong tempi. The real evil is thus hidden for those who are partial to the abuse, but any change in tempo makes the evil apparent enough, and the false execution becomes quite unbearable.

To illustrate this, in the simplest possible way, let us take the opening of the C Minor Symphony:

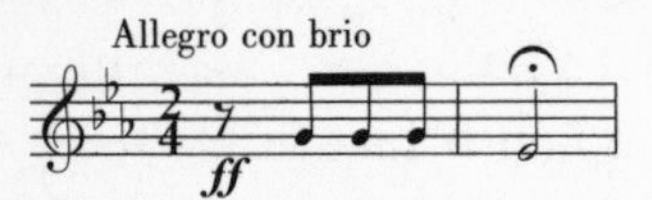

Usually the *fermata* of the second bar is left after a slight rest; our conductors hardly make use of this *fermata* for anything else than to fix the attention of their men upon the attack on the figure in the third bar. In most cases the note E flat is not held any longer than a forte produced with a careless stroke of the bow will last upon the stringed instruments. Now, suppose the voice of Beethoven were heard from the grave admonishing a conductor: "Hold my *fermata* firmly, unyieldingly! I did not write *fermatas* in jest, or because I did not know how to proceed; I indulge in the fullest, the most sustained tone to express emotions in my Adagio; and I use this full and firm tone in a passionate Allegro when I want it as a rapturous or terrible spasm. Then the very life-blood of the tone shall be extracted to its last drop. I arrest the waves of the sea and make its depths visible; I stem the clouds, disperse the mist, and display the pure blue ether and the glorious eye of the sun. For this I put *fermatas,* sudden long-sustained notes, in my Allegro. And now look at my clear thematic intention with the sustained E flat after the three stormy notes, and understand what I meant to say with other such sustained notes." Suppose a conductor were suddenly to ask that an orchestra hold the *fermata* as here described—what would be the result? A miserable failure. After the initial power of the bow of the stringed instruments had been wasted, the tone would become increasingly thinner, ending in a weak and timid *piano:* for—and here is one of the results of indifferent conducting—our orchestras nowadays hardly know what is meant by equally sustained tone. Let any conductor ask any orchestral instrument, no matter which, for a full and prolonged forte, and he will find the player puzzled, and will be astonished at the trouble it takes to get what he asks.

Yet powerful and fully sustained tone is the basis for all dynamics, with the voice as with the orchestra; the many possible modifications of a tone's power, which constitute one of the principal elements of musical expression, rest upon it.

MODIFICATION OF TEMPO

I shall now turn to the question of the modification of tempo; a subject about which our conductors know nothing and for which they consequently profess contempt. Whoever has followed me so far with attention will, I trust, understand that this question goes to the root of the matter before us.

In the course of the argument so far, two species of Allegro have been mentioned; a sentimental character has been assigned to the second, the true Beethovian Allegro, as distinguished from the older Mozartian Allegro, which has a naïve character. I have adopted the expressions "sentimental" and "naïve" from Schiller's well-known essay upon "sentimental and naïve poetry."

It is needless to discuss the aesthetic problems Schiller touches upon. It is enough to state here that I consider Mozart's quick Alla-breve movements as representative of the naive Allegro. The Allegros of the overtures to his operas, particularly to *Figaro* and *Don Giovanni,* are the most perfect specimens. It is well known that Mozart wished these pieces to be played as fast as possible. Having driven his musicians into a sort of rage, so that to their own surprise they successfully rendered the unheard-of Presto of his overture to *Figaro,* he commended them, saying: "That was beautiful! Let us take it still quicker this evening." Quite right. As I have said of the pure Adagio, that in an ideal sense it cannot be taken too slowly, so this pure unmixed Allegro cannot be played too quickly.

The slow emanations of pure tone, on the one hand, and the most rapid figurated movement, on the other, are subject to ideal limits only, and in both the law of beauty is the sole measure of what is possible. This law determines for both extremes (totally restrained and totally unfettered figurated movement) the point at which the desire for taking in the opposite becomes a necessity. It is therefore thoroughly fitting that the order of movements in the symphonies of our masters should lead from Allegro to Adagio, and then by means of a stricter dance form (Menuet or Scherzo) to the most rapid final Allegro. To my mind, however, there are signs of a deterioration of the sense of fitness when composers exhibit their platitudes in the Suite, and attempt to bolster up that old form, with its less thoughtfully arranged succession of typical dance tunes. For these have been fully developed elsewhere and have already been embodied in far richer, more extensive, and complex forms.

What particularly allows us to recognize Mozart's absolute Allegros as members of the naive species is, first, their dynamics, the simple changes of forte and piano, then, their formal structure, the random juxtaposition of certain rhythmic-melodic forms suitable to the *piano* or *forte* execution. In the use of these completely stabilized forms (as in the bustling, ever-returning semicadences) the master shows an astonishing ease. But all such things—even the greatest negligence in the use of commonplace phrases and sections—are explained precisely by the nature of this sort of Allegro, which is not meant to interest by means of *cantilena,* but in which the restless movement is intended to produce a certain intoxication. It is a significant trait in the Allegro of the overture to *Don Giovanni* that this restless movement ends with an unmistakable turn toward the "sentimental." Here—where the extremes meet at the point of contact described above—it becomes necessary to modify the tempo in the bars leading from the overture to the first tempo of the opera (which is also an Alla-breve but a slower one)—and the pace must be slackened accordingly. But our conductors, in their customary crude way, generally miss this point in the overture. We need not, however, be led into premature reflections. Let us merely acknowledge that the character of the older, classical or, as I call it, naive Allegro differs infinitely from the new, sentimental Allegro peculiar to Beethoven. Mozart became acquainted with the orchestral *crescendo* and *diminuendo* at Mannheim, when the orchestra there had acquired it as a novelty. Up to that time, the instrumentation of the old masters shows that as a rule nothing was inserted between the *forte* and *piano* sections of the Allegro movements which were intended to be played with emotional expression.

BEETHOVEN'S THIRD SYMPHONY

Now, how does the true Beethovian Allegro appear with regard to this? To take the boldest and most inspired example of Beethoven's unheard-of innovation in this direction, let us consider the first movement of his *Eroïca.* How does this movement appear if played in the strict tempo of one of the Allegros of Mozart's overtures? But do our conductors ever dream of taking it otherwise? Do they not always proceed monotonously from the first bar to the last? With the members of the "elegant" tribe of Capellmeisters the "conception" of the tempo consists of an application of the Mendelssohnian maxim *"chi va presto va sano."*

Let the players who happen to have any regard for proper execution make the best of it in passages like this:

or these plaintive measures:

The conductors do not trouble their minds about such details; they are on "classic ground," and will not stop for trifles. They prefer to progress rapidly, with *grande vitesse.*

I shall now attempt to describe what I conceive to be the right way of performing Beethoven, and music akin to his. This subject seems inexhaustible, and I shall confine myself to a few salient points.

One of the principal musical forms consists of a series of variations upon a theme. Haydn, and eventually Beethoven, have improved this form, and rendered it artistically significant by the originality of their devices, and particularly by connecting the single variations one with the other and establishing relations of mutual dependence among them. This is accomplished with the happiest results in cases where one variation is developed from another—that is to say, when a degree of movement suggested in the one is carried further in the other, or when a certain satisfactory sense of surprise is occasioned by one variation supplying a complementary form of movement, which was wanting in the one before it. The real weakness of the variation form, however, becomes apparent when strongly contrasting parts are placed in juxtaposition, without any link to connect them. Beethoven often contrives to convert this same weakness into a source of strength; and he manages to do so in a manner which excludes all sense of accident or of awkwardness: namely—at the point which I have described as marking the limits of the laws of beauty with regard to the sustained tone (in the Adagio), and the unfettered movement (in the Allegro)—he contrives to satisfy, in a seemingly abrupt way, the extreme longing after an antithesis. The antithesis, by means of a different and contrasting movement, is now made to serve as a relief. This can be observed in the master's greatest works. The last movement of the *Sinfonia Eroïca,* for instance, affords excellent instruction in this respect; it should be understood as a movement consisting of a greatly expanded series of variations; and accordingly it should be interpreted with as much variety as possible. To do this properly here, as in all similar cases, the above-mentioned weakness of the variation form, and the disadvantage which is felt to result from it, must be taken into account. Single and separate variations are frequently seen to have had an independent origin, and to have merely been strung together in a conventional manner. The unpleasant effects of such careless juxtaposition are particularly felt in cases where a quiet and sustained theme is followed by an exceptionally lively variation.

In the foregoing investigations I hope I have elucidated the problem of the modification of tempo, and showed how a discerning mind will recognize and solve the difficulties inherent in modern classical music. Beethoven has furnished the immortal type of what I call sentimental music. It unites all the separate and peculiar constituents of the earlier essentially naïve types; sustained and interrupted tone, *cantilena,* and figurations are no longer kept formally apart—the manifold changes in a series of variations are not merely strung together but are now brought into immediate contact and made to merge imperceptibly into each other. Assuredly, the novel and diversely combined material of a symphonic movement must be set in motion in an appropriate manner if the whole is not to appear as a monstrosity. I remember in my young days to have heard older musicians make very dubious remarks about the *Eroïca.* Dionys Weber, at Prague, simply treated it as an absurdity. The man was right in his way; he chose to recognize nothing but the Mozartian Allegro; and he taught his pupils at the Conservatorium to play the *Eroïca* in the strict tempo peculiar to that Allegro. The result was that those who heard it could not help agreeing with him. Yet everywhere else the work was thus played, and it is still so played to this day! True, the symphony is now received with universal acclaim; but, if we are not to laugh at the whole thing, the real reasons for its success must be due to the study of Beethoven's music apart from the concerthall—particularly at the piano—where its irresistible power is fully felt, though in a rather roundabout way. If fate had not furnished such a path of safety, and if our noblest music depended solely upon the conductors, it would have perished long ago.

WEBER'S FREISCHÜTZ AND OBERON

To support so astounding an assertion I will take a popular example: Has not every German heard the overture to *Der Freischütz* over and over again? I have been told of sundry persons who were surprised to find how frequently they had listened to this wonderful musical poem without being shocked when it was rendered in the most trivial manner; these persons were among the audience of a concert given at Vienna in 1864, when I was invited to conduct the overture. At the rehearsal it came to pass that the orchestra of the Imperial Opera (certainly one of the finest orchestras in existence) was surprised at my demands regarding the execution of this piece. It appeared at once that the Adagio of the introduction had habitually been taken as a pleasant Andante in the tempo of the "*Alphorn,*"[14] or some such comfortable composition. That this was not "Viennese tradition" only but had come to be the universal practice, I had already learned at Dresden—where Weber himself had conducted his work. When I had a chance to conduct *Der Freischütz* at Dresden—eighteen years after Weber's death—I ventured to set aside the slovenly manner of execution which had prevailed under Reissiger, my senior colleague. I simply took the tempo of the introduction to the overture as I felt it; whereupon a veteran member of the orchestra, the old violoncellist Dotzauer, turned towards me and said seriously: "Yes, this is the way Weber himself took it; I now hear it again correctly for the first time." Weber's widow, who still resided at Dresden, became touchingly solicitous for my continuing success as Capellmeister. She trusted that my sympathy with her deceased husband's music would bring about correct performances of his works for which she had no longer dared to hope. The recollection of this flattering testimony has frequently cheered and encouraged me. At Vienna I was bold enough to insist upon a proper performance. The orchestra actually studied the too-well-known overture anew. Discreetly led by R. Lewi, the cornists entirely changed the tone of the soft woodnotes in the introduction, which they had been accustomed to play as a pompous show piece. The magic perfume of the melody for the horns was now shed over the *Pianissimo* indicated in the score for the strings. Once only (also as indicated) the power of their tone rose to a *mezzoforte* and was then gradually lost again without the customary *sforzando*, in the delicately inflected passage:

The violoncellos similarly reduced the usual heavy accent on:

which was now heard above the tremolo of the violins like the delicate sigh it is intended to be, and which finally gave to the *fortissimo* that follows the *crescendo* that air of desperation which properly belongs to it.

Having restored the mysterious dignity of the introductory Adagio I allowed the wild movement of the Allegro to run its passionate course, without regard to the quieter expression which the soft second theme demands; for I knew that I should be able sufficiently to slacken the pace at the right moment, so that the proper motion for this theme might be reached.

Evidently the greater number, if not all, of modern Allegro movements consist of a combination of two essentially different parts. In contrast with the older naïve unmixed Allegro the construction is enriched by the combination of the pure Allegro with the thematic peculiarities of the vocal Adagio in all its gradations. The second theme of the overture to *Oberon:*

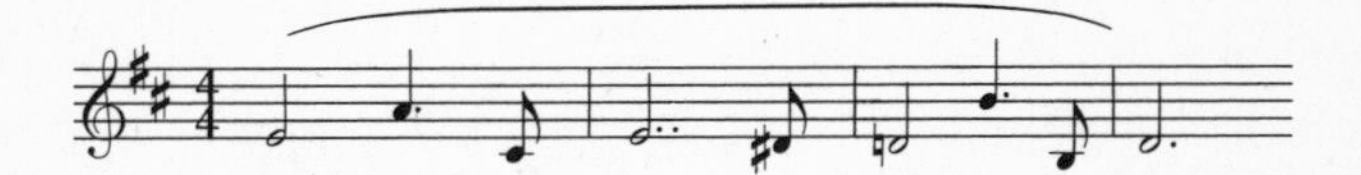

which does not in the least partake of the character of the Allegro, very clearly shows this contrasted peculiarity. Technically, the composer naturally merged the contrasting character of this theme into the general character of the piece. That is to say: on the surface the theme reads smoothly according to the scheme of the Allegro; but as soon as its true character is brought out it becomes apparent to what extent it must be capable of modification, if the composer can consider it suited to both main characteristics.

To continue the account of the performance of the *Freischütz* overture at Vienna: after the extreme excitement of the Tempo Allegro, I made use of the long-drawn notes of the clarinet—the character of which is quite like that of the Adagio:

to imperceptibly hold back the tempo here where the figurated movement is dissolved into sustained or tremulous tone, so that, in spite of the connecting figure:

which renews the motion, and so beautifully leads to the *cantilena* in E flat, we arrived at the very slight nuance of the main tempo, which had been kept up all along. I arranged with the excellent instrumentalists that they were to play this theme:

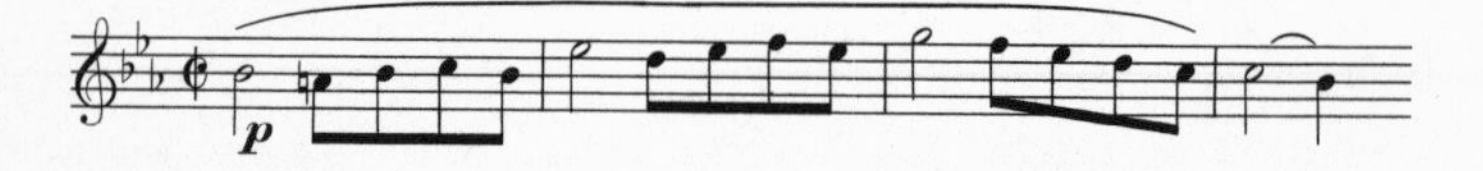

legato, and with an equable *piano*, i.e. without the customary commonplace accentuation and *not* as follows:

The good result was at once apparent, so that for the gradual reanimation of the tempo with the pulsating:

I had only to give the slightest indication of the pace to find the orchestra perfectly ready for the reappearance of the energetic nuance of the main tempo with the succeeding fortissimo. It was not so easy, on the return of the conflict between the two strongly contrasted motives, to bring them out clearly without disturbing the proper feeling for the predominant rate of speed. Here, when the despairing energy of the Allegro is concentrated in successively shorter periods, and culminates in:

the success of the ever-present modification of tempo was perhaps shown best of all.

After the splendidly sustained C major chords, and the significant long pauses by which these chords are so well relieved, the musicians were greatly surprised when I asked them to play the second theme, which is now raised to a joyous chant, not in the violently excited nuance of the first Allegro theme as they had been accustomed, but in the milder modification of the main theme.

This worrying and driving to death of the principal theme at the close of a piece is a habit common to all our orchestras. Very frequently nothing is wanting but the sound of the great horsewhip to complete the resemblance to a concert at a circus. No doubt increase of speed at the close of an overture is frequently demanded by composers; it is a matter of course in those cases where the true Allegro theme, as it were, remains in possession of the field, and finally celebrates its apotheosis. Beethoven's great overture to *Leonora* is a famous example. In this composition, however, the effect of the increased speed of the Allegro is frequently spoiled by the conductor, who does not know how to modify the main tempo to meet the various requirements of the thematic combinations (e.g., at the proper moment to relax the rate of speed), having already permitted the main tempo to grow so quick as to exclude the possibility of any further increase—unless, indeed, the strings choose to risk an abnormal rush, such as I remember hearing with astonishment, though not with satisfaction, from this same Viennese orchestra. The necessity for such an eccentric exertion arose because the main tempo had been hurried too much during the progress of the piece; the final result was simply an exaggeration—and, moreover, a risk to which no true work of art should be exposed—though in a rough way it may be able to bear it.

However, it is difficult to understand why the close of the *Freischütz* overture should be thus hurried and worried by Germans, who are supposed to possess some delicacy of feeling. Perhaps the blunder will appear less inexplicable if it is remembered that the second *cantilena*, which toward the close is treated as a chant of joy, was, at its very first appearance, already made to trot on at the pace of the principal Allegro, like a pretty captive girl tied to the tail of a hussar's charger. It would seem a case of simple practical justice that she would eventually be raised to the charger's back when the wicked rider has fallen off, at which, finally, the Capellmeister is delighted and proceeds to apply the great whip.

As I have related, a number of Viennese amateurs who attended my performance of this poor maltreated overture heard it rendered in a very different manner. The effect of that performance is still felt at Vienna. People asserted that they could hardly recognize the piece and wanted to know what I had done to it. They could not conceive how the novel and surprising effect at the close had been produced, and scarcely credited my assertion that a moderate tempo was the sole cause. The musicians in the orchestra, however, might have divulged a little secret, namely this: in the fourth bar of the powerful and brilliant entrance:

I interpreted the sign >, which in the score might be mistaken for a timid and senseless accent, as a mark of diminuendo ⸻ assuredly in accordance with the composer's intentions. Thus we reached a more moderate degree of force, and the opening bars of the theme:

were at once distinguished by a softer inflection which I now could easily permit to swell to *fortissimo;* and thus the warm and tender motive, gorgeously supported by the full orchestra, appeared happy and glorified.

Our Capellmeisters are not particularly pleased at a success such as this.

Herr Dessoff, however, whose business it was afterwards to conduct *Der Freischütz* at the Viennese opera, thought it advisable to leave the members of the orchestra undisturbed in the possession of the new reading. He announced this to them with a smile, saying: "Well, gentlemen, let us take the overture à la Wagner!

Yes, Yes: à la Wagner! I believe there would be no harm in taking a good many other things à la Wagner."

FELIX WEINGARTNER

About Conducting

Under the same title as that of the present volume, Richard Wagner published in 1869 his well-known *brochure*[15], which, assailing as it did with uncompromising candor the most famous conductors of that epoch, drew upon him the furious enmity of the persons he attacked. In spite, however, of the hatred, open or concealed, of the music-popes whose infallibility was assailed, Wagner's book laid the foundation for a new understanding of the function of the conductor, in whom we now recognise not only the external factor that holds

FELIX WEINGARTNER: Born in Dalmatia in 1863; died in Winterthur in 1942. Though primarily known as a conductor he also composed operas, symphonies, and smaller works, and a number of books and essays. He was Gustav Mahler's successor at the Vienna Hofoper in 1908.

together an orchestral, choral or operatic performance, but above all the spiritualizing internal factor that gives the performance its very soul. Wagner was certainly not the first to realise how much depends on the way a piece of music is rendered. He opines that the reason Bach rarely marked tempi in his scores was because he said to himself, as it were, "If anyone does not understand my theme and my figuration, has no feeling for their character and their expression, of what use will an Italian tempo-indication be to him?" I maintain, on the contrary, that the vigorous old master would have been incapable of looking at art in this resigned way. I believe rather that he so rarely indicated the tempo or gave any dynamic marks only because he always had in view his own presence at the performances. If we picture to ourselves a Bach performance in his own lifetime we must think of himself at the organ with his little band of musicians round him. How many of his innumerable cantatas, now assured of immortality, must in his own day have been sung just once, on the Feast-day for which they were composed, whereupon the manuscript went into the drawer "with the others," and for the next Feast-day the inexhaustible Cantor wrote a new one! His Suites and Concertos, again, are to be regarded as chamber-music works at whose production he himself or a privileged pupil sat at the clavicembalo; the *Well Tempered Clavier* and the Sonatas were intended as studies. Why should he waste time in noting down instructions for execution? It always rested with him to give the correct tempo, and to explain to the musicians the interpretation he wanted. The mighty teacher of the Thomas-School certainly never anticipated a collected edition of his works, in preparing which the editors were often greatly puzzled by the careless figuring of the bass—which again shows that he knew the execution of the *continuo*[16] to be in trusty hands; nor did he anticipate concert productions of them with large orchestras and choruses.

How much Mozart considered the question of interpretation is to be seen in the careful way he has marked his works (especially his latest), and from many passages in his letters. It is not improbable that in Mannheim he heard for the first time an orchestra that could really play *crescendo* and *diminuendo.* Even our best orchestras of to-day need to be constantly told that the increase and decrease of tone is to be done evenly and gradually, not suddenly; and the difficulty of doing this increases with the number of bars over which these variations in volume have to be extended. "*Diminuendo* signifies *forte, crescendo* signifies *piano,*" said Bülow. This is only a seeming contradiction, since to play *forte* at the beginning of a *crescendo,* and *piano* at the beginning of a *diminuendo,* really means the negation of *crescendo* and *diminuendo.* We know that not only Mozart, but Weber, Mendelssohn and Spohr were excellent conductors, and that each of them, from his own artistic standpoint, fought energetically against abuses and errors of taste. How Wagner did this is shown among other things in the book of his I have mentioned. This, however, with all its perfect outspokenness, seems quite mild when we read the flaming words with which Berlioz opens his treatise on "The theory of the art of conducting."*

What experiences Berlioz must have had for this wild cry to be drawn from him can be estimated from the single fact that a conductor who in the first half of the nineteenth century occupied a really foremost position, and of whom both Wagner and Berlioz spoke with the warmest acknowledgement, —that Habeneck of Paris, as Berlioz tells us, conducted not

*Page 22 of this volume.

from the score but from *a violin part,* a custom today confined to beer-garden concerts with their waltzes and pot-pourris. Yet Habeneck, by means of diligent rehearsals with the orchestra of the Conservatoire, must have given performances of a technical perfection that as a rule could not be met with in Germany at the same time; Wagner confesses that it was from Habeneck's rendering that he first really understood Beethoven's *Ninth Symphony,* after having received at the Leipzig Gewandhaus such confused impressions of it that for a time he "had his doubts" even about Beethoven himself. Like so many things in Wagner's writings, these "doubts" must not be taken literally, for a musician of his rank must have been able to judge from his knowledge of the score—of which indeed he had made a manuscript copy for himself—how much of the confused impression was due to the work and how much to the rendering. The fact remains, however, that a bad interpretation can not only completely deceive the uninstructed but also prevent the instructed from listening with full sympathy.

When Wagner, after his first Parisian sojourn, came to Dresden as conductor, he had learned from Habeneck to what perfection orchestral performances can attain under conscientious guidance; and from all we have learned of him as conductor, from himself and from others, he obviously aimed in his own performances not only at correctness but at bringing out that to which the sounds and notes are only the *means.* He sought for the unifying thread, the psychological line, the revelation of which suddenly transforms, as if by magic, a more or less indefinite sound-picture into a beautifully shaped, heart-moving vision, making people ask themselves in astonishment how it is that this work, which they had long thought they knew, should have all at once become quite an-

Felix Weingartner

other thing, and the unprejudiced mind joyfully confesses, "Yes, thus, *thus,* must it really be." Out of the garment of tone there emerges the *spirit of the artwork;* its noble countenance, formerly only confusedly visible, is now unveiled, and enraptures those who are privileged to behold it. Wagner calls this form, this quintessence, this spirit of the artwork its *melos,* which term, later on, was perverted by inability to understand Wagner's own creations into "endless melody." His desire to make this *melos* stand out clearly carried him so far that in some places in Beethoven's works where he held the evident purpose of the composer to be not fully realized in the orchestration—whether because the instruments at Beethoven's disposal were imperfect, or because his increasing deafness sometimes clouded his perception of the relations of the various orchestral timbres—he discreetly altered the orchestration, touching it up so as to bring the hitherto unclear melody into due prominence. Of course the music-popes and wretched literalists screamed anathema. It is certainly open to question whether all these retouchings were happy and deserving of imitation; there is no doubt, however, that he very often hit upon the right thing. I believe, for example, that nowadays no conductor who can think at all will play the *Ninth Symphony* without Wagner's instrumental emendations; the vocal changes, on the contrary, I look upon as both purposeless and tasteless.[17]

Added to this desire for clarity in Wagner was the passionate temperament with which, aided by a keen understanding, he threw himself into his work; he brought to it also a faculty of *immediate communication* with the players and imposition of his will on them—in a word that genius which, in spite of other acknowledgments, he had to deny to Habeneck, but which made some of his own performances historically memorable, in spite of the perishable nature of all reproductive art. *There is no performance of genius possible without temperament.* This truth must be perpetually insisted on, notwithstanding that Schopenhauer has voiced it distinctly enough. Temperament, however, can be given neither by education, nor conscientiousness, nor, by the way, by favor; it must be *inborn,* the free gift of nature. Therefore performances of genius can only receive recognition either by another genius—just as the height and beauty of a mountain are best appreciated from another summit—or by that naïve instinct, often found among non-artists and the people, that gives itself up spontaneously to the beautiful.

I regret that I never saw Wagner conduct. He was described to me; the body, of no more than middle-height, with its stiff deportment, the movement of the arms not immoderately great or sweeping, but decisive and very much to the point; showing no restlessness, in spite of his vivacity; usually not needing the score at the concert; fixing his expressive glance on the players and ruling the orchestra imperially, like the Weber he used to admire as a boy. The old flautist Fürstenau of Dresden told me that often, when Wagner conducted, the players had no sense of being led. Each believed himself to be following freely his own feeling, yet they all worked together wonderfully. It was Wagner's mighty will that powerfully but unperceived had overborne their single wills, so that each thought himself free, while in reality he only followed the leader, whose artistic force lived and worked in him. "Everything went so easily and beautifully that it was the height of enjoyment," said Fürstenau; and the eyes of the old artist gleamed with joyful enthusiasm.

After Wagner had given up regular conducting he sought to transfer his feeling, his insight and his power to some younger, plastic spirits in whom they might live on. His plan of an ideal school, where singers and conductors of the type he desired should be trained,[18] was not realized owing to the indolence of his contemporaries. A few young musicians associated themselves with him, to whom he now imparted of his spirit. Of these, the oldest is the most significant—his intimate friend, at that time his most faithful champion, his *alter ego,* as he himself once called him—the master-conductor Hans von Bülow. After a comparatively short co-operation they had to part company, and Bülow's star first shone brilliantly again when in 1880 he became chief of the Meiningen orchestra. A year later the Duke, whose scenic art had already effectively influenced the dramatic theatre, sent him off with the orchestra on a grand concert-tour through Germany, Austria and Russia. Seldom has such a victory of mind over matter been seen. A rather poorly appointed orchestra, by no means absolutely excellent in its proportions, conquered everywhere the large orchestras, famous the whole world over as possessing the best artists; this was the work of the eminent conductor, who—a second Leonidas—had the courage to defy with a small troop of admirably schooled players the big musical armies that were mostly led by ordinary timebeaters. By dint of diligent, indefatigable practice he had so infused into the orchestra his own conception of the works as to get a perfection of *ensemble* at that time unknown. The most scrupulous rhythmical exactitude was united with so artistic a balance of the various timbres, that the question whether this or that player was the better, or whether this or that peculiarity of the conductor was justifiable, could scarcely be raised. The orchestra seemed to be a single instrument, on which Bülow played as on a pianoforte.

These concert-tours of the Meiningen orchestra were of

inestimable significance. Those whom it concerned recognised that it would not do to go on simply beating time and playing away with the old reprehensible carelessness and thoughtlessness, for that would certainly lower them in the eyes of the public, which, after once having nibbled dainties at the table of the great, would no longer be content with canteen-fare. So these people first of all took pains to cultivate the orchestra better on the technical side, held more rehearsals, followed more conscientiously the dynamic indications, and in general gave more attention to accurate *ensemble.* The capability of orchestras has since then greatly increased, and composers to-day can set problems that even a few years ago would have seemed insoluble, while at the same time a better rendering of the works of the old masters has been made possible. These things represent the *gain* from Bülow's work, and make his name an ineradicable landmark in the evolution of the art of conducting; to him alone, after those great composers who themselves were notable conductors, we owe the diffusion and the strengthening of the consciousness that conducting is an art and not a handicraft.

But Bülow's work also had its harmful features, for which the guilt lies both with himself and a number of his followers; and to expose these and attack them is as much a duty of sincerity as to acknowledge the gains with frank delight. In the first place, it cannot be denied that even while he was leader of the Meiningen orchestra there was often to be detected a *pedagogic element* in Bülow's renderings. It was clearly seen that he wished to deal a blow on the one side at philistine, metronomic time-beating, on the other side at a certain elegant off-handedness. Where a modification of the tempo was necessary to get expressive phrasing, it happened that in order to make this modification quite clear to his hearers he *exaggerated* it; indeed, he fell into a quite new tempo that was a negation of the main one. The *Egmont Overture* was a case in point. Wagner tells us,[19] *à propos* of this motive:

—which, as he says, "is so drastic an epitome of terrific earnestness and placid self-confidence," and which, as a rule, "was tossed about like a withered leaf in the uncontrollable rush of the *allegro*"—that he induced Bülow to play it in the true sense of the composer, modifying "ever so little" the hitherto passionate tempo, "so that the orchestra might have a proper chance to accentuate his dual theme, with its rapid fluctuation between great energy and thoughtful self-content." All who have heard this overture under Bülow must agree with me that at the place in question he by no means made "ever so little" a modification, but leaped at once from the *allegro* into an *andante grave*, thereby destroying the uniform tempo that should be preserved in the *allegro* of the overture, as in general in every piece of music that has a uniform tempo-mark at the beginning. The proper expression can be obtained *without* any change of the main tempo—be it "ever so little"—if the strings, who have the first two bars of the theme, are told to bring them out energetically and very precisely by a uniform down-bowing of the crotchets, thus preventing the last quaver of the first bar from being turned, as often happens, into a semiquaver, whereby indeed, as Wagner says, the effect of a dance-step is given; and when we consider that the tempo of the main part of the overture is just *allegro*, not *vivace,* there can be no danger of an "uncontrollable allegro-rush" if the tempo is correct. It is a common source of trouble that introductions are taken very slowly and the main sections very fast, and the numerous gradations of these broad tempo-differences scarcely observed. We often hear the beginning of the *Seventh Symphony* taken *adagio,* whereas it is marked *poco sostenuto;* the finale of the *Fourth Symphony* is usually taken *presto,* whereas the humor of the movement only comes out when attention is given to Beethoven's marking, which is "*allegro ma non tanto*". The introduction to the *Egmont Overture* is marked *sostenuto, ma non troppo,* which does not at all signify an actually slow tempo; while the next section is marked *allegro,* that only increases to *allegro con brio* at the end—which again, however, does not imply an immoderately rapid tempo. The maintenance of an essentially easy tempo just suits the tragic weight of the work, that is completely destroyed by hurrying. The only way I can express the distinction between the introduction (that should be taken with three moderate beats), and the main portion, is that one bar of 3/4 section is about equivalent to a minim, and so to a third of a bar in the 3/2 section, whereby the crotchets at the entry of the *allegro* do not become about half what they are in the introduction. In this way any *ritenuto* at the place in question is superfluous, and the "terrific earnestness" of the:

and the "calm self-confidence" of the two following bars are made perfectly clear.

Wagner quite rightly contended against the scherzo-tempo in which it had become usual to take the third movement of the *Eighth Symphony*, and claimed that it should go in comfortable menuet-time. Under Bülow, however, I heard this movement played so slowly that its humorous cheerfulness was replaced by an almost disagreeable seriousness.

It certainly belies the titanic character of the *Coriolan Overture* when, as usually happens, the chief theme:

and all that follows it are taken in a flying *presto* instead of *allegro con brio;* but Bülow began it almost *andante* and then increased the tempo until the pause in the seventh bar, to begin again *andante* and accelerate the sequence in the same way. In the first place, taking the incredibly characteristic theme in this way robs it of its monumental strength; in the second place, I hold that if Beethoven had wanted these subtleties he would have indicated them, since he always gave his directions for performance with the greatest precision.

Bülow's *purpose* as such was always clearly recognizable and also quite correct. It was as if he said to his audience, and more especially to the players: "This extremely significant passage in the *Egmont Overture* must not be scrambled through thoughtlessly; the comfortable, easy-going menuet of the *Eighth Symphony* must not be turned into a scherzo; the main theme of the *Coriolan Overture* must be given out in a way conformable to the dignity of the work." But in the effort to be excessively clear he often went too far. His quondam hearers and admirers will recollect that often when he had worked out a passage in an especially plastic form he turned round to the public, perhaps expecting to see some astonished faces, chiefly, however, to say, "See, that's how it should be done!" But if the Venus of Melos, for example, were suddenly to begin to speak, and to give us a lecture on the laws of her conformation, we should be a good deal sobered down. Art works and art performances exist only for the sake of themselves and their own beauty. If they pursue a "tendentious" aim, even though this should be instructive in the best sense, the bloom goes off them. From "tendencies" of this kind Bülow's interpretations were seldom quite free. Thence came also his proneness to make details excessively prominent. In an art work, indeed, no one part is of less significance than another, and *each* detail has its full *raison d'être,* but only in so far as it is subordinated to a homogeneous conception of the essential nature of the whole work—a continuous conception that dominates all detail.

It is this homogeneous conception of the essential nature of a musical work that constitutes what there is of specially artistic in its interpretation; it originates in a deep feeling that is not dependent on the intellect, that cannot, indeed, even be influenced by this, while it itself must dominate everything that pertains to the intellect—such as routine, technique, and calculation of effects. If this feeling is not strong enough, then the intellect usurps the foremost place and leads, as was often the case with Bülow, to a propensity to ingenious analysis. In the contrary case the feeling becomes unwholesomely powerful and leads to unclearness, false sentimentality and emotional vagueness. If neither feeling nor intellect is strong enough, then we get, according to the prevailing fashion, either mere metronomic time-beating or a senseless mania for *nuance,* a mania that chiefly prompted me to write this book. Neither, however, has anything to do with art, which is at its best when that exceedingly delicate balance—more a matter of intuition than of calculation—is attained between the feeling and the intellect, which alone can give a performance true vitality and veracity.

Here I must digress to contradict sharply an opinion that has considerable vogue. The interpreter—in our case the conductor—is *not* able to *increase* the worth of a work; he can merely diminish this occasionally, since the *best* that he can give is simply a rendering on a par with the real value of the work. He has done the best that is possible if his performance expresses just what the composer meant; anything more there is not and cannot be, since no conductor in the world can, by his interpretation, make a good work out of a bad one. What is bad remains bad, no matter how well it is played; indeed, a particularly good performance will bring out the defects of a work more clearly than an inferior one.

The pedagogic element I have referred to in Bülow's performances became more prominent in the last years of his life; it was linked with a capriciousness that was probably increased by his physical sufferings and his consequent spiritual distemper. This capriciousness led him into eccentricities that had no object, not even a pedagogic one, and that could have been thought fine only by those who, having quite lost the capacity for thinking for themselves, fell at Bülow's feet in blind idolatry, and pocketed his insults submissively when he now and then treated them as they deserved. Through his habit of making speeches at his concerts he committed such errors of taste that it was difficult to maintain unimpaired the feeling of esteem that could in the most heartfelt way be given to the earlier Bülow. It was sad to see the public rushing to his concerts with the question, "What will he be up to today?"

It almost goes without saying that the striking phenomenon of such a conductor as Hans von Bülow was bound to lead to imitations. A whole tribe of "little Bülows" sprang up, who copied the great Bülow in everything they could—his nervous movements, his imperial pose, his stabs with the baton, his furious glances at the audience when anything disturbed him, his half-instinctive, half-demonstrative look round at some special *nuance,* and finally the *nuances* themselves. His concert speeches alone no one dared to imitate. I have ventured to label this kind of conductor, whose manner was a more or less complete caricature of his master's, the "tempo-rubato conductor." Wagner speaks of "elegant" conductors, at the head of whom—whether with justice I rather doubt—he puts Mendelssohn—conductors who skip in the fastest possible tempo over passages that are difficult and at first sight obscure.[20] The tempo-rubato conductors were the exact opposite to these; they sought to make the clearest passages obscure by hunting out insignificant details. Now an inner part of minor importance would be given a significance that by no means belonged to it; now an accent that should have been just lightly marked came out in a sharp *sforzato;* often a so-called "breath-pause" would be inserted, particularly in the case of a *crescendo* immediately followed by a *piano,* as if the music were sprinkled with *fermate.* These little tricks were helped out by continual alterations and dislocations of the tempo. Where a gradual animation or a gentle and delicate slowing-off is required—often however without even that pretext—a violent, spasmodic *accelerando* or *ritenuto* was made.

I would here insert a rule, the observance of which I

hold to be indispensable for a right apprehension of the *limits* of tempo: No slow tempo must be so slow that the melody of the piece is *not yet* recognizable, and no fast tempo so fast that the melody is *no longer* recognizable.

The rhythmic distortions to which I have referred were in no way justified by any marks of the composer, but always originated with the conductor.

I would add the admonishment always to observe most precisely whether an accent comes in a *forte* or in a *piano* passage, which will determine quite different grades of strength and expression for it. It is also of the utmost importance whether a *succession* of accents occurs in a passage proceeding in uniform loudness, or during a *crescendo* or *diminuendo,* in which latter case the accents also must of course have their own gradual increase or decrease. Obvious as this may seem, it is necessary even with good orchestras to point out emphatically *where* the accents come, and so prevent their being continually hammered out in the one style.

If many of the above-mentioned errors could be supposed to be "proofs of ardour" and of good intention, it was in the end regrettable that by the behaviour, artistic and personal, of some "new-modish Bülows" so much attention was directed to the person of the conductor that the audience even came to regard the composers as the creatures, as it were, of their interpreters, and in conjunction with the name of a conductor people spoke of "his" Beethoven, "his" Brahms, or "his" Wagner.

The saddest part of the business was that the chief arena chosen for all these varieties and experiments was our glorious classical music, especially the holiest of all, that of Beethoven, since Bülow had acquired the reputation of a master-conductor of Beethoven, and his followers wanted to outbid him even there; though one would have thought that reverence—to say nothing of love—for this unique genius would have put all vain thoughts of this kind to flight.

To take only one example, how the C Minor Symphony has been tampered with! Already the gigantic opening has brought into being a whole crowd of readings, notably that according to which the first five bars (with the two *fermate*) are to be taken quite slowly. Even the "spirit of Beethoven" was cited to justify this misguided attempt at emendation, for which, however, not Beethoven's spirit but that of his first biographer, Schindler, is entirely responsible. Schindler, the key to whose character, I think, is sufficiently given by the fact that after the master's death he had visiting cards printed with the title "Ami de Beethoven," has told in his biography so many anecdotes whose untruth has been proved by Thayer, that we may unhesitatingly reckon among them the story that Beethoven wanted the opening of the C Minor Symphony to be taken *andante,* and the faster tempo to come only after the second *fermata.* Is there even a moderately satisfactory explanation why Beethoven, instead of specifying so extremely important a change of tempo, should have marked the passage *allegro con brio* when what he wanted was *andante?* Liszt's opinion on the point will be of interest. . . . He told me that the "ignorant" and furthermore "mischievous fellow" Schindler turned up one fine day at Mendelssohn's, and tried to persuade him that Beethoven wished the opening to be *andante*—pom, pom, pom, pom. "Mendelssohn, who was usually so amiable," said Liszt laughingly, "got so enraged that he threw Schindler out—pom, pom, pom, *pom!*" . . .

I need mention no names in order to point out that several conductors of importance have refused to have anything to do with these perversions of style. I may also say that my remarks refer for the most part to an epoch now somewhat removed from ours. When I published this book in 1895, my object was to try to show how much the art of conducting had developed up to then, since the time when Wagner had given it a new basis both by his deeds and his words. If on the one hand a decided progress could be noted —greater competence in the orchestra, a more perfect *ensemble,* more feeling for vital phrasing than hitherto, thanks to Bülow and some excellent conductors who had become great under Wagner's direct influence—on the other hand there was imminent danger that the vanity, egoism and caprice of younger conductors should make fashionable a style in which the masterpieces of music should be merely pegs on which to hang a conductor's own personal caprices. This is all the more dangerous as an audience with little artistic education may, in its astonishment, take the arbitrary for the genuine thing, and, its healthy feeling once perverted, always hanker after these unsound piquancies, so that finally it thinks the trickiest performance the best. Wagner's treatise combated the philistinism that suffocated every modification of tempo and therefore all vitality of phrasing in a rigid metronomism; my own book on the other hand combated the errors that had arisen through exaggeration of these modifications after the necessity for them had gradually come to be admitted. It was therefore no plagiarism of Wagner's, as was of course asserted, but its counterpart, or, if you will, its continuation in the spirit of our own day. If Wagner opened new paths, I believed it my duty to warn people against mistaking a senseless trampling of the grass for progress along new paths.

But when I saw that my conduct was looked upon merely as unprofessional and prompted by the desire for self-exaltation, that my right to enter into literature was denied, and that in the end, in spite of the rapid spread of my book, all I had fought for was wilfully ignored and I myself described as the worst of the tempo-rubato conductors, I consoled myself with Goethe's fine saying, that it more becomes the good man to do the right than to be concerned whether the right is realized. So in the first place I sought by conscientious self-education to remove from my own conducting everything that, externally and internally, might savor of false attempt to be a "genius," and laboured to become an ever more faithful interpreter of the masters by intimate comprehension of the peculiar style of each of them. I had the joy finally to succeed with what I had recognized as right. My taste must indeed have received thereby a powerful purification, which alienated me from many things I had thought significant, and drew me towards many things that I had misjudged. In the last few years I have heard very little. I sometimes see in the journals one of the younger conductors specially praised for his "simple" and "grand" readings, from which I conclude that the "tempo rubato" is not at such a premium as formerly, and that its unhealthy excrescences represent a fashion that is gradually dying out if not yet quite extinct. We know, however, that fashions may return, and so when a third edition of this book was called for, I felt that I ought not to shirk the trouble of a careful revision, and then send it out into the world once more.

There remain some special points for me to discuss—in the first place, conducting from memory.

This makes a great impression on the audience, but I do not place too high a value on it. In my opinion a conductor may really know a work by heart and yet fear that his memory may play him a trick, either through pardonable excitement or some other disturbing influence. In such cases it is always better to use the score; the audience is there to enjoy the work, not to admire the memory of the conductor. I recommend doing without the score only when knowledge of it is combined with such a mastery of oneself that reference to it is more a hindrance than a help, and the conductor, though he may read a page now and then, yet feels that to use the score throughout the whole work would be putting a needless fetter on himself. It is all a purely personal matter, however, that has nothing to do with the perfection of the performance. If the conductor is so dependent on the score that he can never take his eyes from it to look at the players, he is of course a mere time-beater, a bungler, with no pretension to the title of artist. Conducting from memory, however, that makes a parade of virtuosity is also inartistic, since it diverts attention from the work to the conductor. Now and then we see a conductor put a score on the stand *although* he conducts from memory, his object being not to attract too much attention—a proceeding that I think commendable. But I hold that it is entirely the conductor's own concern whether he will use the score or not. A good performance from the score has value; a bad one done from memory has none. For instrumental artists also, playing from memory is in my opinion a matter of quite secondary importance; it can be done by anyone who has a quick and reliable memory. But if a player has difficulty in learning by heart, it is better for him to devote his time to mastering the intellectual and technical structure of the piece and to play from a copy at the concert, than to be in continual dread of a lapse of memory and of having either to stop or to pad with something of his own, which means disfiguring the work. I have even heard Bülow, who had a remarkable memory, "improvising" in this way in his piano recitals. Here, as in so many other cases, it only needs someone with the courage to begin and the others will follow.

Bülow, in his witty way, divided conductors into those who have their heads in the score and those who have the score in their heads. I might distinguish them, perhaps rather more deeply, by means of the following antithesis—some conductors see only the notes, others see what is *behind* the notes. Then again there are conductors who destroy the unity of a work that is one and indivisible, and others who can shape the *apparently* fragmentary into a unity.

Some conductors are reproached with making too many gestures—not without reason, for the mechanical element in conducting is by no means beautiful in itself, and the black dress-coated figure with the baton-wielding arm can easily become ludicrous if the arm gesticulates wildly instead of leading the men, and the body also twists and curves in uncontrollable emotion. A pose of assumed quiet is however just as repellent. In our music there are, thank God, moments when the conductor must let himself go if he has any blood in his veins. An excess of movement is therefore always better than its opposite, since—at any rate as a rule—it indicates temperament, without which there is no art. We should not laugh at a talented young conductor whose vehemence prevents him bridling himself, but exhort him in a friendly way to keep his body quiet, and to train himself *not to make any more movements than are necessary*. The expression of each passage will then generate an appropriately great or small motion of the baton. A complete harmony between music and gesture will indeed only come with the years; but as a general thing it may be pointed out that short, quick motions ensure greater precision than very extensive ones, since in the time taken up by the latter the strictness of the rhythm may easily be deranged.

Some demands that I made at the time of the first publication of *this* book I still hold to be valid to-day, wherefore I repeat them here:

The conductor must before all things be sincere towards the work he is to produce, towards himself, and towards the public. He must not think, when he takes a score in hand, "What can I make out of this work?" but, "What has the composer wanted to say in it?"

He should know it so thoroughly that during the performance the score is merely a support for his memory, not a fetter on his thought.

If his study of a work has given him a conception of his own of it, he must reproduce this conception in its homogeneity, not cut up into pieces.

He must always bear in mind that the conductor is the most important, most responsible personality in the musical world. By good, stylistic performances he can educate the public and promote a general purification of artistic perception; by bad performances, that merely indulge his own vanity, he can only create an atmosphere unfavorable to genuine art.

To have given a fine performance of a fine work should be his greatest triumph, and the legitimate success of the composer his own.

RICHARD STRAUSS

Ten Golden Rules

FOR THE ALBUM OF A YOUNG CONDUCTOR

1. Remember that you are making music not to amuse yourself but to delight your audience.

2. You should not perspire when conducting: only the audience should get warm.

3. Conduct *Salome* and *Elektra* as if they were by Mendelssohn: Fairy Music.

4. Never look encouragingly at the brass, except with a short glance to give an important cue.

5. But never let the horns and woodwinds out of your sight: if you can hear them at all they are still too strong.

RICHARD STRAUSS: Born in Germany, 1864; died there in 1949. A leading composer (*Don Quixote, Rosenkavalier, Till Eulenspiegel, Salome*), he was a gifted conductor as well.

6. If you think that the brass is not blowing hard enough, tone it down another shade or two.

7. It is not enough that you yourself should hear every word the soloist sings—you know it off by heart anyway: the audience must be able to follow without effort. If they do not understand the words they will go to sleep.

8. Always accompany a singer in such a way that he can sing without effort.

9. When you think you have reached the limits of prestissimo, double the pace.

10. If you follow these rules carefully you will, with your fine gifts and your great accomplishments, always be the darling of your listeners.

On Conducting Classical Masterpieces

It is decisive for the technique of conducting that the shorter the movements of the arm, and the more confined to the wrist, then the more precise is the execution. If the arm is allowed to be involved in conducting—which results in a kind of lever-action the effects of which are incalculable—the orchestra is apt to be paralyzed and misdirected, unless it is determined from the start (and this is frequently the case with conductors whose down-beat is imprecise) to play according to its own judgment, in tacit agreement, as it were, without paying too much attention to the antics of the conductor.

The left hand has nothing to do with conducting. Its proper place is the waistcoat pocket from which it should only emerge to restrain or to make some minor gesture for which in any case a scarcely perceptible glance would suffice.

It is better to conduct with the ear instead of with the arm: the rest follows automatically.

In 50 years of practice I have discovered how unimportant it is to mark each crotchet or quaver. What is decisive is that the upbeat which contains the whole of the tempo which follows should be rhythmically exact and that the down-beat should be extremely precise. The second half of the bar is immaterial. I frequently conduct it like an *alla breve.*

It was Richard Wagner who demanded that conductors should grasp the fundamental tempo correctly, since this is all-important for the proper performance of a piece of music; especially in slow movements, he said, distinct bowing of, let us say, a melodic phrase consisting of eight bars was essential. A conductor who interprets aright the *adagio* theme of Beethoven's *Fourth Symphony* will never allow himself to be led by the rhythmical figure accompanying the first bar into chopping this fine melody up into quavers. Always conduct periods, never scan bars.

At a music festival in the Rhineland 80 years ago Franz Liszt, when conducting the last movement of Schubert's C Major symphony, adapted his beat to the period, i.e., he only used a down-beat once in every four bars. The poor orchestra, unused as it was to the ways of genius, was at a loss how to squeeze in its triplets and concluded that this was no conductor. Second-rate conductors are frequently inclined to pay too much attention to the elaboration of rhythmic detail, thus overlooking the proper impressive rendering of the phrase as a whole and the insinuating lilt of the melody as a whole, which should always be grasped by the listener as a uniform structure. Any modification of tempo made necessary by the character of a phrase should be carried out imperceptibly so that the unity of tempo remains intact.

We have no authentic metronome figures for the works of our classical masters. Only our music critics seem to have received authentic information on this point straight from the Elysian Fields.

It is probable that the pulse of the present generation beats faster than it did in the age of the post-chaise. This is proved by the fact that the younger generation of today and the Latin peoples rebel against Richard Wagner's 'longueurs,' obviously incapable of making themselves at home in the emotional and spiritual atmosphere of an earlier age.

Richard Wagner once wrote that Mozart's allegros 'should be played as fast as possible.' Quite, but not *twice as fast* as possible. The *Figaro* overture, the two great finales, *Cosi fan tutte,* Act 1, *Figaro,* Act 2, are usually played far too fast.

The following tempi should not be exceeded:

Cosi fan tutte finale: metr. 𝅗𝅥 = 136 (D major)
Figaro finale: metr. 𝅗𝅥 = 128 (E flat major)

Let us not forget that Wagner, with his 'longueurs,' could not in 1850 in his worst delirium have meant 'as fast as possible' to denote the insane tempi we hear today. That good old conductor Franz Lachner, whom it is a little unfair to remember as a pedant, once remarked quite correctly to my father: 'In fast movements, when conductor and orchestra have become all too excited, the conductor's art consists in guessing with accuracy the point at which the mad rush can be stopped either by gradual slowing down to the *tempo primo* or even by a well-motivated sudden retardation.' There is such a movement in the D major passage in the finale of *Cosi fan tutte.* There must be a restrained entry of the dominant after the two sustained notes. I myself have known so-called geniuses of the baton to rush headlong into these Beethoven and Mozart finales as if their horse had shied and was pulling the reins. I would also mention in connection with this the finale of Beethoven's B flat major symphony which is always played far too fast and should be a comfortable allegretto: *Heiter* does not mean a speed record!

Just before exciting moments or dramatic outbursts (second movement of the *Fourth* and *Fifth Symphonies*) Beethoven frequently interposes almost playful 'pianoforte passages,' as a man might mechanically and apparently apathetically tap the table with his fingers at times of high nervous tension. These passages should accordingly be played quite loosely, thus the final cadence in the adagio of the B flat major symphony.

The slackening of pace just before a great *fortissimo* is, for all its popularity, quite unbearable. This is just as amateurish as the drawing out of loud brass passages (e.g., the E-flat major in the Funeral March of *Götterdämmerung*) or the energetic up-beats. Subjects which the composer himself has drawn out should not be drawn out further (e.g., the woodwind passage in the *Third Leonore* overture just before the prestissimo). Dreadful also in the wonderful overtures by C. M. v. Weber are the *ritardandi* in the bars leading to the second subject—especially abominable is the sentimental slowing-down of the cello passage in the *Euryanthe* overture, and the cheap *ritardando* in that vivacious melody:

and especially of the subsidiary subject in A major of the *Oberon* overture which offends entirely against the style of these virtuoso pieces.

The *Tannhäuser* overture usually offers an example of the false broadening of coda phrases. Keep up the presto to the end without any slowing-down. This also applies to the overture of *The Flying Dutchman.* There must be no slowing-down in the trombones before the last *meno mosso* which must be strictly in tempo without *ritardando* (and not too slowly at that).

MOZART

In Mozart we must distinguish between (usually fast) pieces which present a lively pattern of sound—in these the *cantabile* subsidiary subject should generally be taken a little more quietly (*Figaro* overture, first movement of the G minor symphony)—and (usually slow) movements in which the play of the emotions is frequently carried to heights of passion, e.g., the *andante* of the *Sinfonia Concertante* for violin and viola, a passage which can only be achieved (like so many of Mozart's slow movements) with extremes of rubato. With the exception of Beethoven there is hardly a composer whose tempi are more mistreated or who requires so much delicacy in this respect.

Special rules: *Andante* or *Adagio* 𝄵 to be carefully observed: Introduction of *Don Giovanni* overture, *Andante con moto,* a fairly lively tempo: Cherubino's second aria. No change in tempo in the second half of Zerlina's two arias, above all no allegro, the first half therefore to be taken comparatively fast. This applies also to the duet 'Reich mir die Hand, mein Leben.' The slow movements of the last three great symphonies (G minor, E flat major, C major) should be interpreted and if possible conducted in crotchets; I usually slow down in the last concluding passage (as also in the andante of Schubert's great C major symphony and in Beethoven's *First Symphony*). In some very quick movements it is advisable to relieve the tautness of concentration by slowing down a little at the end. The final fugue of the *Jupiter* symphony and the finale of Brahms's *Second Symphony* are cases in question. Mozart's final fugue belongs to the category of movements which Wagner wished to be taken 'as fast as possible': at the beginning of the second part after the development and at the beginning of the third part I retard strongly. In order to allow the fugue to retain a distinct shape at *presto* speed it is necessary to reduce the volume of brass and timpani, and these reductions should be clearly marked in the score. Mahler made the first violins in the first *Figaro* duet play staccato. I made them play cantando, half legato.

During a rehearsal of *Il Seraglio* in the 'nineties in the Munich Residenztheater, Cosima Wagner said to me, 'Your first violins don't sing enough.' In Mozart and in his symphonic opera orchestra the first violins should always 'lead' and should never be allowed to lapse into an expressionless 'soft accompaniment,' which in Mozart is usually mistaken for 'orchestral discretion.' Almost invariably in performances of Mozart's operas the sustained middle parts of the woodwind and the high horns in A and G are too loud, thus drowning the quick parlando of the singers. It is therefore impossible to mark too many *pianissimos* in these woodwind parts, which should, moreover, be observed. The symphonic texture of the string quartet must not be obscured or bungled, since the singer must not only be accompanied but also supported. Mozart writes *ff* on rare occasions only, and only on very rare occasions should his *f* be treated roughly. Beauty of sound is the most important factor here. In Haydn's and Mozart's symphonic works the *forte* passages are subconsciously conceived as *tutti* in the manner of the *concerti grossi,* in which the passages played piano by the solo instruments alternate almost automatically with *forte* passages repeated by the whole orchestra.

In Mozart and Haydn these *forte-tutti* are, as it were, architectonic pillars framing emotional passages, the *fortes* with their natural trumpets, horns and timpani are therefore more the expression of a heightened enjoyment of life than are Beethoven's, whose trumpet octaves and timpani *sforzatos* represent explosions of wildest despair and of defiant energy, only rarely mitigated by the use of the darker and softer trombone. The trumpets, horns, and timpani in the Commendatore's scene in *Don Giovanni* are Beethovenesque; this is far more incisive without trombones which should not therefore be used in this scene. One should also differentiate carefully between *sfz* in Mozart and in Beethoven, and between *sfz* in a *piano* and in a *forte* passage.

Producers of opera usually make the mistake nowadays of translating each particular orchestral phrase into terms of a movement on the stage. In this matter one should proceed with a maximum of caution and good taste. There is no objection to bringing life into the production by changes of position and new nuances of acting during repetitive passages of music, especially in arias. Preludes of one or two bars frequently, and especially in Mozart, clearly express some gesture on the stage. But each trill on the flute does not represent a wink of the prima donna, nor every delayed chord on the strings a step or a gesture. Whole passages, especially in the finales, are pure concert music and are best left undisturbed by 'play-acting.'

But the worst thing of all is if in *The Magic Flute* the sets are made to clash stylistically with the work especially by the use of lavishly modernized décor. Such new décor, properly speaking, would involve rewriting the libretto in the 'modern' style and re-orchestrating in the style of the *Götterdämmerung.*

HANS VON BÜLOW AS AN INTERPRETER OF BEETHOVEN

The exactitude of his phrasing, his intellectual penetration of the score combined with almost pedantic observation of the latter, his analyses of the period structure and above all, his understanding of the psychological content of Beethoven symphonies and of Wagner's preludes in particular have been a shining example to me to this day, although I myself have at times modified his incisive dissection of some movements—e.g., of the first movement of the *Eroïca*—and although I endeavor to achieve a greater uniformity of tempo. I found particularly memorable the rigid slow tempo he used in the *Coriolan* overture, the slow beginning of various scherzi (*Eroïca:* bridge passage leading to the funeral march; *Ninth Symphony:* the great working up to the *fortissimo furioso*). Thus he took the three repetitions of the scherzo of the *Seventh Symphony* a little faster each time, not reaching full *prestissimo* until the third time. He started the finale of the A major symphony like a peasants' dance with minor modifications, but took the coda as a tremendously exciting *stretta*.

The only thing he did not correct was the tempo of the *Egmont* overture, which should not be faster than the first movement of the *Eroïca,* if only to judge by the indications of speed. It was left to me to bring out the mood of depression and obstinacy implicit in this tragic piece. The wrong tempo would seem to have originated with Mendelssohn. The decisive factor for the fundamental tempo is the second subject of staccato crotchets which Bülow recognized correctly but played too slowly as compared with the first subject (contrast between Klärchen's tragic fate and Egmont's levity). This is immediately followed in the A flat major development by the Klärchen episode.

In the sixth volume of his letters, page 54, Bülow mentions that Wagner had conducted the *presto* of the *Third Leonore* overture *poco a poco accelerando*—'lest the *presto* rush too impetuously into the climax'—I consider:

to be better, stronger, and more Beethovenesque, and maintain that the whole passage is built on the C major tonic and not the dominant. Nor should it ever degenerate into a mad rush. I effect the real final *accelerando* only four bars before the *ff*. In the whole passage it would be important to stress clearly the rising scale of the respective lowest notes. This is therefore to be rehearsed as carefully as possible.

TWO OVERTURES

Freischütz. I do not agree with Richard Wagner that the great final C major of triumphant innocence should be played entirely piano; this is too much against Weber's intention. But Wagner is quite right; the *fortissimo* brass is too brutal for this beautiful poetical melody. For this reason I make the strings play their melody *forte,* all the brass accompanying piano, and only when I come to the high A do I let the strings play *fortissimo* and the brass *forte.*

Third Leonore: people constantly overlook the fact that the transition in the first *allegro* passage to the E major cadence should be kept *piano* for four bars:

until *forte* is really marked in the score. It is a bad mistake to slow down the last bar in the development before the entry of the trumpet on the stage.

On the contrary, this whole passage is to be played *accelerando:* after all, Pizarro, as he rushes at Leonore, knows nothing of the B flat of the trumpet. It is further a serious blunder to allow the whole of the woodwind passage before the last *presto* to slow down. If the composer himself draws a theme out, the conductor should not slow it down further. Bülow and I maintain throughout the full tempo of hopeful expectation. I am inclined, if anything, to accelerate so that the violin passage enters in the main tempo—not as a mad rush—and only accelerates four bars before the *fortissimo.* Above all, the melodic line must be brought out with the greatest clarity. These things should be obvious to anybody who can read a score—but what is obvious nowadays?

Die Meistersinger: Ever since it has been dubbed 'opera comedy' after the Wagnerian 'longueurs' of the other operas, people have taken to conducting this wonderful work like an operetta, doing the greatest possible violence to the style of the opera. Alexander Ritter once explained to me that each act of a Wagner opera has a uniform symphonic tempo, violent divergencies from which are admissible only in rare (dramatically motivated) exceptions. Thus the score of *Die Meistersinger* stresses the uniformity of the fundamental tempo practically every time a new tempo is introduced by means of signs like 𝅗𝅥 = ♩ of previous tempo, and correlates the various parts clearly one to another.

Metr. 𝅗𝅥 = 56–60: The main tempo indication especially of *Die Meistersinger:* very moderate—moderate, moderately fast—characterises exactly the fundamental note: Cultured bourgeois comfort and contentment, fundamental decency, Hans Sachs towering above it all—superiority involves restraint!—interrupted only by the passionate utterances of the lovers and the malicious outbursts of Beckmesser. But even these must be brought into some sort of connection with the fundamental tone of the opera and must never be allowed to assume the proportions of Tristan's passion.

Overture: Very moderate *allegro,* a slight modification in the last bar before the entry of the flute—but the whole of this small episode should be kept within the character of the fundamental tempo and should not be allowed to relapse into an *adagio* and into endless *ritardandi* before the violin passage. The centre movement in E major has the following legend: Main tempo as in the passionate whispers of the love duet. Even the Beckmesser episode (E flat major) is inscribed 'Mässiges Hauptzeitmass.' Beware of taking the chorale which follows too slowly. The scene between Evchen and Walter should be taken with minor modifications to suit the words. It is usually taken far too fast so that the hurried dialogue becomes obscure.

The ensemble passage of the masters, 'Das heisst ein Wort,' is inscribed *Vivace ma non troppo,* otherwise the tempo must be slowed down too much when Pogner speaks. Walter's 'Am stillen Herd' is usually started too slowly. The little *ritardandi* and sustained notes prescribed are sufficiently restraining. Not until Sachs's reply, 'Halt Meister,' should there be a noble restraint showing intellectual superiority. This passage should not be taken too fluently nor should the intonation be too strong. The following are dreadful nuances: Pogner's indignant 'Dass nur auf *SCHACHER* und Geld' and Sachs's sentimentally stupid '*ARME* Poeterei.' Simple, oh so simple! Second act beginning 6/8 and following therefrom 2/4 conversation between David and Magdalene usually too fast and hurried. Likewise the conversation between Pogner and Eva 2/4: moderate and then very leisurely—this is usually taken too fast.

The Cobbler's songs are also usually taken a little too fast, with too little character. Possibly the same tempo as in the overture: Wagner's 'Andante' 'alla breve.' At the end of the second act the bad mistake is frequently made of letting Beckmesser get faster and faster, starting from the moment at which he sings without interruption so that when the fisticuffs start it is impossible to implement the 'a little faster' and the whole scene becomes complete chaos. From the beginning ('Darf ich mich Meister nennen') Beckmesser must maintain the same uncompromising pace.

It is also a mistake to begin Pogner's B flat major 'Will einer Seltnes wagen' as an *adagio* aria. Nor should there be any trace of *adagio* mood about Sachs's lilac monologue and no unnecessary drawing out of:

which is after all right from the beginning an impetuous motif going through the head of a worried, meditative Sachs. Our conductors are always inclined to conduct in accordance with the musical phrase as such, instead of in accordance with its dramatic emotional content. (*Cf.* in this connection the E flat major passage in my own *Elektra,* which is always sung as a mellifluous *cantilena* instead of being sung in highest excitement after the tremendous experience of recognition.) If the audience is bored with Wagner, it is the conductors who are to blame: they lack the wider view of the dramatic line of a Wagner act and are unaware that it must be sustained until the curtain drops.

The prelude of Act III is inscribed *moderately* drawn out—it is often played like a true *adagio.*

First act Beckmesser's 6/8 'Ei! Was kümmert doch Meister Sachsen' in the tempo of the first prelude: Metr. 116–128.

Tristan: Cosima Wagner once said—quite rightly—that in *Tristan* the actor's gesture always occurred exactly one bar before the word, and that this had been followed out faithfully in the orchestra and constituted a special *Tristan* style: 'Wohin Mutter'—'Zerschlag es, dies trotzige Schiff'—''Wie lachend sie mir Lieder singen,' etc.

After a production of *Parsifal* (Summer 1933): When studying the score with the orchestra I particularly noticed the *ritardandi* which have become traditional: thus in the first subject of the prelude, whose wonderful perfect rhythmic form is positively destroyed when it is played with a sentimental *ritardando.* It becomes unbearable unless it is played with metronomic exactitude, with liturgical 'indifference.' When conducting *Parsifal* one should distinguish between three clearly defined groups of expression, whose style and content must determine the tempo:

The liturgy: This applies especially to:

to be sung without sentimental *ritardandi* with sistine 'objectivity': the purely ecclesiastical element.

The narrative group: personified in Gurnemanz who, as a kind of 'evangelist,' should be maintained throughout in an objective instructive manner. In his part we find the words which are otherwise very unusual in Wagner: 'Do not drag.' It demands much tact and dramatic intuition on the part of the conductor not to impede the steady flow of music in this part.

The immediate experience (Amfortas, Kundry, Parsifal): This allows free play to a purely emotional presentation to achieve the most immediate effect, provided always that the greatest rhythmical exactitude of declamation is not impaired.

Conducting is, after all, a difficult business—one has to be seventy years of age to realize this fully!

HANS PFITZNER

Judgment about the Conductor

Since, by the nature of their activity, the stage director and the conductor are dependent on a group of human beings as intermediaries between themselves and the audience, I consider them "indirect" artists, as opposed to the "direct" artists, the singers and players of all kinds. Any judgment of the respective achievement of these two types of interpreters must therefore acknowledge the great dissimilarity between them; it must take into account their essential difference, or better still, their different essences. This is an easier task with

HANS PFITZNER: German composer born in Moscow in 1869; died in 1949. His best-known opera is *Palestrina* (1917); his works include a number of choral works and over ninety *Lieder,* as well as articles and books.

the invisible stage director. But with the visible conductor one tends to forget that the major portion of his achievement is indirect; his preliminary work, study, rehearsing, and the actual execution of the piece by the living human group under his influence. One first judges, as a rule, by what one sees at the performance: gestures, or what amounts to the dot on the *i* of his actual achievement, and, on the other hand, by what is audible from the orchestra or other performing group. How much of the success, failure, good or bad playing can be put to the conductor's account? To be able to judge requires a great deal of knowledge.

One must understand this clearly, even though it really seems self-evident. Daily experience shows, however, that what should be self-evident is not always so, and that justification exists for the question: how is the achievement of a conductor to be judged?

In matters of art the judging organism and the activity judged are the two parts of judgment.

Whatever the conductor himself does at the performance is something which is only seen; what is heard is produced by other living beings. What one sees of him are gestures, signs, glances, cues, although these are closely connected with the resulting sounds. Yet so many details go into the chasm between sight and sound that we must first of all study them closely.

In making a distinction between the grounds for judgment of the direct and the indirect performer (for instance, pianist and conductor), we start out from the same premise: our unconditional reaction to the achievement of the one and to the other at the performance. We shall assume that the critic is equally able to evaluate either type of performer and eliminate from consideration all irrelevant or incidental differences. Likewise, the quality of the inanimate tools—things which have no will—can be made equivalent: the piano of the performer can be thus or so, as can the instruments of the orchestra. In both cases there is preparation: here, practicing, learning, work with piano, violin, etc.; there, study of the score, or preparation by oneself, which must be distinguished from the subsequent preparation with others. And what is now left is the factor which creates the real difference between the direct and indirect performer, a factor which can never be equalized because it exists only in indirect interpretation. The living unit, orchestra, theater ensemble, choir, or whatever it may be, is the intermediary between conductor and audience, influenced by the conductor's movements and actions during preparation, rehearsal, and study, and eventually by his gestures and signs at the final presentation. This presentation must always be seen as made up of these two separate but equally important activities.

Only on this basis is it possible to talk sensibly about conducting and the judging of it.

Thus the attainment of the conductor consists solely of this dual manner of influencing living instrumentalists, other artists. Accordingly, one could classify conducting personalities as those whose strength lies more in preparation and those who are at their best at the time of performance. As a matter of fact, there are good conductors who ruin their excellent preparations by impossible gestures or other inabilities at the performance; and those who evade study, and yet can, at the concert, captivate the audience, if not the experts. But the master conductor must be on an equal level at rehearsal and performance.

If the silent gestures at the performance are to be more than mere mechanical time-beating or giving of cues, then the motions made by the man with his little baton must serve as reminders of his previous preparation. They must represent the renewed transfer of his will by means of mute signals. This will he previously tried to transfer to the artists over a period of time, with the help of word, explanation, study, rehearsal—in short, all that belongs to preparation with this group of human beings.

In order to judge the performance of a conductor one must first know something about how it is achieved. What can one say of a conductor by merely listening to the performance?

Almost nothing.

To judge a conductor by his behavior on the podium is the fashionable yet the most unreliable method. It is judging a matter of the ear with the eye instead. To what extent his gestures, his facial expressions are genuine, an involuntary outgrowth of his enthusiasm, or to what extent they are affectation, calculated mannerism—all this is difficult to determine. The calmest orchestra leader can be lured into excessive motions at the performance if he had no rehearsals, or if he has to cope with human problems in the group he is to lead. The most intense, excitable, devoted artist might succeed in giving the audience the impression that his influence on the orchestra is nil. Gustav Mahler, the prototype of the great conductor and one of the most strong-willed persons I ever knew, trained himself, in the course of his life, to the deepest calm on the podium. The "small gestures" which he acquired through self-discipline have unfortunately become dogma, and have led, by way of the customary exaggerations, to the worst kind of indistinctness. And in most cases, they are nothing but pretense.

The Frankfurt Opera director Otto Dessoff originated the fine saying: "The conductor who best performs his task is the one whose outward activity is the least noticeable at the performance."

In all artistic endeavors, particularly in the theater, everyone feels qualified to pass judgment without understanding the least thing about them. Yet not only the outsider but also the experienced critic must thoroughly try to understand what the conductor's apparatus really is. Let us imagine, in jest, that by some magic all the keys of a piano were turned into living beings, with their own will and own abilities. Thus the high C sharp would be gifted and have a beautiful tone; the F sharp might be stubborn and hostile to the intentions of the fingers; the D unwilling to produce a strong tone, only soft ones; the C absent-minded, not remembering that it should sound together with the E; the F filled with the greatest wish to obey the player. At the concert, the performer goes to his instrument—but all his pressing and hammering and finger motion have become virtually devoid of responsibility, half-useless, and are a reflection of his intentions only in so far as the living keys are able and willing to make it so.

Every orchestra, every opera ensemble, is such a bewitched piano.

Under the most favorable circumstances, an orchestra can almost represent such a magical piano in the good sense only—that is, when the entire orchestra is filled, to the last man, with performers of the greatest ability and the best will. When it has absorbed its leader's conception to the smallest detail in plentiful rehearsals, then the conductor can mount the podium with virtually the same feeling with regard to his instrument as that of the virtuoso sitting down at his compliant piano. He, himself, can be calmer than the virtuoso, because the main job will be done by the orchestra, not by him. He has only to remind it of his intent by moving his baton through the air—in effect a supporting action. His major task is completed—studying and rehearsing. How much can still be spoiled by unclear signals or wrong beats, or to what extent the performance can be enhanced by the right support, through personal influence (I would almost use the word hypnosis) on the orchestra, need hardly be mentioned.

To group together a certain number of living persons means to combine an equal number of different abilities and dispositions. The most telling illustration of this is the opera ensemble. The unified orchestral body again seems to be the bewitched piano when compared to the people who appear individually on stage and yet belong to the whole. To the responsible conductor, in the context of the work of art, they are at one with the orchestra, and the mute markings in the score do not differentiate among them.

Ability and inclination—to be able and willing. To estimate the limits of an opera director's responsibilities rightly one must think of the entire scale of ability and degrees of willingness in the persons moving about on stage while singing from memory. It would be impossible to give even a partial account of all the possibilities and mixtures of unwanted and wanted deviations from the intent of the conductor. Does any opera conductor who takes his preparatory work seriously not know the feeling, a mixture of despair and resignation, with which he mounts the podium, realizing full well that certain important passages will certainly come out differently from what he wants and knows to be right; that all his rehearsing was in vain, and that his signals will be useless, because this singer will drag terribly, that one will rush, the third will sing so unrhythmically that he will never be together with the orchestra. Another will turn his back at the moment of an important cue; there will be lapses of memory, so that the leader will have to help, to jump along, and thus distort the music. There will be a thousand such things which will make it impossible to obtain the right musical execution of the work by the singers. Now, the signals of the conductor represent his will in the eye of the audience. Of what use is listening or even watching, in making a judgement, when the signs are in large part not the result of the conductor's actual concept, but of entirely different exigencies? It takes, in a complicated situation, a really good judge, one who thoroughly knows the entire company, the opera, and the conductor, and can observe the latter from the closest proximity. Then he might be able to determine to a certain extent, from mere feeling and hearing, whether this mishap or that error are the conductor's fault or the singer's, and whether the conductor leads or only accompanies, and what he could have done better in the given circumstances, and what not.

I hope that the foregoing has made it clear that one cannot judge a conductor, even if one sees him, if one is unaware of all the circumstances. The judgment on a conductor requires not only what is heard and what is seen, but also knowledge.

SERGE KOUSSEVITZKY

On Creative Conducting

When we remember that Berlioz, Mendelssohn, and Wagner were the first conductors who *interpreted* works, we realize that the art of interpreting music, and especially the art of conducting, is very young. These musicians founded a new school. To the best of my knowledge, Wagner was the first to lead the orchestra with his back to the audience. Previously, conductors assumed a position facing the audience from a three-quarter angle. One can imagine how little influence a leader could have on his players if he stood with his back to them. But in those days, conductors were mainly time

SERGE KOUSSEVITZKY: Born in Russia in 1874; died in Boston in 1951. A doublebass virtuoso as well as conductor, he was conductor of the Boston Symphony from 1924 until his retirement in 1949.

beaters who did not even take the trouble to rehearse, but left that to the concertmaster. At the performance the piece was simply played through, and no attention was paid to details or to a complete realization of the work. If the orchestra had a virtuoso instrumentalist who had to play a solo passage he did this entirely to his own taste, without consideration for the inner structure, overall sense, or line of the work.

Wagner and Mendelssohn unleashed a veritable revolution in the field of conducting. They no longer beat time but build up the musical phrase. Nevertheless this was still far removed from the modern art of conducting. Mendelssohn's style was perhaps closer to the practices of our period than Wagner's since his approach was more abstract. But almost the entire younger generation followed Wagner and not Mendelssohn, since the former reflected the era infinitely more strongly.

And now we come to the problem of interpretation. Prior to World War I, the art of interpretation was greatly influenced by the Romantic school. That is, the interpreter of music looked at a composition as a painter did at a landscape; it was for him a "picture of nature." He rendered this picture as he saw, felt, and understood it. Therefore the same landscape might be rendered in two different ways by two different artists; in addition, the form of the same object would receive different highlights and shadings.

It has been proven repeatedly that the executant has the right to a free interpretation of a musical piece. This right is given to him by the composer. In Bach's works, for instance, there are hardly any nuances. Does that mean that Bach wanted his music performed without nuances? Definitely not. The great Bach leaves this to the performer. Or, in the Classical concertos of Mozart or Beethoven, the composer only rarely wrote out the cadenzas, but left to the artist the freedom to improvise them. In Wagner's scores we find no exact tempo indications after *Tannhäuser* and *Lohengrin.* He omitted them deliberately, and said in his book, *About Conducting,* that it is unnecessary to give the exact tempo, since a gifted conductor will find the right one and the untalented one will never grasp it regardless of what the score says. That is why Wagner only indicates his tempi in general terms, such as "*bewegt,*" "slower," "faster," and so on.

Personally, I believe that a composer not only infuses his work with the power of his musicianship, but also with the entire meaning of his life, of his being. For this reason we must find a "basic idea" in the work of each composer—this is the meaning of his life and of his ideals, which he transmits to us through his music.

With Bach this basic idea was religion; Haydn's was gaiety and humor which he wanted to share with others; Mozart gives us limpid harmonies, the absolute purity of musical form. In Beethoven's work, we might say that the basic idea is the unifying element of universality. The last composer I shall list here is Wagner, whose entire work is imbued with the idea of love and faithfulness.

The truth of the interpreter's art grows out of precisely this. When the artist succeeds in grasping the inner sense, the basic idea of a composition, he finds within himself the right inspiration for its proper rendition. It may not be difficult to determine the basic idea externally, since there is a comprehensive literature about the life and work of every composer. It is also easy for a musician to analyze a score externally, its form, its melodic and harmonic structure, its architecture. But this is only half of the basic idea, its façade, which does not give us a true understanding of the work or its creator. The most significant part cannot be learned or read: it lies within the interpreter, in his own experiences, depths, and emotions.

Nowadays we can often hear "authorities" exclaim, in reviewing a performance: "Let the music speak for itself!" The danger of this maxim lies in its paving the way for mediocrities who simply play a piece off accurately and then maintain that they "let the music speak for itself." Such a statement is not right, in any event, because a talented artist renders a work as he conceives it, according to his own temperament and insight, no matter how painstakingly he follows the score markings. And the deeper the interpreter's insight, the greater and more vital the performance.

A perfect rendition of a work can have two different aspects which are equally faithful to the score. One part can be called mechanically perfect, the other organically perfect. The first gives the listener the beauty of mathematical balance, symmetry and clarity, the second the complete, vital, pulsing *élan vital* of the composition. The one wants to present a pretty façade, while in the other the musical creation—its basic idea—comes to life. The one may be compared to a completely symmetrical building, the other to a great Gothic cathedral, in parts asymmetrical and yet an organic unit. The one is always friendly and pleasant, but always retains something superficial, like a lovely stage set. The other touches the listener, arouses him, fuses him with the reality of the basic idea, and allows him to experience the *élan vital* of the composition.

Examining further the quality of orchestral rendition I must state that the level of performance has never been so high as it is today in America. European orchestras did not, even in the good old days, have anything approaching the

Serge Koussevitzky

possibilities which we have here. Nor did they ever have the same intensity in work and interest. The Berlin Philharmonic Orchestra, one of Europe's oldest, in its most brilliant period gave ten concerts under Nikisch; the rest of the season was led by various conductors of no consequence. And yet it was the most eminent orchestra of its time. A particularly interesting period in Vienna's musical life, rightly called "the heroic period," was the time when Mahler was director of the Vienna Opera. Its orchestra also gave symphonic concerts, then calling itself "the Philharmonic." But it was primarily an operatic orchestra, and the concerts were fitted in; it gave perhaps eight or ten concerts in a season, led by various conductors. The possibilities in America are incomparably greater and give the listener a new idea of an orchestra's achievements.

The notion that the development of America's musical life is due solely to the wealth of the country is wrong. Musical activity grows steadily because we have a need of music. This need of our time is easily explainable: people search for something which will bring out their best and deepest emotions, and find it in music.

What is the musician's actual standing in the life of our time? To find the answer we must look into the past. In less than two hundred years his position has gone through three clearly defined phases.

In the first stage we find him nothing more than a man "who is to provide entertainment" at some European court and advertisements for a lackey or valet who was also a good accompanist were not unusual. In spite of these conditions, musicians showed an amazing intellectual independence, individuality, and great creative power; this, after all, was the time of Haydn and Mozart, and in part even that of Beethoven.

The second phase extends to the post-Romantic era. The

musician, clad in the cloak of exclusiveness and the aureole of the blessed, was the *enfant gâté* of society which took pleasure in his eccentricities. But the artist became aware of the artificiality of his position, and struggled for acceptance not as a jester, but as an equal.

Now we are in the third phase, a period marked by great artists who are also great human beings. Men like a Paderewski or a Schweitzer announce a new era in which the external perfection of virtuosity no longer suffices, but in which one seeks a new dimension, the limitless fourth dimension of one's inner self.

A student of music who decides to become a musician must ask himself whether he has the true talent and abilities to step onto the podium. There, thousands of eyes will be on him, in expectation of the message which he will bring them through his art. Will he really be able to fulfill this expectation?

As one chosen by destiny and endowed by nature, the artist must have a feeling of obligation toward those who do not possess such gifts, and must in all humility dedicate himself to the fulfillment of this obligation.

PABLO CASALS

A Conversation

Pablo Casals talks about conducting, in answer to questions by his friend, J. Ma. Corredor.

In your opinion, which are the principal qualities a conductor should possess?

Before anything else, a great conductor must be a great performer. The most convincing proof of his value can be found in his ability to get in touch with his musicians in order to communicate and convince them of his personal ideas. An absolute necessity is that each word of the conductor

PABLO CASALS: Born in Spain in 1876. Primarily known as one of the world's foremost cellists and interpreters of Bach, he has been conducting since his youth, and has also composed.

must be understood and accepted by the orchestra. If this condition is fulfilled he can rely on the good will and enthusiasm of his musicians; in this way there is no necessity to be overforceful, a practice which I utterly condemn.

What about the lack of rehearsals?

On that subject I have always been uncompromising. If I am asked to conduct a concert I ask for three long rehearsals. Even when you deal with a good orchestra, it is not enough to "conduct" it. All the details must be gone into and absorbed into a harmonious whole. This requires time. I want to do with an orchestra what I do with my violoncello.

And what of the routine, which is so characteristic of orchestral players?

This is one of the principal dangers. The conductor must know how to fight against the bad habits which can always creep into an orchestra, the feeling of automatism which always ends in routine. To counteract this, the conductor must know how to preserve the artistic feeling of his players so that they all end by putting technique at the service of music. The highest aim is to *make the music speak.*

All this requires a great deal of patience. Yours is proverbial!

The thing which counts for the conductor is that he must be very severe towards himself and ask himself if he has succeeded in making his ideas comprehensible. One cannot expect everything from others.

The rehearsal work must often be irksome.

Not for me. Rehearsing is the sort of work I like and enjoy. It is the moment when I can communicate my views and my feelings. I have never been disappointed in the reactions of my players. They realize very soon that I look on them as collaborators instead of slaves. And in that way the work of a rehearsal becomes a pleasure to all.

But when you conduct an orchestra which is not yours?

When you are on tour and you have to deal with an unknown orchestra, I think you realize right away if your authority is going to tell or not. One look sometimes is enough to judge the new "boss."

Do you ever conduct from memory?

No, for I do not see the use of useless accomplishments. Richter was of the same mind.

I see that your scores are covered with notes.

I never start rehearsing a work until I have studied every note of it, and marked all the points I think necessary.

What should one do to become a great conductor? I have read that Toscanini began to conduct by accident, so to speak, at Rio de Janeiro during a performance of Aïda. *You cannot become a good conductor if you cannot use a good orchestra, and a good orchestra will not be lent to you if you are not a good conductor. The problem seems impossible to solve.*

If a musician feels he has a vocation for conducting he can begin with a group of amateurs, or a modest orchestra in the provinces. It is a necessary training and it becomes an excellent way of practising. Supposing the orchestra is a bad one and the new conductor succeeds in making it improve a little, it gives an indication that he is capable.

Herman Scherchen declares that the conductor has at his disposal three principal means: "representative gesture," "expressive mime," and "explanation by word of mouth." What do you think of "expressive mime" to help the musicians in finding the kind of expression suitable to the music they play?

I agree with this as long as the mime is a natural one and not studied.

One day a young musician asked Furtwängler, "What is, in fact, the role of your left hand when you conduct?" Trying to answer this question, the great German conductor said: "After over twenty years of conducting, I must say that I had never thought of it."

Neither have I. It seems to me a trifling question. The conductor's left hand, as well as his right one, contributes towards the expression of the work he wishes to convey to the orchestra.

I have read that your old friend Bruno Walter sometimes stops a rehearsal and instead of making observations to his players, he just says—please let us play this again, it sounded so lovely.

I do understand that—and it reflects the sweet nature and the cordiality of Bruno Walter. It is a pity he has abandoned his piano playing, because I think that besides a very great conductor he is also a very great pianist.

Toscanini and Furtwängler are the two conductors you admire most?

I admire a great many conductors, even if I don't always agree with their rendering, but I certainly place Toscanini, Furtwängler, and Stokowski at the top of the living conductors.

Howard Taubman, who wrote Toscanini's biography, says

that Toscanini "holds his tempi." Sometimes when a performance of a Classical symphony was timed with a stop watch, it was discovered that there was only a difference of one or two seconds in performances of the same work given many years later.

I don't understand what conclusion should be drawn from this assertion. Toscanini, like all great artists, does not lack in creative fantasy. And since a musical work does not always appear to the artist in exactly the same way, without the slightest difference, it follows that a great interpreter can be carried away by some inspiration of the moment, where the idea of the stop watch has no place at all.

Which works did you like to conduct best?

Besides the well-known ones, any work that has a musical interest.

BRUNO WALTER

The Conductor

PREFATORY NOTE

I remember gratefully how as a young musician I was helped and stimulated by Richard Wagner's essay *On Conducting*. I am far from considering my deliberations as, in any sense, a continuation of, or complement to, the teachings of a creative genius. But what Wagner has handed down to us in the way of instruction is comparatively scanty; in general, advice is scarce in this wide and important field of the re-creative musician. At the same time, we must remember that in our age creative achievement in music has become of lesser,

BRUNO WALTER: Born in Berlin in 1876; died in California in 1962. He was a close friend and disciple of Gustav Mahler, and succeeded Felix Mottl as general music director in Munich in 1913. He conducted throughout Europe, and was mainly active in New York after the outbreak of World War II.

musical interpretation of greater, importance. Therefore I assume that young conductors and other readers of this may perhaps be glad to be acquainted with my professional experiences and my thoughts on conducting. Whatever the value of these insights may be, they are the result of my continuous, many-sided activity as executant, and I would rejoice in being able to give to the fruits of my life-long endeavours a profounder, supra-personal meaning and a new lease of life by putting them at the disposal of young and prospective conductors, and of all young musicians. With this practical aim in mind, I have not always been able to eschew in the subsequent *chapters*—as far as they deal with the special tasks or training of the conductor—an occasional didactic tone, which I have been at pains to avoid in the rest of this *book*. But as I felt under an obligation to make myself understood to the more inexperienced reader as well, I was compelled to address him as a person of experience. This has made necessary some digressions which the more mature among my readers are likely to find superfluous. I trust to their forbearance if, on occasion, I expatiate on matters that must for long have been self-evident to them.

An orchestral player once told Hans Richter, the great conductor of the Vienna Imperial Opera, that he had recently had his first opportunity of conducting an orchestra. 'How did it go?' asked Richter. 'Very well indeed,' replied the player; 'but you know, Herr Hofkapellmeister,' he added with some astonishment, 'this business of conducting is really quite simple!' From behind a shielding hand, Richter whispered back, 'I beg you, don't give us away!'

That conducting is not only easy, but unnecessary, was the belief of the 'orchestra without conductor' which for some time gave concerts in Russia—in Leningrad, if I am not mistaken—in which the orchestra played without the guidance of the conductor. Simultaneous entries were achieved by a gesture from one of the musicians, and ensemble-playing by thorough rehearsing and intense concentration on the part of everyone.

'Yes, but is it really of any importance who is standing up there wielding his baton?' I have, in fact, been asked. 'In the end, it is the orchestral musicians who play, give expression, and overcome the technical difficulties. Their parts, lying on their stands, tell them what to play. What more has a conductor to do than to keep them together with his movements?'

This question, as well as the naïve statement of the Viennese player and the experiment of the Russian orchestra, is based on the same assumption: that the most essential task of a conductor is beating time, and that, therefore, his is a purely mechanical function. That this in itself should be a negligible, easy, or unnecessary activity will perhaps become doubtful to the devotees of this persuasion on attending, not the performance of some relatively simple piece, but one, let us say, of Wagner's *Götterdämmerung*, or of any symphony. But whether they believe the function of the conductor to be an easy or difficult one, an important or unimportant one, a necessary or expendable one, there remains the fundamental error of assuming that the foremost task of a conductor is to keep the players together.

This error is fostered by appearances: one sees a single person in front of all the fiddling, blowing, beating, singing musicians, and to the superficial observer, his task seems to be to bring unity and order into these masses; the eyes of all participants are directed at that one man, he raises his hand and stick and moves them, thereby keeping the many together and leading them. No wonder the 'spectator' believes such a function to be mechanical. What he does not see is the transmission of spiritual impulses from the conductor to the executants; and he does not see anything of the preceding rehearsal-work during which musical and emotional understanding has been established, either.

No one, however, who is in the least susceptible to music, will let himself be deceived by these visual impressions; his ear tells him, and his musical feeling corroborates it, that —contrary to appearances—it is in actual fact that single person who is making music, playing on the orchestra as on a living instrument, and transforming its multiformity into unity, and that he is concerned with the technical as well as the spiritual aspect of the music. The musical feeling of the listener perceives that the conductor's conception and personality sound forth from the playing of the orchestra, that his re-creative inspiration reveals, by means of the executants, the inner meaning of a work of music. The truth of this is proven by every performance under the direction of a great conductor. But even true music-lovers and connoisseurs rarely have a clear idea *how it comes about* that his personal interpretation of a composition sounds forth, perceptibly and convincingly, from a massed effort—or, in other words, what the proper sphere of the conductor's work is.

Therefore, I believe that I should try—notwithstanding the jocular injunction of the revered Hans Richter—*to give away* our professional secrets to the best of my ability. I would like to show how the general problems of musical interpretation apply in the special case of the conductor. Although my reflections are intended primarily for the young or prospective generation of conductors, they are also directed at all true music-lovers, and are meant, in particular, to satisfy

1960

those among them whose serious interest in the work of the conductor prompts them to glance into his workshop.

PECULIARITIES OF HIS TASK

What distinguishes the activity of the conductor from that of all other musicians? That he does not play himself, but guides and influences the playing of others. It is not before he enters on the professional phase of his vocation that he can really come to know the handling of his instrument, the orchestra; practice alone will teach him to master it; only by practice can he learn.

How different it is with the instrumentalist! He has been alone with himself and his instrument during his years of study—and who would deny that one had better be alone and undisturbed when one wants to learn. He has been able to practise to his heart's content, to develop his technique, to become familiar with his instrument, to gain mastery, during years of study, of his own resources and those of his instrument.

The conductor is denied these years of quiet, preparatory exercise, in which he could become familiar with his many-sided instrument and develop his technical mastery of it. He never could, and never can, be alone with his instrument—for it consists of a great many persons—and there is no solitude among many. To him alone, of all executant musicians, is denied the inestimable advantage of being able to try out matters in the quiet of his study. Of what benefit to him are those few years of small-scale opportunities for conducting which, if all goes well, are granted to him by a friendly fate? Or even several years of wider possibilities? It is the complicated character of his instrument and indirect way in which it has to be played, and above all, the unavailability of the instrument at the time of his training, that prevent the conductor from setting out on his professional career with a degree of assurance and technical proficiency akin to that attained by other musicians.

OF CORRECTNESS

Correctness is the indispensable condition and prerequisite for any musical interpretation that bears witness to the spirit and soul of a work. Exactness, cleanliness, orderliness, i.e. rightness of notes and time, clarity of sound, and compliance with dynamic and tempo indications: these are the demands of correctness, and it is only from such a basis that meaningful music-making can evolve. Even the most fiery expression cannot do justice to a passionate composition if the spirit of order is lacking in its execution, if its passages are played untidily and its rhythm inexactly. Nor can the most soulful rendering of a violin or woodwind passage make its impression unless the other instruments or instrumental groups are adapted or subordinated to it.

One may speak, by way of comparison, of the *body* and the *soul* of a musical performance, meaning by the former the actual sound that is produced by the player and makes the physical impact on the ear of the listener, by the latter the musical and emotional meaning of the performance. The saying 'Mens sana in corpore sano' can be applied figuratively to music-making: the absolute correctness of the performance stands for the healthy body from which the soul of the work, unencumbered by *physical* imperfections, can roundly and clearly sound forth.

In his elementary striving for correctness in music-making, it will become apparent to the conductor that his task is, right from the start of his career, much more involved than that of an instrumentalist. If his ear detects a wrong note he cannot, like the instrumentalist, make his own fingers put it right. Clearness in passage-work must be wrung by him from the technique of his players and not from that of his own hands. The dynamic gradation of tone, for the soloist a simple, if not always easy, task, frequently presents great difficulties to the conductor.

With the instrumentalist, the double function of execution and supervision forms an undivided and concurrent process, since in both there is at work the same ego; its powers of volition are closely geared to those of control; his own ear will teach his own hand; it will tell him instantly of mistakes in playing, and he will be in a position to correct these instantaneously, and mostly does so unconsciously. With the conductor, the striving for the same aim takes a much more complicated form—in his case, there is no organic connection between the executive and the supervisory organs: it is not with his own resources but with those of others that he must maintain a state of bodily health in his music-making; the goal of correctness, which the soloist approaches by a direct route, must be pursued by him on circuitous paths; the homogeneity of an individual's musical powers gives place, in his case, to the endeavour to communicate with those others, the executants.

EAR AND HAND

It is by studying a composition, whether by way of playing it or reading it through, that the mind of the student forms an aural conception of how it should sound. Among the most important aims of studying is the gradual acquisition of a distinct, inner sound-image, or rather, sound-ideal; this will establish itself in the ear of the interpreter as a criterion that exerts a guiding and controlling influence on his practical music-making. In less independent musicians or those whose internal ear is weaker, this sound-ideal derives not from their own aural imagination, but from the impressive performances of others. Not only does the sound-ideal actively influence a performance, it has also its share in receptivity by providing a standard by which the critically listening interpreter can judge his own performance. On this dual function of the ear—namely, to give direction according to the dictates of the ideal, and to exert supervision under its influence—depends, in actual fact, the success of every musical performance. While, with the instrumentalist, this dual function usually operates within the realm of his musical *instinct,* that is subconsciously, it must emerge into consciousness with the conductor: for he has to explain to his musicians in the clearest possible terms—sometimes by singing—'what is missing,' i.e., in what respect his testing ear has remained unsatisfied.

The training of the ear for its two-fold task rightly belongs to one's schooling, at least as far as its first part is concerned, that is, the acquiring of vivid, inner sound-images from the study of the score. The young musician should be able, at least to a certain degree, to hear a score inwardly before setting out on his professional career. It is only afterwards, of course, that he will be able to embark on the second part of his task: of listening critically to what comes from the orchestra and of estimating in what respects this differs from his intentions.

Even when studying, the conductor must be *all ears;* in his rehearsals and performances, as I think I have now established, he must be *all ears twice over.* Technically, his achievement will depend, in corresponding degree, on his hand. Without its purposeful functioning, neither that correctness which I have called a prerequisite of spirited music-making, nor the entire gamut of lifelike tempi and expressions, the shaping of which depends on the conductor's gestures, can be attained.

Just as there is such a thing as a good piano-hand, a favourable physical disposition for violin-playing, a natural aptitude of the lips for horn-playing, there also exists a specifically manual talent for conducting, an innate skill for keeping together and guiding an orchestra by means of hand movements. The notes and indications of the score decree that the multiplicity of executant musicians should become an ideal unity; the hand of the conductor makes an actual unity of them during practical music-making. His spiritual mediation, drawing inspiration from the work, is then needed to give an individual stamp to this actual, that is sounding, unity; the seal of personality must be set upon it.

The practice of every art has a basis of craftsmanship; only if he is sufficiently gifted as a craftsman and this gift has been sufficiently trained, can an artist become master of his art. If this elementary gift is lacking or has remained neglected and undeveloped, his achievement will be imperfect, even if he has considerable artistic talents. A highly talented musician without the specific gift for conducting or without technical experience, is bound to be *thrown;* the performance will come to grief, or at least not run smoothly; the orchestral players will feel insecure under his direction and will not take him seriously. The truest understanding of a work on the part of a conductor and the deepest musicality cannot make up for a lack of material correctness and technical precision in a performance—the clumsiness of the hand will prevent the work from making the right impression.

I cannot say in what specific physical trait the manual aptitude for conducting lies, any more than I can pinpoint the physical disposition for a craft such as, let us say, joinery. But if we closely watch an artisan who is specially gifted for his craft we see how naturally and purposefully, and with what sure instinct, he handles his tools. They appear to be part of his own body—his nerves do not seem to end under the skin, but seem to continue through the tool he uses, directly affecting the object on which he works. More than that, a tool is not only *innervated* but seems *inspirited* when it is employed in the service of an artistic purpose; I am thinking of the knife of a woodcarver, cutting out of the dead wood the vividly devout face and the touching posture of an apostle. The same goes for the sculptor's chisel and mallet, and similar conditions surround every tool that is wielded by the hand of a master in the service of spiritual—not necessarily artistic—purposes. But I repeat that this oneness of hand and tool, this inspiriting of the latter, can only occur in the case of an artist whom nature has granted, besides his artistic talent, that specific aptitude for craftsmanship.

In the hands of the *born* conductor, the baton gradually becomes a tool of this kind. To all appearances, its function is mechanical and similar to the metronome. In reality, the beat of the metronome could never produce precise orchestral ensemble-playing just because it is purely mechanical, lacking any personal energy-impulse. The concept of musical precision has by no means only a mechanical significance; it has also a mental and qualitative significance; a beat that was nothing but mechanical could not achieve an exact ensemble, except in march-music, which, because of its regularity, is not really in need of any external direction and, besides, is held together with precision by an energy-impulse peculiar to its kind. The impulse fraught with personal energy, however, which brings to life the mechanical function of the baton and is indispensable for attaining musical precision in orchestral playing, must join hands with other mental forces before the conductor can fulfill his elementary task of achieving correctness by the wielding of his baton. For his beat is meant to achieve the musical precision of orchestral playing in the tempo conceived of as right by him, in all its ramifications as well as in *ritardando, accelerando, rubato,* etc. Such lively shaping of the tempo is among the most important requirements of musical execution; in it, the musicality of the conductor must convincingly prove itself; in the baton's function of precisely holding together the orchestra in so freely shaped a tempo, an abundance of musical and spiritual impulses must join with the mechanical gesture. This is the manner in which the tool in the conductor's hand becomes inspirited; thus it helps him in mastering his instrument—always provided that an inborn manual talent has smoothed the way towards such perfect harmony between soul and technique.

Here, some comment seems indicated on the custom of conducting without a baton, fashionable of late. Personally, I see in the renouncement of the baton the surrender of a highly developed technique of craftsmanship, which carries the seeds of decay. The baton, extending as it does the obviously restricted beat of the bare hand, and magnifying it to distantly visible proportions, provides, in view of the enhanced clarity and plausibility of its movements, a better aid to precise orchestral playing than the empty hand. Every orchestral musician will affirm that he feels much less secure under the guidance of empty hands dispensing mesmerism than under the clear beat of the baton in the conductor's right hand, which thus provides for clarity, while the left effectively looks after dynamic gradations. I regret that this technique of leading an orchestra, which has been developed to perfection, is being relinquished, and I have yet to encounter or discover conclusive arguments in favour of this. To be sure, the orchestras have got so used to stick-less hands that they are now able to follow their gestures, and I myself have heard, not without astonishment, precise performances of this sort. But I have often asked myself whether a certain crampedness and nervous restlessness frequently met with in these performances does not, at least in part, derive from the loss of that security which a baton wielded by a practiced hand used to give the players. Or—to put it positively—whether it is not the *magic* of a manual direction lacking the clarifying participation of the mute tool, which produces that element of restlessness in the emotional curves of the performance? I would also like to mention that the more extended movements of the baton to left and right leave the musician in no doubt as to what beat of the bar—whether, for instance, the second or the third—is being given; this orientation, which is needed particularly in passages with frequent changes of time, can certainly not be provided with the same clearness by the empty hand as by the stick. Not to mention the directing of large forces, including orchestra and choir, as is frequent in opera: here, the more distantly posted musicians or singer will not be able to follow the movements of an empty hand with any certainty.

As to the handling of the baton, I think it is neither possible nor necessary to impart practical advice. He who has manual talent for conducting will soon wield his baton in a way that can be followed by the orchestra. It will help the beginner to watch the handling of the baton by first-rate conductors. One remark, however, I believe could be of assistance to the inexperienced: while conducting, never think of the movement of hand and baton, only of the playing of the orchestra. In the former case, one's attention would be directed at the mechanism of conducting—but this can never be an aim in itself; it is one's musical intentions rather, that should, by the skill of one's hand, be translated into movements whose mechanical meaning is wholly immersed in their musical significance as the transmitters of the impulses for expression, tempo, and precision. It is to these impulses, which are in the service of one's general conception, that one's attention must be directed in conducting, even if the hand should prove clumsy and refuse to do what the head wishes. I am speaking from personal experience, for during my first years in Vienna I suffered for some time from technical shortcomings, and my mistakes only increased when I concentrated my attention upon the use of the baton. I have related in my autobiography how, in those days, every *pizzicato* chord of the strings and every freely entering upbeat of an orchestral group, was a problem to me. My difficulties became more acute the more I endeavoured to find a mechanically correct set of gestures. Experiences like these usually occur at a fairly advanced stage in the development of a young conductor, and this proved true in my case, too. For at the beginning, the technical side of conducting seems easy and unproblematic —if one has manual talent to a certain degree. I should like to put on record here that in my experience every innate talent—in music as in many other fields—usually goes through three phases of development: in the first, one can do everything; in the second, one becomes unsure of oneself, loses one's ability, searches, doubts, experiments, learns, matures; the third begins when the assurance of the first gradually returns, now enhanced and made conscious by the experience one has gained. Thus, at my début at the age of eighteen, when I conducted Lortzing's *Waffenschmied* at the Cologne opera-house, I was not aware of the slightest difficulty. I knew the score in its vocal and instrumental sections by heart, likewise the words; was thoroughly familiar with the events on stage; and had achieved, during my piano rehearsals with the singers, complete agreement on matters of music and expression. In the orchestral rehearsals and in the performances my hand took over the technical direction quite as a matter of course and I was not conscious of any difficulties; and henceforth a firm balance within the orchestra itself and between it and the stage was maintained. As far as I remember, my technical assurance in conducting lasted for some years. I was bent on gaining musical command and spiritual penetration of the works, on studying with singers and orchestra, on influencing the dramatic expression of the singers, and the stage-action; the technical function of conducting gave me no trouble since in this first phase my hand seemed to know, all by itself, what to do. My explanation of this common and deceptive phenomenon of a young conductor's unaffected assurance is that the multitude and variety of the technical problems facing the conductor, the floods of sound that inundate his ear, make such extreme demands on his powers that he cannot but be *active:* he wills, he gives, he overflows, his instinct helps, the ego operates as an undivided unity. This state of overwrought activity of course impedes the calm, critical functioning of his ear: he hears what he expects to hear, what he wants to hear—for he is entirely caught up in velleity—and it is only very gradually that his powers of judgment become equal to those of his will, that his ear learns to listen and to collate the actual sound with the standard set up by his imagination.

And thus begins—and began in my life, too—the second phase in the development of the conductor: in it the ear emancipates itself from its primitive adhesion to the complex of executive forces. This complex could only stand up against one's growing experience and self-observation, and the rising demands one makes in one's musical performances, as long as the vehemence of the active, extroverting forces was able effectively to silence one's receptivity, observation, and judgment. It goes without saying that cruder offences against correctness or other elementary musical prerequisites have from the beginning been noticed by the conductor; these can be settled without effort by word and hand. But considerable time and ample experience are needed for his ear to develop into a superlative observer and his consciousness to shed its light on the ways of his talents and instincts. When this time arrives, he will want to account for himself, to explore the whys and wherefores of the right way. He will find himself immersed now in the unavoidable second phase of artistic development: the phase of conflict between activity and observation, when his actions have to account for themselves before the court of his self-criticism. Without such rendering of account, however, there can be no progress on the artistic, moral, or even general human plane; it is not likely that the life of any aspiring personality has ever been exempted from the crises of this period. At this time, things that have at first seemed simple often become problematic; we are no longer able to do what we used to do; our assurance dwindles, the ground wavers under our feet. This may lead to doubts in our talent threatening our vitality. The impact of this shock may differ according to the character and disposition of the person concerned; but scarcely any artist is wholly spared these growing pains, and in some cases they may continue well into the third phase, in which conscious ability is developed. If there should be artists who have never known crises of this sort—a fact that need not be held against their talent and artistic conscience—I would have to consider their life as an exception from the law of development in three phases which, as I have said, seems to govern the growth of every talent.

This second phase, in which the hand loses its former assurance, and in which we search, err, experiment, and alternate between competence and incompetence, is essentially ruled by the tyrannical demands we make on our conducting technique in order that it may find the precision corresponding to an ever subtler shaping of the tempo. What happens is that technique is being gradually inspirited. For the freer the shaping of the tempo, the harder it is for our hand to achieve a technical precision in orchestral playing that accords with it. Sufficient natural talent provided, the spirit cannot fail to develop the technique it needs. For this is indeed essentially a spiritual task since, as I have said before, precision is only to a very limited extent of a mechanical nature—at bottom, its claims are musical, and the technique required to achieve it must, therefore, arise and evolve from spiritual-musical impulses. By concentrating on precision, one arrives at technique; but by concentrating on technique one does not arrive at precision. And as it is with precision, or rather, with that musical quality that expresses itself as precision, so it is with all musical qualities up to the subtlest and highest: if only our inner wish for them is intense enough, they will create in the course of time and experience the conducting technique that can lead the orchestra towards them. To put it more clearly: inner musical feeling is converted into technique, becomes technique. Yet this can only happen very gradually, for our intentions grow ever more refined and intricate, and our technique has to absorb refinements and intricacies in equal measure.

While, in the course of the second phase described above, the ear at last turns from a critic of technique into its helper, problems may arise from a different quarter, the like of which I myself have often found vexing and unsettling. How often I have neglected precision in my struggle for intensity of emotional expression! How often my conducting technique has failed me when I was concerned with modifications of tempo on emotional grounds to which my gestures proved unequal! Here, we are faced with an opposition that is essentially a permanent one: supreme intensity of feeling, such as is needed in music-making, will always take possession of the entire personality—thus, our emotional exaltation will diminish our attention to technical perfection, and on the other hand the striving for the latter will lessen our intensity of feeling; it is only complete mastery that is able to reconcile these opposites. But just as, in the opera house, my advice to singers was never to force the voice for the sake of dramatic expression but rather to forego an extreme of dramatic power for the sake of vocal technique, so I must entreat the conductor never to neglect technical perfection, even though this may lead to a compromise with expressive intensity. I am aware that this advice must sound strange coming from me; but, as I have said before, correctness is among the elementary prerequisites of music-making which must be satisfied under all conditions, for emotional effusiveness together with technical inadequacy constitutes one of the most common forms of dilettantism. My own struggle has been a long one and I speak from an experience rich in conflicts when I say to conductors: give all your soul in music-making, but never allow the transports of feeling to benumb your spirit of observation and your sense of control.

In the third phase of development, when the conductor

matures towards mastery, he will be able to devote his energies entirely to the higher problems of musical interpretation, untroubled by technical difficulties. His technique, having gone during the second phase through the school of consciousness, has regained the former happy state of *unconcern;* now, however, it is on the higher level of competence. The guiding hand and the probing ear have been trained to be reliable servants of the spirit—now it is the demands of the *desiderating* ear which, having insinuated themselves, during the second phase, with growing urgency into those of the *probing* ear, govern the music-making of the conductor and his intercourse with the orchestra. . . .

OF THE PRACTICE OF CONDUCTING

Let us imagine the young musician standing at last as a conductor before his orchestra, about to take his first rehearsal with musicians who are entrusted to his guidance. The step to practical conducting is made—he is beginning his career. But what he experiences now, with a fast-beating heart, is very different from the idea of an orchestral rehearsal he has dreamed about during his studies or formed from actual observation. Then, the conductor, bearing the responsibility for work and performance, had seemed to him the absolute ruler, the supreme commander of the musicians who had responded with devotion to the bidding of the practical, experienced hand of the master. But already the fast beating of his heart will not fit in with this radiant idea of kingliness: these palpitations betoken the excitement of an inexperienced person who, far removed from any dreams of sovereignty he might have cherished, and deeply troubled by his lack of routine and self-assurance, finds himself face to face with the calmness and habitual assurance of professional musicians. However thorough his general training may have been, however vivid may be his inner image of the work to be played, he is a beginner in rehearsing and conducting—above all, in rehearsing. In conducting itself, he may perhaps be helped over the first difficulties by manual skill and vigorous musicianship; the special knack of rehearsing, on the other hand, comes to the conductor only after years of professional experience. Thus the young rehearsing conductor will constantly have the sobering awareness of being a novice thrust at him. How different from what he had imagined, or experienced as a listener, does everything sound in close proximity to the orchestra—a confused and confusing jumble of sounds envelops him. What should he do or say to achieve dynamic balance and clarity? When will the right moment have come for stopping and correcting? Will he then be able to find the *mot juste,* the *right tone,* the effective approach, for gaining his musical ends with the orchestra? These and similar *acute* worries of the new conductor during his first professional contacts with the orchestra—everyone, according to his personality, will experience them in a different way—take on, after a while, a milder, *chronic* form; but they will, greatly diversified, and often assuming the proportions of serious problems, accompany the conductor over a good part of his career. For all these worries are indicative of the above-mentioned essential point of the conductor's profession, in which it differs from that of all other musicians: he has to accomplish the most personal exercise of our art, music-making, by means of exerting his influence as a man and musician on others; his task is a personal one as much as an artistic one. He who cannot deal with people or exert his influence on them is not fully qualified for this profession.

The problem of dealing with people, as it presents itself

to the conductor, can only be grasped by him if he comes to understand the profound difference of his task from that of the orchestral musicians: his is the will, theirs the obligation; and since such passive obligation, being in the nature of a depersonalization, cannot yield artistic results, it must, by means of the conductor's persuasive force upon his musicians, be transformed into willing participation.

I should advise the conductor to make himself conversant with the thought—one which should be readily intelligible to a young conductor of growing perspicacity—that every orchestral rehearsal demands of him an active effort of will power, whereas the most he can expect of the orchestra, to start with, is a basic attitude of ready good-will and equability. To be sure, this is a relative statement, for every good orchestral musician will certainly be as keen and attentive as his task demands. This fact in itself, however, means that there will be some considerable differentiation even within the orchestra, for the soloists—the leaders of the string and wind sections, the harpist and the drummer—will be keyed up to a higher state of tension by the greater responsibility of their task than the rest of the players. The importance of the executant's task is thus a determining factor for the degree of his activity or passivity. How greatly and fundamentally therefore, must the conductor's state of mind differ from that of the orchestral musicians! Their task is, in each case, a partial one; the conductor, on the other hand, bears and feels the total responsibility for work and performance, and for the latter's spirit and details.

By reason of the high tension and activity with which this responsibility invests his whole being, the conductor will be affected in his work by the orchestra's equability—that is, its lesser degree of tension; this will be like a heavy, pressing weight, the daily shifting of which may well remind him of the lot of Sisyphus. What must come to his rescue here, is an intense empathy with the mind of the players that will teach him to put life into the orchestra, raise its tension towards his own, fire the musicians with his own fire, and kindle their activity by his.

Such empathy will help him make the orchestra into an instrument on which he can play with the freedom of a soloist. But what are the artistic means of realizing those highest orchestral achievements in which his conception, his own self, can find audible expression? I shall not trouble to try and explain the strongest and most effective means, for it is, at the same time, the most obscure: I mean by this the forcible, direct influence which the born conductor, by virtue of his inner musical intensity and the sheer power of his personality, exerts on his musicians. The forces that emanate from him create an atmosphere of spiritual communion which gives elemental spontaneity, completeness, and conclusiveness to the musical performance. Every truly sympathetic observer will have perceived in this collaboration of conductor and executants the workings of deep, instinctive forces of the soul, together with such as are elucidated by consciousness. At the very least, he will have received an intimation of an irrational element subsisting in the influence of that single one on the many.

This instinctive faculty for immediately transmitting one's own musical impulses to the orchestra is the sign of true talent for conducting. Especially in opera, where singers and chorus, too, come under its sway, it has brought about astonishing improvisatory feats of musical and dramatic expressiveness. (Opera companies in particular, incidentally, with their scheduled repeats of performances after intervals without rehearsal, have to rely on the invigorating, improvisatory flair of such conducting talents.) But our symphonic music, too, lives—as far as its life is dependent on interpretation—from the vitality of such natures. And yet, although a strong talent of this sort may be able occasionally to improvise an excellent performance without sufficient preparation, it will only in very rare, exceptional cases be in a position to dispense with thorough rehearsing. No doubt one can, from the conductor's desk, incite the participants to responsiveness, one can bring one's influence to bear on the work as a whole and in detail, one can, by the shaping of the tempo, induce the rising and falling of the emotional floods, thus reaching, moving, and shaking the souls of the listeners by way of the executants and in concord with them; yet unless the execution of details has previously been established with meticulous care, unless dynamic gradations, subtle nuances in expression, and so forth, have been thoroughly rehearsed, even the most buoyant performance will disappoint a truly musical listener. Enthusiastic scurrying over disorderly and neglected details is the hall-mark of dilettantism. If, however, a non-dilettante, but rehearsal-shy conductor makes himself guilty of this, he is behaving unscrupulously and will, in consequence, undermine the artistic morale of the executants. Loving care and impulsive intensity must be combined with unceasing industry if the demands of the work are to be satisfied in performance.

But rehearsing has a purpose yet deeper than the preparation of single performances: the gradual establishment of a musico-personal relationship between conductor and orchestra. This must sustain, supplement, and enhance the improvisatory, impelling influence of a strong conducting personality—without such increasing artistic familiarity as can only result from continuous rehearsing, the immediate influence of the conductor during performances would gradually weaken and in the end fail.

In rehearsing, then, the conductor has to give detailed expression to his musical intentions; and he must do this in a manner that will intensify the general psychological readiness of the players to fulfill these wishes.

Among the difficulties he has to overcome on his road towards this goal, one of the most serious—and it is a far more serious one than the understandable equability I have mentioned above—is the power of habit and complacency which I am constrained to call a professional disease of orchestras. How well do I remember from my first years as a conductor the frequent reply made by older musicians to my corrections: 'Well, I have always played it this way.' Whether their resistance to a change or innovation expressed itself verbally or—which was almost worse—in the passive form of standing by their convictions in hostile silence, I experienced what a great, inimical power I was challenging in my fight against habit.

There are people for whom life begins anew every morning. It is they who are ever more deeply touched by every renewed encounter with Schubert's *Unfinished,* it is they whom the perusal of a familiar Goethe poem moves with the force of a first impression; people over whom habit has no power; people who, in spite of their increasing years and experience, have remained fresh, interested, and open to life. And there are others who, when they watch a most glorious sunset or listen to the Benedictus in Beethoven's *Missa Solemnis,* feel scarcely more than 'I know this already'; and who are upset by everything new and unusual—in other words, people whose element is habit and comfort. It is for the former that our poets have written, our artists created, and our musicians composed; and it is for them, above all, that we perform our dramas, our operas, oratorios, and symphonies. As regards the latter, we artists must try, time and again, to burst open the elderly crust they have acquired, or with which many of them may have been born; our youthful vigour must call upon theirs or revive whatever is left of it. And in exactly this consists the task of the conductor when he deals with musicians who suffer from the said professional disease. The dull reluctance in which this disease expresses itself points to its mythical sire, Fafner, and his words: 'Ich lieg' und besitz'—lasst mich schlafen!'[21]

It is exactly in his belief of possession that the error of the routinist lies. For a possession that is not being constantly striven and worked for crumbles and melts away. There exists a habitual *espressivo* in the rendering of a musical theme as well to habitual nuances of expression in the declamation of poetry that consist in the memory of former, spontaneous interpretations and their tempo, expressive contents and fall of voice. But rendering and interpretation have gradually become stale, the true, heart-felt content has vanished, and only the manner has remained. A highly-esteemed actor once boasted to me that he was able to re-create, with the utmost success, the passionate agitation of a certain scene he had often played, without any inner participation, purely from the memory of his former performances and their points of detail, such as excessive resonance, wild gestures, sobbing, and so on. I had attended the performance which had, of course, deeply depressed me, much as I admired its virtuosity. Surely we must all realize that in artistic competence, in the mastering of the means of our art, there lurks the danger of falling into routine, and that, the more often we perform a work, the better we know it, and the more brilliant our technique has become, the more carefully we must beware of a habitual performance, and the more imperative it is for us to keep in touch with live emotion. Perhaps I may venture to instance my own life here: the more often I had to perform a work, the more care did I take to revive in myself the feeling of my first enthusiasm, and ask myself time and again whether the first spontaneity had yielded to a routined expression. There can have been scarcely a performance of *Tristan* or *Don Giovanni* or the *Eroïca* in my life that was not preceded or succeeded by such self-searching—thus, the works of music have remained for me 'glorious as on the first day.'[22] Paradoxical as it may sound, the greatness and beauty of the masterpieces of all the arts is to me nothing static and definitive: they live, they *become* greater and more beautiful with every encounter, just as works of smaller stature become duller and paler. To the question whether I know Mozart's G minor symphony, I should have to answer, in all honesty: 'Today I think I know it, but tomorrow it may be new to me'; for I have often thought before that I have known it, only to find later that it was new to me.

From this ever-intensified tendency to self-examination there arose, by necessity, my resolution to carry my war against habit and indolence into the camp of my collaborators. I was hindered in this—as in every conflict of my life—by a natural tendency of mine to see how other people feel; when I put myself into the place of an *opponent,* who in this case usually was a routined, over-worked orchestral player, it dawned on me what it must mean for him suddenly, at the bidding of a young, inexperienced conductor, to *change his ways;* that is, to play this or that in a different way from that which he had been used to and considered right. Thus, as a human being, I understood only too well what as a musician

I could not tolerate, and felt, in consequence, not only artistically but also morally impeded. Besides, I realized soon enough that there was nothing in me of a Siegfried who could, sword in hand, boldly attack the dragon. I therefore essayed to find a method of rehearsing that was in accordance with my character and yet capable of over-coming the dully passive, and occasionally active, resistance of the Fafner mentality.

In this endeavour, so-called discipline could hardly be of help to me. By its application, one can suppress open opposition in the orchestra, but not silent rejection; it may uphold good manners, but cannot contribute to the artistic communication between conductor and players. Quite apart from the fact that the harsh orchestral discipline of former days has long since given place to a socially more dignified form of orderly co-operation, the concept of discipline—in its general connotation of dutiful obedience—is of a negative nature: discipline prevents disturbances. By doing this, to be sure, it creates the social basis for an artistically fruitful relation between the orchestra and its head, but the more it is stressed, the more detrimental it becomes to the spiritual rapport between them. It was really only in the most extreme cases that I made use of disciplinary measures; nearly always I succeeded in achieving order and obedience by direct, personal influence.

Here, I should like briefly to mention the traditional notion of a kind of discipline that has been found to be sufficient for regulating the relation between guidance and execution in all those cases where the higher musical or spiritual aims are not even sought after. The demands of hard-boiled mediocrity easily attain their mediocre fulfilment by means of conventional discipline.

I must, however, categorically declare myself in favour of order, in general conduct as well as in music-making itself.

For the lofty intrinsic order that is an essential feature of all art and its representation cannot be approached in an atmosphere of external disorder. An adequate degree of external discipline is as indispensable in the artistic workshop as cleanliness and orderliness are in a well-run household.

This external discipline is, however, neither able, nor supposed, to achieve more than the creation of an undisturbed atmosphere for musical work; what is needed for this work itself is the agency of an inner, higher, that is, artistic, discipline; the true supervisory power in music-making, which has scarcely more than the name in common with 'discipline.' Its province comprises attention to the directions of the composer, exactness of time and rhythm, fidelity to the laws of music in general—it is the pre-condition for the productiveness of the conductor's work with the players, and its maintenance must be his constant concern.

In order that they may be able to satisfy the practical demands of this higher, artistic discipline, conductor and orchestra are, to be sure, in need also of that special form of experience which we call routine. This last is the precious fruit from the barren field of habit: valuable, nay, necessary, since, being adjuvant to practical execution, routine renders feasible or facilitates the overcoming of such difficulties as arise in instrumental technique, sight-reading, and other tasks of the executant musician in the mastery of which experience plays a part. Routine is essential for the practical, day-to-day business of artistic institutions; but it cannot claim a higher place than that of a useful servant of musical practice—from the proper artistic sphere of music in which the spirit should reign supreme, it must most definitely be kept away.

There is no doubt that, over the years, Fafner's resistance gives less and less trouble to the conductor; it retreats before the conductor's growing experience and competence which, in turn, enhance his self-assurance; altogether, one can say that the increasing respect, sometimes mixed with fear, that the players feel for a rising personality greatly facilitates the work of the conductor with the orchestra in all its aspects. I myself, perhaps, had a particularly difficult stand with the orchestra since, as I have said, my all-too-selfless empathy in others critically reduced the assurance and energy of my self-assertion. Eventually, however, it was my very recognition of this moral impediment that showed me the way most accessible to my nature. I realized that I was certainly not cut out to be a ruler or despot, but rather to be an educator who, as we know, methodically uses his empathy with others for gaining influence over them. My task was now to enforce the powerful, nay, irresistible demands of my musical personality by means of that empathy; to uphold my own ideals uncompromisingly without violation of other people's.

In retrospect, I can state today that the artistic results of my work with singers, choirs, and orchestras in the opera-house and on the concert platform must be ascribed, if we pass over my musical and dramatic influence, to these educational endeavours. I think my musicians and singers will acknowledge that, far from being put under any pressure or compulsion, they were encouraged to obey their own inner urge in their playing and singing, and that my constant inspiriting served to stimulate them to give of their best in the common effort, and to participate in my intentions.

But far be it from me to recommend as a panacea a method that was indicated for me by my character. Every approach that enables the conductor to project himself and his musical intentions onto his collaborators has, by this very fact, proved its individual merits. Gustav Mahler, undoubtedly one of the greatest conductors of our age, effected his masterly performances by dictatorial means—unforgettable, incomparable achievements in the opera-house and on the concert-platform were wrought by his eruptive, violent personality. Strictly speaking, Mahler's results and those of kindred natures are not reached by following a method; the means employed, which are, if anything, instinctive and prompted by the moment, are revealed and justified by the loftiness of the interpretation.

But it would be a mistake to believe that I am prepared to sing the praises of despotism *per se.* For the conductor as absolute ruler is usually as much dictated as dictator; his passionate artistic intensity forces him to exert force; the demands he makes on himself are even more inexorable than those he makes on his collaborators. Besides, it is perfectly possible for this sort of artistic character to go hand in hand with goodness of heart, love of humanity, mental agility, and catholic interests, as was the case with Gustav Mahler. In its interpretative activities, such a nature is subject to an inner pressure which, in turn, compels it to seek its aims by means of subjugation.

However, it is only in extreme cases that this is a matter of apodictic contradistinction: the educator may, particularly in his younger days, develop a temperamental streak of impatience, or, when older, on occasion adopt a dictatorial attitude after mature consideration of its efficaciousness; the more violent nature, on the other hand, when dealing with very gifted or particularly obliging artists, may often be able to achieve his aims by the mildest forms of communication. Since, moreover, the methods, or 'non-methods,' of influencing singers and players are not only as numerous and varied as the personalities of conductors, but also undergo development and, not infrequently, fundamental changes during a conductor's career, our sole criterion for their value will be the results they achieve: the performance. Now, it is true that I have heard excellent performances that resulted from violent methods not less often than I have encountered equally great achievements that were reached by a more educational approach. Perhaps the former were rather staggering and shattering, the latter rather up-lifting and edifying; perhaps the former were mightier in their general impact, the latter richer and lovelier in details. This being so, it will depend on the specific emotional sphere of a work which conductor is more suited to it; the listener, too, will have to decide which kind of execution comes closest to his heart.

In general, however, it can be said that a violent manner of dealing with people will either be defeated by their resistance or result in their intimidation. On the other hand, the milder methods of psychological empathy, persuasion, and moral intermediation will have an encouraging and productive effect. Of course, it is more the individual effort in orchestral music-making that is favoured and promoted by these methods, whereas sharper ones often produce an amazing intensification of group-feelings, of the communal striving for achievement. The aim of the educator—in the family, in the school, and wherever human beings are entrusted to his care—is to develop the individual to his highest potentialities, to educe what is latent in him. In the music-making of an orchestra, however, is contained more than such individual efforts; apart from his individuating activity, the preponderant part of the conductor's work is in raising a community to its highest potentialities, that is, to collective efforts in which those individual elements find their organic place. Whenever, therefore, the common effort as such is to be influenced, the conductor must adapt his method to this task; his method must become as efficacious in ministering to the individual as to the collective spirit.

In these endeavours, he will experience how much easier it is to win the heart of an individual player, as for instance, the first 'cellist or the first trumpeter, than to strike enthusiasm into, shall we say, the third bassoonist or a second-fiddle player at the fifth desk. For musicians such as the latter, cited here as the representatives of the *compact majority* of the orchestra, the conductor cannot really be an educator, if education is to signify the modeling of the individual. What will be instrumental in the modeling of a group, such as is requisite here, is not any method, but rather that compelling, direct influence of the born conductor which I have instanced above as the mark of true talent for conducting; to it, the 'tutti' of the orchestra, inclusive of all second fiddlers and bassoonists, will be just as amenable as is a large meeting to the words of an eloquent leader—for strong is the binding force of group spirit, particularly under the influence of an impressive personality. Incidentally, I believe that the instinctive effect made by the conductor on the totality of musicians springs from a propensity in his nature that is, all being said, allied to that for teaching; like the conductor's educating influence on the individual, the teacher's influence is directed to the advancement of talents, and mental attitudes, and the encouragement of achievement.

A moral danger which, at the same time, is an artistic one, lies for the conductor in the power he has over others—if it is given to him, that is. It is in his interest as a human being, as well as in that of his musical achievements, to resist the temptation to misuse it. Tyranny can never bring to fruition artistic—or, for that matter, human—gifts; subordination under a despot does not make for joy in one's music-making; intimidation deprives the musician of the full enjoyment of his talent and proficiency. Yet I should certainly not want to impugn the employment of earnest severity—or even the occasional borrowing of the bolt of Zeus; the latter, if the hand knows how to wield it, can in exceptional situations bring surprisingly good results. Severity is a quite legitimate, even indispensable, means of dealing with people, which the conductor cannot well forego. But the basis of the conductor's relation to the orchestra, as of all human relationships, must be tolerant benevolence, the *bona voluntas;* combined with complete sincerity, this creates the right climate for fruitful work and will suffuse the orchestra's achievements with its warming glow.

The orchestral musician needs this warm climate for the full unfolding of his artistic abilities; under the chill of unfriendliness or mordant scorn, under the heat of impatience or anger emanating from the conductor's desk, they freeze or wither. Yet the moral force of real benevolence and sincerity is sometimes strong enough to find its way to the player's heart despite a superficially unfriendly or violent manner, whereas false friendliness or affection, arrogance or vanity, have a vitiating, nay, destructive effect on the relation between conductor and orchestra.

If it is possible, nevertheless, for a conductor of distinguished musicianship and strong personality to achieve great, or even overwhelming results in spite of a character that predisposes him to the above-mentioned, or even worse, defects, the cause of this must be sought in a curious propensity of music: in acoustic representation, music becomes a transmitter of personality, in the sense that metal is a transmitter of heat. It transmits the ego of the performer more directly to the listener than can any other medium of direct communication from one human being to another. This explains the unequaled personal success of executant musicians of strong individuality, and their breathtaking, though transitory, impact which overwhelms the listeners and makes them oblivious of the work itself. To be sure, these enthusiasts often scarcely realize that they have succumbed not so much to the music as to the dynamism of the personality that communicated the music to them. Moreover, these mass-effects may sometimes exemplify a variation of a psychological phenomenon encountered in many other fields; namely, the urge felt by natures lacking in self-reliance to subject themselves to a strong personality. A multitude of those who are inclined to submissiveness—which may often be the cloak of worthier aspirations—respond and succumb to the tyrannical impulse to rule over the souls of others. Surely, such personal successes of certain interpreters are in no wise a yardstick of true musical culture, as a misled public opinion often believes they are. Not on successes, but on achievements, depends the standard of the public cultivation of the arts. The value of an art-offering in the opera house or on the concert platform can only be determined by inquiring whether this interpretation has revealed the wealth and greatness of the work and the significance of its creator. In proportion as the conductor attempts, and is capable of, satisfying this true purpose and aim of re-creation, he has proved himself the chosen apostle of creative genius and the faithful servant of his art.

At all events, personality is of decisive importance in the realm of musical interpretation, and its expansive force means more in the matter of influencing the orchestra than a spate of rational explanations. And yet, the musical achievement will be a higher one if the conductor's moral faculties allow him to be 'his brother's keeper' in relation to the orchestra, rather than its task-master. For if, to take two examples, the soli of the bass clarinet after King Mark's entrance in *Tristan*, or the themes of oboe and clarinet in the second movement of Schubert's *Unfinished* are to be instinct with the personal sentiment of these woodwind players, then the conductor must grant his players certain musical rights of their own; what is more, he must extend a helping hand to them. Wherever personal sentiment shows itself in the orchestra, it will—in careful coordination with the conductor's intentions—serve to enrich the performance. Conversely, if individual taste or personal, emotional participation are ruthlessly suppressed, the result will be a sort of emotional impoverishment of the performance. The conductor should strive to encourage every sign of emotional participation in the orchestra, he should explore and employ to the fullest degree the capacities of his collaborators; he should excite their interest, advance their musical talents; in short, he should exert a beneficial influence on them. In this way, the orchestra will not be a subjugated, that is, artistically inhibited, mass of people, but a harmoniously attuned, live unity of individuals who will gladly follow the conductor's guidance; the work of art in all its facets will receive its due, and the conductor will have at his disposal an instrument from which his soul sounds forth.

The contrast between the two extremes of the re-creative character is shown by the egotistical tendency in the one case, and the selfless manner, in the other, in which the ego is affirmed. The egotist strives, consciously or instinctively, to conquer, to dominate, to triumph; that *other one*, and those *others* are for him but a means of his unlimited artistic aggrandizement, of attaining his ends with ruthless energy. Under the egotist's direction, a certain *sameness* will descend on all works; one that will detract from the wealth and variety of their creative content; but one which, at the same time, is capable of giving a strong, nay overwhelming, impression of personality. Selflessness, on the other hand, with an equal investment of personal dynamism, wishes to convince, help, advise, and teach; such an ego does not prey upon others, but seeks to give of itself to that other one, the composer, and to those others, the players, and thus to wield the influence of an educator; it means to do justice to the manifoldness of the works. The selfless ego strives to extend its power over others, the self-centered ego to incorporate others into itself. Between these two extremes in the realm of reproductive art—let us call them the conqueror and the guardian—there is, of course, every possible kind of gradation and mixture, and the resulting differentiation between the various types of musician serves to enrich our musical life. It offers to us a plenitude of works in a plenitude of different expositions, none of which is of necessity *wrong* because it differs from the others. If the talented and experienced conductor strives faithfully to explore and reveal the spirit of a work; if he, with this aim in mind, works with the orchestra in all simplicity and sincerity, the very truthfulness and seriousness of his approach will ensure that his conception shall seem no less authentic than other, different, interpretations.

I have already pointed out in a previous context that a work is capable of different interpretations and that, moreover, our own repeated performances of it need not, when allowance is made for spontaneity, entirely agree with each other. Faithfulness to the spirit knows of no rigidity—it is not faithfulness to the letter—the spirit of a work of art is flexible, *elastic,* hovering.

Once more: what matters, apart from talent, is the convictions and intentions of the conductor—his musical abilities and his character together affect the method of his practical work with the orchestra, and together they determine the artistic standard of his achievements and the strength and persuasive force of their message.

Gustav Mahler

... Past understanding are God's works and fair as at the birth of light"—thus, in *Faust,* the Archangel sings the praises of the creations of God, and the same enthusiasm for the masterpieces of music lived in the soul of Mahler. "Fair as at the birth of light" were they to him at every moment, did they sound in his playing, and did they appear to the listener, a prominent trait of his interpretation being this very impression of newness, improvisation, and spontaneity. Only the most profound understanding of a work reveals that remnant of incomprehensibility which is the property of the great creations of art and of nature and the mark of their greatness. It alone is able to kindle ever anew the flame of interest and enthusiasm, while the shallow-minded, thinking that they understand this composition to the very last or know that one thoroughly, soon lose their sense of proportion and become the victims of routine and triviality. His growing familiarity with the works of the masters but served to increase Mahler's amazement at and his admiration for that which was "past understanding" in them, and to give nourishment to his capacity for a constantly renewed relationship. Just as only constant wooing serves to keep love vigorous, so he, too, never ceased to woo the works of art and was ready at any time to revise his conception, or to improve and deepen it.

And that is the reason why none of his performances ever sounded hackneyed—every one of them, even the thirtieth repetition of the same work, took place "for the first time." It goes without saying that at the bottom of his apparently uncontrolled and impetuous production of music there was an inexorable exactness. He rendered strict obedience to the musical score, to the value of its notes, and to its directions concerning time, delivery, and dynamics, and demanded it of all his co-workers. He asked for an instrumental correctness from his singers and was never satisfied until the last measure of precision had been achieved by all. His insistence upon absolute musical clearness was commensurate with the clearness of his conducting and the exemplary beat of his baton, the distinctness of which was not impaired by even the most violent emotion. In the numerous performances under his guidance witnessed by me I may have noticed a mistake, now and then, on the part of the singer or a musician, but never a lack of precision or an inaccuracy in the ensemble, for the unfailing accuracy of his beat always knew how to keep stage and orchestra in perfect accord with each other.

At the same time, he never gave the impression of

machine-like precision, and I cannot recall that his exactitude was ever particularly mentioned either by his audiences or by the critics. The reason for this was that his precision was to him but a means to an end, and this end was—soulfulness. Without a sacred sense of order, leading almost to pedantry, the gifts of a genius were to him but an empty sound meaning nothing. When, however, he had succeeded, by his persistent demands upon singers and musicians, in achieving absolute distinctness and precision, the soul was permitted to spread its wings freely upon this secure foundation, and thus his performances produced the effect of spontaneous improvisation.

There was no arbitrariness at all in his interpretations. That he was accused of it merely proves the difference between his inspired presentation and that which was traditionally accepted. If he did make changes in classical works they were directed against the letter and in favor of the clearly recognized spirit. In that sense is to be explained, for instance, his much discussed retouching of the instrumentation of Beethoven's *Ninth* and other works. With his thorough knowledge of the orchestra, he interfered wherever the instrumentation was likely to mar the distinctness or the realization of Beethoven's intentions and, when he was attacked for it in Vienna, he defended his changes in a public declaration by pointing to the difference between the power of Beethoven's conception and the instrumental limitations of his day, the example set by Wagner, and to the duty to provide for a clear flow of the orchestral voices. The fanatical obedience to the score, which I have mentioned, did not blind him to any contradiction existing between its directions and the composer's actual intentions. I dare say that people are today generally convinced of the necessity of such retouching and the views diverge only as to the manner. At any rate, Mahler was actuated, in this respect, by the acuteness of his ear, which made him sense the musical meaning of vaguely instrumented passages.

"Your Beethoven is not my Beethoven," he replied resentfully to a well-meaning friend who had interrogated him on the unusual character of his performances. And that, indeed, explains the whole matter. His Beethoven had nothing in common with the polished classic habitually heard in routine-like concerts of the day. His relationship to him was born of experience, and fraught with experience was his interpretation. His *Fidelio* with the *Leonore Overture* and his indescribably fine rendition of the overture to *Coriolanus* have remained sufficiently clear in my memory to enable me to testify to the "Beethoven-nearness" of his nature. For in him were the thunderstorms of Beethoven's soul, its vigor, and its love; and in him, too, was simplicity and truth and the sense of the symphonic which, no matter how much care he bestowed upon details, always gave precedence to the organic form.

A look into the depths of the work, as piercing and full of divination as his, made arbitrariness and subjective conception impossible. Complete was the picture that stood before his inner vision and there was no gap to be filled on one's own authority. The frequent crime of arbitrary changes and subjective alterations of the meaning of works of art has its cause—where downright presumption or a craving for originality are not to blame—in the defective spiritual vision of an interpreting artist who has not been given the key to the heart of the work. What is there left for the poor fellow to do, if he wants to avoid a shallow performance, but to fill up the gaps arbitrarily on his own authority?

Mahler's clear vision of the works of the masters was not,

however, the clearness of daylight. Music is by no means a daylight art and its backgrounds and its last depths are not disclosed to the man of the bright soul. From dark underground regions it springs and in dark underground moods is it understood and felt. Not the clear blue Mediterranean, but the darkly surging ocean, is kin to it. Dark, too, was the surging in Mahler's soul. Is it surprising, then, that it felt at home in the kindred element and was able to pierce the depths of music by virtue of its nocturnal vision?

"What is best in music is not to be found in the notes," Mahler was in the habit of saying. And this best and soulful element which surged with eloquent force from the music he performed produced so elemental an effect and one of so personal an avowal that doubts were entertained at times whether it was still the composer himself who spoke or whether Mahler's impetuous soul had not perhaps seized upon the musical language of the other man as a means of pouring out his own feelings. That Mahler desired nothing but to disclose to his very depths "the other man"—i.e. the work to be performed—is beyond any doubt. The question, however, whether, from such a production of music, the soul of the composer spoke, whether it was that of the interpreter, or a mixture of both, touches upon the real secret of musical re-creation. Only a positive avowal of one's ego, whether it be in life or in music, is able to carry conviction and to stir up deep emotions by the full force of its directness, and it is the failing of even the most sincerely meant mediocre interpretation that the identities of composer and interpreter are lacking, that an "I" tells us of a "he." How different is it in the case of an inspired interpreter! The expression of being "beside oneself" gains its most impressive meaning in the transports of his enthusiastic production of music. Ecstasy loosens within him the fetters of individualization and the re-creation of the other becomes a co-creation and almost a creation of his own. His gift resembles the ability of Proteus. Heart and imagination are so filled with "the other" that, in an excess of fellow-feeling, a kind of amalgamation takes place: the barriers separating the creating and the re-creating artist seem to disappear and the conductor now rules as over a work of his own. His it is to say "I," his to feel "I," and this very feeling of egoism gives to his interpretation its directness and its convincing power. It is for that reason that, in musical re-creation, serving loyalty and ruling license go hand in hand, and only he who understands that, under Wagner's baton, the *Ninth* sounded entirely in the spirit of Beethoven and that yet Wagner's own personality fully lived in it—nay, what is more, that only the unstinted pouring forth of Wagner's substance was able to set free the spirit of Beethoven—comprehends the essence of musical interpretation. And that is how it was with Mahler's conducting. By the full power of his great personality the work of the other man arose pure and strong and received its potent vital glow from the amalgamation of the two souls.

But even in cases where difficulties of understanding or the lack of an inner contact stand in the way of a complete absorption of the other's individuality, subjective assurance and a realization of one's own individuality need by no means imply that violence is done to the composer. Mahler succeeded in presenting faithfully and, at the same time, with a full assertion of his own personality, even works which were somewhat foreign to his nature, much to the surprise of the composers themselves who were fully conscious of the gulf that separated them. Of decisive importance, if such endeavors are to be successful, is the "will to the other," in which Mahler, as an interpreter, was never lacking. In the presence of this serving loyalty—to allude to the teaching of that scholastic, mentioned by Jean Paul, according to whom forty thousand angels could dance on the point of a needle—all manifestations of the collaborating imagination may find room at every point in the firm structure of a genuine work of art without constricting the space taken up by the work itself, and it may even be said that without this wealth of sympathetic vibration of the mind and the soul its convincing realization cannot be achieved at all.

The visible picture of Mahler's conducting became very considerably simplified in the course of years. Boehler's excellent silhouette caricatures show the violent and drastic nature of his motions during his first years in Vienna. Although he was seated when conducting at the Opera, his agility at that time and also previously, in Hamburg, was astonishing. But it never produced the effect of exaggeration and superfluity, but rather that of fanatical adjuration. As time went on, his attitude and gestures became quieter. His technique of conducting had become so spiritualized that he was easily able to achieve a combination of unfettered playing and unfailing precision by his seemingly simple beat, his body remaining otherwise almost motionless. His powerful influence upon singers and musicians accomplished by a look and the most sparing of gestures what he had formerly endeavored to convey by violent motion. In his last years, his conducting presented a picture of almost uncanny quiet, although the intensity of expression did not suffer by it. I recall a performance of the *Sinfonia Domestica* by Strauss under Mahler's direction at which the contrast between the uproar of the orchestra and the immovable attitude of him who had unleashed it made a most eerie impression.

In spite of his absorption in the purely musical work with singers and musicians, on the occasion of stage rehearsals with orchestra the dramatist within him watched with the hundred eyes of Argus, and nothing on the stage, whether connected with the dramatic performance, with the lighting, or with the costumes, ever escaped him. Everything was under his observation at all times. By precept or teaching, at times in a quiet form and, then again, by violent attack, he accomplished the whole of his purpose with the performing artists. Not, however, because he set out to accomplish it, but because he must; and this powerful compulsion that governed him forced his co-workers through him to unquestioning obedience.

Let me once more refer to his warmness of heart as the most striking characteristic and strength of the conductor, a quality that imparted to his interpretations the impressiveness of a personal avowal and made one forget all the painstaking rehearsals, all traces of his educational work, all virtuosity and perfection of execution, and made the music he produced into a spontaneous message from soul to soul. In this borderland of artistic and human endeavor the nobility and strength of his soul proved true; the secret of the glory of the Opera's director and musical leader, which shines as bright today as ever, is explained by an ideal combination of artistic gifts and the emotional power of a great heart.

LEOPOLD STOKOWSKI

Conducting

Conducting is little understood and greatly misunderstood. Often the superficial and exterior aspects of conducting are exaggerated, and the inner realities of the art of conducting completely unperceived. As music is for the ear and not for the eye, the visual part of conducting is relatively unimportant. The only visual part essential is for the players to be able to see clearly the notes they are reading, and at the same time to be able to see easily the conductor's beat and his eyes. Also, the conductor should be able to see the players' eyes so that there can be understanding and

LEOPOLD STOKOWSKI: Born in London in 1882. He was conductor of the Philadelphia Orchestra from 1912 to 1936. Later, he organized orchestras of his own, and was a guest conductor of numerous orchestras.

comradely co-operation among all those in the orchestra.

A good conductor is an integral part of the orchestra. He co-operates with all the players of the orchestra in rhythms—tempi—phrasing—accentuation—the modeling of melodies—the combining of counter-melodies—the gradual growth of the music—the relating of all the parts of the musical structure—tonal climaxes—architectonics—the feeling of the style of the music—the fullness of its emotional expression—the freedom of its imagination—its purely musical quality. These and many other things are the function of the conductor. If a conductor is separate or remote from the orchestra, he is not a living part of that great instrument—not a warm and vital channel for the music being played.

Conducting is only to a small extent the beating of time—it is done far more through the eyes—still more it is done through a kind of inner communication between the players and the conductor. If this inner communication does not exist, a conductor is only a time beater, and any good orchestra can keep time perfectly without such a time-beating conductor. In fact, such a conductor disturbs and depresses a good orchestra. Some believe that to beat time correctly is the main part of conducting—others, that to reproduce the score exactly as it is printed is the chief aim of conducting. Some conductors are in such a state of nervous excitement that they have little control over themselves and none over the orchestra—the result is a dull and blurred tonal picture of what should be clear and eloquent. Good conductors have control of themselves and the orchestra—they are sensitive to many kinds of feeling—they have within them many kinds of imagination—they are alive to the poetry of music and the poetry of all life—they bring to music a creative, dynamic power. These are born conductors.

A violinist may have the good fortune to have a Stradivari instrument—or a pianist a Steinway—but a conductor must form his own instrument. He must know how to choose each player, recognizing in him his degree of mastery of the instrument—his flexibility in fitting his part to all the other parts of the orchestra—the beauty and variety of his tone—his understanding of the principles of phrasing—his general musical culture—intelligence—emotional qualities—imagination. The conductor must choose not only the players but their instruments. Some instruments are good for solo playing but unsuitable for orchestras. The conductor must understand the psychology of the players and know how to unify all the greatly varying characters of the players into one harmonious organism—which is a combination of many instruments, but still more of many psychological and emotional personalities. All these must be fused into *one.*

Whether or not a conductor uses a baton is of little importance. Personally I find a baton unnecessary—I am convinced that unessentials should be eliminated. But other conductors like to use a baton. It is of no importance—only the music—its deepest essence—is important.

Equally unimportant is whether a conductor reads from a score. Some conductors like to conduct everything from score—others conduct always from memory—still others conduct sometimes from score, sometimes from memory. Conductors use several kinds of memory. One is photographic—the conductor can see each page of the score in his mind—it is a *visual* impression. Another kind of memory is musical—the conductor can hear in his memory each melody, harmony, rhythm, and the interrelation among all the other elements of the music—this is an *aural* impression. In the thoughts of some, music and memory are confused. A man may be a

great musician and yet have a poor memory for music—conversely, a man may have a remarkable memory and yet be literal and mechanical as a musician. To a discriminating mind, music and memory are totally different. In my opinion the ideal way is to conduct with the score, and yet know the music from memory. This protects the music from a lapse of memory, which might happen to anyone, and yet gives the conductor perfect freedom. Personally I like to conduct concertos for violin, piano, and cello from score, because they seem to me like chamber music on a larger scale. But more impulsive emotional music I like to conduct without score. It is all a matter of individual preference and is of little importance. But there is one factor of vital importance in conducting—to achieve the most complete and eloquent expression of the inner spirit of the music and all the potentialities lying dormant on the printed page of the score. These dormant potentialities are like seeds which sometimes lie for years in the soil until the right combination of sun and water, the right minerals and fertilizing elements within the soil, awaken the life in the seed so that stems and leaves and flowers and fruits unfold themselves. A conductor should fully express all the potentialities of the music he is conducting. Often there is much more in the music than is expressed by a performance that is technically perfect, but mechanical and unimaginative.

Conductors are born, not made. No amount of academic education can make a real conductor out of someone who is not born with the necessary qualities. But musical education and general culture are of inestimable value to the born conductor. The following aspects of conducting can be taught, provided the conductor already has a deep and broad musical culture—

How to beat time
How to read orchestral scores
The nature of the orchestral instruments—their various technical resources—how they sound separately—how they sound when related together in various groups.

All the above are connected with the material side of conducting. But another aspect of conducting is difficult and perhaps impossible to teach. This has to do with imagination—emotion—suggestion—the power to visualize a whole composition so that its proportions and varied musical qualities are seen in relation to each other in one glance. To be able to evoke the poetry of the music—to give vitality to every phase of its expression—to understand and project the inner meaning of the music—its deepest essence—its soul—these and many other of the highest qualities of conducting are born in a man. They cannot be taught.

A conductor should have great range of sensitivity to different kinds of music. He should enter into and live those different phases of music. He should understand all the instruments in the orchestra—what they can do—what they cannot do—their different registers—their different timbres—how all instruments relate to one another in groups—and how those groups make the whole tonal design of the orchestra. A good conductor feels with each player in the orchestra. He feels the motion of each bow of the string instruments—the intensity or relaxation or speed of motion of the left-hand technique of the string instruments. He feels the breathing and lip tension of each wood-wind and brass player. He is sensitive to the differing capacity of every player each day—because that is never twice the same. He must be a leader of men and yet simple. The players must have confidence in him—believe in his sincerity—and be willing to co-operate with him so that they give all the musical powers in them to the music. He must devote and concentrate all his life to conducting and to music. It must mean everything to him. He must have musical intuition—he must know instinctively the inner invisible powers of music—through imagination he must be able to reveal remote, yet intensely stimulating and inspiring, possibilities and moods in music. When a truly great violinist plays the violin concertos of Beethoven or Brahms, he not only plays all the notes and rhythms correctly, but he conveys through those notes and rhythms an immense range of profound emotion—he suggests states of feeling and illumines visions we have all experienced and know to be among the highest possibilities of music. With an orchestra these possibilities are sometimes greater, and therefore demand an even wider range of expression. A true conductor must be able to fulfill the creative side of this responsibility. In addition, a conductor must have a complete understanding of the music's emotional content—its range of imagination—the quality and subtlety of its psychic suggestion—because great music has the power of suggesting moods in us which are remote from this life and utterly different from the outer world in which we live. The more a conductor can—through his imagination—intensely evoke these remote and subtle states of feeling, the more is he a worthy collaborator with the composer.

WILHELM FURTWÄNGLER

About the Handicraft of the Conductor

The artistry of leading an orchestra is exercised, like virtually nothing else in music, in full public view. Like the technique of various instruments, whose preparation demands a great deal of time—in part a lifetime if they are really to be mastered—the technique of conducting is no mystical science. The audience has the opportunity of witnessing all the secrets of communication flowing to and fro between conductor and orchestra, because conducting is an art of "transference." Here the rhythm, the sound, the expression of the entire ensemble are determined in their most minute details

WILHELM FURTWÄNGLER: Born in Berlin, 1886; died in 1954. The successor of Arthur Nikisch as conductor of the Leipzig Gewandhaus Orchestra, he conducted with great success throughout the world.

through relatively simple gestures. The how is open to the observation of anyone who cares to think about it. One sees the musicians, the way they look at the conductor (and often do not even seem to look); one sees the motions of the conductor. These, because they are linked to the realization of the rhythmical pattern, do not vary much. And yet: can anything produce a greater change in an orchestra than different conductors? I am not speaking of interpretation, which naturally will vary according to the personality of the orchestra leader. I am speaking about the "material" qualities of the playing which appear earlier—and often much more decisively—than interpretative intentions. First of all, there is the sound in itself.

Why does the same orchestra sound full, rich, and smooth under one conductor, and brittle, hard, and angular under another? Why does it play legato—an important quality when required—under one, but not under another? Is it not often as if the purely tonal difference of one and the same orchestra under two conductors were barely smaller than the difference between two violinists, or even two singers? There are orchestra leaders under whom the smallest village band plays as if it were the Vienna Philharmonic, and there are those under whom even the Vienna Philharmonic sounds like a village band. It has become customary in such extreme instances to speak of "suggestion," "power of personality," and the like. All that is nonsense; no power of personality enables one conductor to make the smallest phrases sing, sound rich and well-balanced, while with another conductor they are stiff and wooden when they can be heard at all—assuming that both have the same tempo and the same interpretative design.

No. In fact, and now it must be stated openly, there is no art kept more secret than that of the real conductor. This is true not only for audience and critic, who are more or less dependent on general impressions, but also for the so-called "professionals," the conductors themselves. How long it took me, a young conductor, starting out like other young conductors, to discover why every orchestra sounded so changed under the simple beats of Arthur Nikisch; why the winds played without the usual exaggerated sforzati, the strings with a singing legato, and the sound of the brass fused with the other instruments, while the general tone of the orchestra acquired a warmth which it did not have under other conductors. I learned to understand that this beauty of unified sound under Nikisch was not an accident; that this phenomenon, to put it more accurately, was caused by the way in which Nikisch "beat into" the sound. That it was, therefore, not a result of his personality, his suggestion—this term does not exist for sober professionals—but of his "technique."

The technique of the conductor is naturally connected with the person in so far as it is shaped by the expressive needs of the man. The imagination of a Stravinsky conceives an orchestral sound different from that of a Richard Strauss, and his conducting technique will involuntarily reflect it. Incidentally, there is nowadays a conducting technique which is taught in books and is practiced everywhere—a standardized technique, as it were, which produces a standardized orchestral sound. It is the technique of routine whose aim is simply precision. Here something which should be a natural prerequisite to the proper leading of every orchestra is made into a final purpose, an end in itself. Such a technique will never really do justice to the true requirements of music. Something summary, mechanical, will always adhere to it; the "apparatus" burdens the spirit and chokes it. Tolstoi says: "Ninety-five per cent of all artistic activity is routine, can be learned; that is not important. What is important, alone and exclusively, are the remaining five per cent."

Conducting concerns itself in the first instance with the transference of the rhythmical elements. The conductor first of all indicates the tempo, from which everything else—precision, ensemble playing, and so on—follows. This tempo is, to begin with, something abstract, as, for instance, telegraphy is abstract, and is rendered through the Morse code. The metronome shows a tempo in abstract numbers. Nevertheless, it is never a matter of abstract tempo in this sense, but of an actual realization of the music through tones, through definite, ever-changing melodies, and so forth. It may happen that such music is in itself of a more abstract nature—that is, somewhat staccato in rhythmical emphasis. In such instances, gestures which concentrate on the rhythmical nucleus are in order. It may also be that the music flows forth in broad melodies; then precise gestures, emphasizing the basic rhythm, are a necessary contrast. In this case, the orchestra must play the melodies as coherent phrases, as *melodies,* in spite of the fact that the conductor's gestures are only capable of indicating the points, the corners, the rhythmical intersections. And here we have the entire problem of conducting technique in essence: how do I, the conductor, who can only wave my baton through the air, get the orchestra to render a singing phrase in its proper nature—as song? In other words: how can I, considering the transfer—mechanisms which are based on rhythmical points—make an orchestra sing? To a certain degree, it can be done in a mechanical way; because singing too takes place within a definite rhythm it is harnessed into a rhythmical entity. To that extent, even a conductor who is exclusively rhythm-oriented could give it its proper place. But no more than that. Because, in truth, song, the singing phrase,

Furtwängler

is something quite specifically different from music resolving itself only in rhythm. It is not only a chain of connected points, but it is an entity. As such, even in the rhythmical context, it detaches itself from the rhythm of the whole, then adjusts to it again. The song, the singing phrase, is different in principle from all rhythm; but—and this must be stated here once and for all—it is something no less basically important than rhythm for the art of music, as we understand it in Europe. Only here does the problem of hearing and music-making, and thus of conducting, actually begin. The question of the "technique" of the conductor, from which we started, is then in short: how do I get the orchestra not only to play together with rhythmical precision, but also to sing, to sing with all the freedom which belongs to the realization of every living singing phrase? Mechanical rhythmic precision and the freedom of singing—seemingly irreconcilable opposites—how are they to be reconciled? Or conversely: how do I get an orchestra that sings (with all those innumberable, inexpressible rhythmical singularities which can never be fixed at rehearsal, and which yet belong to all genuine singing) to play together in a rhythmically precise manner in every last detail. Here we have the reason for the effect of Arthur Nikisch's conducting, which I had occasion to experience myself. Nikisch had precisely the capacity to make an orchestra sing. This—and one may be certain of it—is a most uncommon talent. This "singing" does not mean only those relatively easy passages, where the music actually streams forth in broad, easily perceptible melodies; it also refers to those infinitely varied formations, as they appear principally in the classical literature, where the singing line (the "melos," as Wagner called it), is ever present, but is constantly changing in pitch, position, voice, even within fractions of single bars. It is no less important for the understanding of contemporary works, but is naturally more difficult to recognize there in its thousand disguises.

The gesture which corresponds to the rhythm, to the point, is by nature itself rhythmical, itself like a point, and given with the utmost precision. But, and this is the practical problem of all conducting, this point, this precision, cannot be attained with an orchestra when one makes such a point in the air, because what induces a group of people to come in at the same moment needs a certain optical preparation. It is not the moment of the down-beat itself, nor the accuracy and sharpness with which this down-beat is given, which determines the precision achieved by the orchestra, but the preparation which the conductor gives to this down-beat. That the down-beat itself is short and accurate has at most an effect on the succeeding down-beats, since it marks the pulse of the rhythmical entity. But it is meaningless for the first note, for which this down-beat is after all intended. This is not known to those—and this includes 90 per cent of all conductors—who only conduct in points; that is, with sharp down-beats. There is no doubt that the sharp down-beat has its disadvantages. It means fixing the gesture at the one point, and results in a reduction of the expressive possibility that the living flow of the music demands. A point always remains a point; it is obvious that an orchestra which is conducted with points will also play with points, that is, everything rhythmical will be rendered with the required precision. But everything melodic, everything that lies between the individual beats (and that is sometimes quite a lot: one only has to remember the abundance of signs of expression, crescendo, and decrescendo which are so important in the works of some composers) will not be influenced. It is characteristic of such an interpretation—and this is frequently the case nowadays—that the rhythm, the meter come into their own, but not the music.

It cannot be sufficiently emphasized that the possibility of influencing a tone lies entirely in the preparation of the beat, not in the beat itself—in the brief, often tiny moment of the down-beat, before the point of unified sound is reached in the orchestra. The manner in which this down-beat, these preparations are shaped determines the quality of the sound with the most absolute exactness. Even the most experienced conductor is forever astounded by the unbelievable precision with which a well-coordinated orchestra reflects his smallest, most minute gestures. This is precisely the reason why a conductor who *really* is one has no opportunity, at concerts, to make gestures "for the audience." It used to be asserted that a conductor like Arthur Nikisch had affectations. Now I can certify from personal knowledge of this conductor—and this knowledge is quite thorough—that any kind of pose was entirely foreign to him. On the other hand, other orchestra leaders who, in contrast to Nikisch, conducted in a pedantic way were not free of artifice; their rather simple focus on technique gave them time to think of the audience. This would never occur to a conductor like Nikisch. After all, he was engrossed in the sound as such, with the shaping and realization of that sound.

Thus, the conductor's opportunity for influencing the character of the interpretation and the orchestra's way of playing lies entirely in the preparation of the beat at least to the extent to which this influence is immediate, and not a matter of rehearsing. Here I would like to remark parenthetically that in general the actual work at rehearsal is overrated in this era, in which everything mechanical is held in such high esteem. What one can teach an orchestra in rehearsals, even extended, highly concentrated, and very precise rehearsals, is little in comparison with what can be done right from the start and in a few moments, through the type of beat and the related instinctive (that is subconscious) method of communication. And this is also the reason why different conductors —at least those deserving the name, and not mere timebeaters—get such a different sound from the same orchestra. It is on this that the instinctive appreciation which the public bestows on a conductor is based. If, as I stated before, the preparation (the beat itself and not its final point) is that which most strongly influences the sound of the instrument, could not one imagine a style of conducting which would renounce the final points of every beat, the knots, the pointing signals which might be likened to the peaks of telegraphy, and make use only of the beat, of the preparation as such? I might mention here that this is not mere theory, but that I myself have tried to practice this method for many years. This is the reason why many spectators, accustomed to the usual technique taught at conservatories, do not understand my gestures. They call them unclear, and go so far as to assert that I engage in "camouflage." Recently a critic wrote about a concert of mine with the Vienna Philharmonic: "With the unclear gestures of the conductor, it is impossible to understand how the orchestra could achieve such flawless ensemble playing. There is only one solution to the puzzle: endless rehearsals." No, that is precisely not the solution. My rehearsals do not exceed the customary number and hardly touch on questions of technique, that is, of precision. This very precision is much more the natural consequence of my "unclear" conducting. That this unclear conducting is not unclear after all, is shown by the fact that the instrument functions with flawless precision. It is, so to speak, the acid test. I can only repeat:

there are no conducting gestures as such, but only those with a practical goal, namely the performance of the orchestra. Conducting gestures must be judged from the aspect of the music, and then my gestures will be understandable, as, after all, the reaction on the orchestras which I lead everywhere clearly proves.

Great composers are not always conductors, but they are great musicians and as such significant for the conductor. A composer who was more of a conductor than most of the others, Richard Strauss, once mentioned to me, at a performance of Nikisch: "Nikisch has the ability to get a sound out of the orchestra which we others do not possess. I don't know what this is based on, but it is an undeniable fact." Strauss here touched on the problem that I have tried to illuminate in these pages, a problem so particularly difficult to elucidate because conducting, which takes place in full view of the public, must remain open to the comprehension and judgment of this public, even in its technical aspects. But experience shows that even seasoned professionals, persons who have been intensely concerned with conducting and questions related to it, are baffled at the sight of a real conductor. Were this not so, there would be many more orchestra leaders trying to imitate that style of conducting of which Nikisch was the exponent in the previous generation.

SIR ADRIAN BOULT

Arthur Nikisch

Eloquent pens have mourned in many languages the loss of Arthur Nikisch. We have in the last few weeks been reminded of the marvellous power of exposing the beauty of any work he touched, of the personal charm and influence over those with whom he came in contact and of the broadness of view which caused him to study and follow the music of many nations and many periods; and it is these qualities which have endeared him to audiences in many countries. But it may not be without interest to examine for a moment the side of him which some of us would venture to assert was

SIR ADRIAN BOULT: Born in England in 1889 and knighted in 1937. He has conducted major British, European and American orchestras.

the greatest of all—his power as a conductor in the narrowest and most technical sense of the word.

We know that technique in all things is the ability to make use of our means with the least effort and the greatest effect, and here surely Arthur Nikisch was supreme. His loss must seem to other conductors almost comparable to the loss of the dies at the Mint or the destruction of the standard measures at Greenwich; or even worse than this, for the means of reproduction or replacement are more complete in these latter cases. Consciously or unconsciously—and we are inclined to think it was instinct and the effortless outcome of long experience that brought him to this perfection—he always seemed to secure his results in the simplest way possible with the slightest movement and the greatest beauty. I can remember the most thrilling performance of the Brahms C Minor Symphony that I have ever heard—we are not now discussing whether Brahms should be thrilling or not—and at the end, when the orchestra and audience had been worked up to a white heat and the movement had finished in a blaze of triumph, it occurred to me that Nikisch's hand had never been raised higher than the level of his face throughout the whole movement. The long stick held by those tiny fingers almost buried beneath an enormous shirt-cuff had been really covering quite a small circle the whole time, though the range of expression had been so wide; and surely if the arm had ever been stretched to its full length, some catastrophe must have occurred, like an earthquake or the destruction of the building.

He did not spare only his own physique, but also the strain to the forces he controlled. Two interesting examples of this may be quoted. In Amsterdam in 1920 I was present at all the rehearsals before his first concert—he had not been there for 24 years. He began rehearsing the D Minor Symphony of Schumann. All was quiet and restful, even cold; a great deal was shown by gesture though always with the utmost restraint, and of real excitement there was none. Suddenly, where the last movement becomes "schneller" near the end, his wrist seemed to start a dynamo and there was an unexpected dramatic intensity about the two crashes and intervening silences. The second pause in particular seemed endless, when with a whispered "Eins, zwei," he led the basses off into their final passage, and the excitement of those last 26 bars of Presto so roused the orchestra that they got up and cheered. By this time the master was quite calm again and for the rest of the three rehearsals there was no other moment of tension. He had taken the full measure of his orchestra in those few moments and there was no need for anything but quiet work until the concert. A still more remarkable instance of this was at Leeds Festival in 1913. The interest of the chorus at the arrival of the great Nikisch was intense, and he, as usual, perfectly sure of himself, knowing every member of the orchestra and trusting the reputation of the chorus, took a risk that none but he would have taken and started the rehearsal with a work with which he had obviously the very slightest acquaintance—Richard Strauss' *Taillefer.* He went right through the work with hardly a stop and at a very deliberate pace, and I do not think he looked up from the music more than six times. He then played a few passages again and shut up the score. The chorus were obviously in despair, as he had not once given them the slightest "lift"; and a distinguished musician who was sitting next to me said, "Surely to goodness he is not going to leave it in that state?" He then went on to the familiar first-act selection from *Parsifal,* when he was able to get on intimate terms with the chorus, and I am told that the performance of Strauss' battle picture was as full of fire and excitement as anyone could have wished.

At home in Leipzig in his own hall with his own orchestra Nikisch had reduced everything to the lowest possible output of effort. The weekly arrangement there was a private rehearsal on Tuesday evening (to which we students were given cards of admission); the public rehearsal on Wednesday morning, which was filled with the musical people of Leipzig, who used to tell you it was "exactly the same as the concert, only the audiences were much more intelligent"; and the fashionable subscription concert on Thursday evening, where seats and boxes were handed down from father to son and for which it was very difficult to buy a single ticket. It was an accident that took me to the second Gewandhaus concert of the season during which I was a student. I had been to the Wednesday morning rehearsal and had there been disgusted to hear the violins play the opening tune of the slow movement of the *Jupiter Symphony* in canon *divisi,* the second half playing the tune at a quaver's distance from the first half. Various other things, notably continual exaggerations of expression and an extraordinary looseness of ensemble, were all swallowed by the complacent "musical" audience with complete equanimity. Coming to the conclusion that if Nikisch treated Leipzig audiences like this I preferred to hear him in London, I almost refused the kind offer by a friend of a ticket for the evening concert. However, I went, and was rewarded with one of the most perfect Mozart performances I have ever heard. From then on I went whenever possible to both rehearsals and the concert, and it was often amusing to note how Nikisch would finish the private rehearsal in an hour or so, perhaps not touching a big work like the Schubert C Major; how he would then blatantly rehearse the Symphony in front of his Wednesday audience, which happily drank in the absurd *rubatos* and other exaggerations; and how these things would all drop into proportion at the concert and fine performances result, even though one did not perhaps go all the way with the master in his "readings" of Beethoven or the Slavonic—or rather Magyar—passion he infused into Brahms.

Particularly at the time when Nikisch first came to London a great deal was said about his mesmerising the orchestra, and the Press contained quotations from statements of orchestral musicians to the effect that they "felt unlike themselves" when playing under his direction. Such things are difficult to discuss and even more difficult to gauge, but it may be possible to think of certain causes contributory to this impression. One of our most distinguished orchestral players whom I happened to meet a few minutes after he had finished rehearsing recently with Dr. Strauss said to me, "I have been playing the passages in *Don Juan* and *Till Eulenspiegel* for the first time for many years." The meaning of this was, of course, that although Strauss' beat looked rather wooden, it was in fact most sympathetic and flexible, and he would give a little time wherever it was needed to avoid a scramble; but so little that the ordinary hearer would be unaware of any *rubato*. In things of this kind Nikisch was quite remarkable; his long experience as an orchestral player, coupled with a remarkable sympathy which also showed itself in his conducting of concertos and opera, made it easy for him to do things that would never occur to most people. Another example of this was the way he would let the length of a pause or a *ritardando* depend on the bowing of the string players. Again, his experience helped him to glance always at the right man in the orchestra, however they were grouped and however deeply they were concealed behind a voluminous music stand. The curious slow gaze with which he seemed to take in the whole orchestra at the beginning of most rehearsals and of every concert gave him an opportunity of noticing everything and at the same time of getting on to terms with everyone.

Under such conducting it is easy for players to "feel unlike themselves" and for observers to think they are being mesmerised, but no amount of technical competence will account for the fact, agreed on by everybody, that from the first note of any performance the actual tone of the instruments seemed different from the tone produced by any other conductor. This shows a remarkable personal power, and there are few others of whom it is true. No one will forget the extraordinary way in which he compelled his audience to listen and made concentration child's play from beginning to end of a long concert or opera. This is, of course, a power common to all great artists, although the nature of the attraction varies. I can remember the impression made by Paderewski, who seemed to plunge us into the very presence of Beethoven or Chopin or whoever it might be. Nikisch rather brought us face to face with Nikisch, and it was only when his temperament matched that of the composer that the greatest performances would result. I would almost go so far as to say that there were few works that I would not have felt could have been better given by other conductors, in spite of the marvellous fascination of Nikisch's art.

But whatever he touched was alive and warm, and vitality is the alpha and omega of executive music. In all Wagner (except perhaps *Die Meistersinger*), often in Mozart and Haydn and always in Weber, his performances were supreme, and another landmark was the Verdi *Requiem* at Leeds in 1913. Even when we felt we must disagree there was such poetry and beauty, not to mention technical mastery, that we were held spellbound; and now all musicians and music lovers can only mourn together the loss of a great personality, a lovable man and a marvellous artist.

HERMANN SCHERCHEN

On Conducting

THE TEACHABLE TECHNIQUE OF CONDUCTING

Imagination and Reproduction

The significance of ideal conceptions in music. The art of conducting is governed by the fact that the conductor's instrument is a live one, consisting of a number of performers playing a number of different instruments. The conductor's task is to make this complex machine serve the art of music.

As he is playing upon a live instrument, he must understand not only the laws of his art, but also the idiosyncrasies of this instrument; and he will find perforce that he has

HERMANN SCHERCHEN: Born in Berlin in 1891. Conductor, writer, violist, and teacher, he is particularly known for his advocacy and performances of contemporary music.

to form a higher and more spiritual conception of these laws in consequence.

More than any other artist, the conductor must be a master mind, with an imagination capable of conceiving and materializing a musical image. Only when a work has come to absolute perfection within him can he undertake to materialize it by means of the orchestra.

We have to distinguish, then, between the preparatory process, by which the conductor evolves the highest possible ideal conception of a work, and the realization in sounds, the actual conducting (which consists in making things clear to the orchestra and in achieving the performance of the work).

The practice of conducting calls, firstly, for a manual training which is the first step towards acquiring the actual capacity to play on the orchestra. Here, again, the conductor and the orchestra remain apart, and at this stage artistic activity is restricted to a theoretical sphere. To acknowledge that the conductor's domain is largely spiritual is to realize the exceptional character of his art; one can then appreciate the great artistic and human attributes which must be possessed by the true conductor.

Music as the most spiritual of the arts. The main defect in musical life today is lack of imagination on the part of artists. Performers acquire a knowledge of the instrument they play, but never of the works they wish to perform. The technique of the instruments has become an end in itself. The player devotes the whole of his labour to this, but has practically no acquaintance with the technique of composition. And he knows even less of the creative forces.

Music is the most spiritual of arts. Triumph over matter marks the opening of music's greatest era. Werckmeister, when he evolved the tempered semitone system, reduced to order, and subjected to a human, an intellectual law, the unlimited diversity of the materials of music. That which had been sought in vain for nine centuries—the disposal of sounds in proper array, the central form-principle of music—followed, of necessity, upon the new logical hypothesis; the most elusive of materials was captured by the intellect of man.

The secret of art is the secret of personality, whose infinitely various possibilities cannot be counted. But the materials of art can be reckoned up. There is no secret in ordered sound but the secrets of man and of human nature; music proceeds according to human laws, it exhibits an orderliness which is human. Tones and the relations between them can be reckoned up; they have measurable, unequivocally representable values. Good music and good musicians understand one another without aid—without signs indicating dynamics and phrasing, or tempo, expression, and rubato. But that most autocratic of artists, the conductor, is only too often most willing to renounce his power: instead of obtaining his vision of his art from within himself alone, he usually becomes acquainted with musical works through an intermediary. Hence they are obscured by the instrument upon which he plays, and disfigured by the shortcomings of its instrumental technique.

The conductor has to materialize his ideal conceptions. The conductor, when representing a work to himself, must hear it as perfectly as the creator of this work heard it. A creative artist relies upon the acuteness of his own artistic perception; he hears new tone-colors, he views his materials in a new light, he stamps his own personality upon the music.

1930

Of all the human means of musical expression, singing is the most living or vital. Singing comes from within ourselves. The conductor's conception of a work should be a perfect inward singing. And if the work lives within him as an ideal, undimmed by obstacles of mechanism, then is he worthy to bear the conductor's responsibility. To conduct means to make manifest—without flaws—that which one has perfectly heard within oneself. The sounds must be commanded, and to conduct is to give them shape. The instrument which the conductor uses for this purpose is most sensitive, most richly and diversely equipped and articulated, inexhaustible and most inspiring: it is an organ of which each pipe is a human being. To be able to play this organ is to be a magician; to command it requires almost superhuman powers. But these powers live only in the innermost focus of the ego, at the very source of feeling and inspiration.

The ego must radiate all that it has felt in terms of music; and its radiations must be translated into tones of this magic organ. Only a man who can achieve this mediation in all its purity, in whom are combined the greatest powers of receiving and of giving out again, whose conception of the work does not dwarf it and who is capable of lifting up his medium to the level of that work, is worthy of the name of conductor. . .

Preparedness in Music

Being ready to play. It is important that the players should be ready, both outwardly and inwardly, at the moment of beginning to play and in view of all the problems that crop up in performance. In music (which is the only art whose presentation takes place in time) not enough importance is given to this 'beforehand' attitude in the matter of the players' imagination and self-observation. Luminous, spirited performances are invariably ascribed to instinctive genius. Instinct is one element of the organic, basic secret, of personality; and it cannot be 'learnt.' But it remains helplessly restricted in its manifestations if its possessor is unable to master the needful technique. And in order to master it, he must be aware of all artistic events and actualities past or new.

Significance of the Beginning. The beginning of a piece may be *p*, or *pp*, or *f*, or *mf;* it may be gentle, agitated, buoyant, or hard; dark and restrained in colour, or bright and exuberant; its character may be that of an insignificant accompaniment; it may give out the constructive energy of the piece in motto-like unison; it may, in short, be as diverse as life itself, and reflect any of life's variations.

How to achieve this. The conductor must, in one act of tense concentration, immediately seize the personalities of the orchestra and get them under his sole control. When he is ready to raise his stick, every player must have his instrument, ready to play, in front of him. And the conductor's first movement must be so precise, so charged with the required volitional power, as to take effect with the inevitability of a switch turning on electric light.

Technical aids. Should the music begin with an imperceptible *piano,* the players should be made to start moving their bows (though hardly noticeably) before they actually have to touch the string; the bow, gliding through the air, will gently start impelling the string to vibration. If the beginning is in a natural, simple, singing tone, let the usual practice of accentuating the attack be avoided. If the beginning is energetic, and has to gather up all the forces from the outset, let adequate preparations bring out these forces with the very first note. All these externals should exhibit the accuracy of perfect machinery set in action by the guiding will power of the conductor.

Leader and Orchestra

Educational activities. It is the duty of the leader, by his influence and watchfulness, to do away with all the usual habits of the string-players and the usual effects of their bad technique. The following are important points:

Downbowing must not emphasize, nor accentuate, nor end in *decrescendo.*

Upbowing must produce no *crescendo;* in upbeats the whole length of the bow need not always be used.

Changes of bowing should never occasion caesuras or accents.

The bow must be used in all suitable ways, all lengths and parts of it being resorted to (nut, point, middle, upper half, lower half).

The various types of *non legato* should be accurately differentiated: *spiccato* should never become *portato,* nor *portato* become *legato.*

As a general law, the stroke in orchestral playing should be the whole-length stroke, in *p* as in *f*, in *dolce* as in *appassionato;* it should resolve all melodies into elastic subdivisions, according to the structure of each one.

The tone must always be intense, never dull—to this effect, the part played by the left hand is vital.

Any technical process must be applied simultaneously by all players: few are the cases when a variety of processes is admissible.

Regulating the divisi, *etc.* The leader (in association with the principals of the second violins, violas, celli, and double-basses) has to regulate the allocation of *divisi* and the distribution of chords and double stops which are impossible to perform undivided. He must come to an agreement with his colleagues on matters of fingering and bowing so far as these are not prescribed by the conductor.

The natural starting-point of the motions of Conducting. All the advice given in this book for the technical solution of definite problems sets forth single tested possibilities of satisfactory execution. Carefully studied, it will safely lead the student to the point at which, by thoroughly studying cases as they occur, he will speedily discover the modifications that correspond to his own individuality.

The natural starting-point of all conducting motions is that where the fingers come to rest when the right arm, half extended, is raised forwards, shoulder-high. This raising naturally results in a slight curve of the elbow, which curve is restricted by the fact that when the arm moves thus, the elbow is slightly raised sideways and to the right. This position makes possible the performance of motions upwards, downwards, away from the body or towards it, and sideways to the right or left. Motions downwards, to the left or right, and upwards, are to be used exclusively for indicating the metre; but when they are brought closer to or farther away from the body, they acquire a power for expressive presentment. Unconsciously, we associate the notion of greater volume of tone with larger gestures, and that of a decreasing volume with a decrease of their compass. Hence the rule for indicating *f* or *p*, *crescendo* and *decrescendo:* motions that start from the natural starting-point and revert to it indicate the most neutral type of volume and intensity, that is, the *mf*. For a *crescendo*, the motions not only increase in amplitude, but their starting-point is carried farther forwards, away from the body. Conversely in *p*, not only are the gestures smaller, but the starting-point is brought closer to the body.

All this shows how wide a diversity of combinations are available. It is the conductor's sensitiveness and his capacity to conceive clearly and thoroughly that will enable him to use them all discriminatingly and always unambiguously.

A way of 'extinguishing' sonority is to bring the motion quite close to the body. Conversely, the amplest and most concentrated gestures must be reserved for dynamic and expressive culminations. It is therefore important always to keep in mind the neutral centre of tone-volume and of amplitude of gesture, and most carefully to proceed thence in the one direction or the other. And especially one should try to keep in reserve, in their unimpaired freshness, the most intensified or reduced gestures for the extreme points to which they correspond.

The Conductor's Bearing. Conducting should never be confused either with dramatic acting, pantomimic presentment, or gymnastics. Its ideal should be that no part of the body except the right arm should move. There is no need to resort to distorting emotional grimaces; on the contrary, the eyes should be kept quite free, alert, and ready, for they must watch, help, indicate, and encourage the players, and keep the conductor in touch with every one of them.

If all the rest of the body keeps in repose, attention is automatically restricted to the right arm, to which all movement is practically confined. A natural, easy, fixed position of the feet will prevent the lower part of the body from moving.

So far as possible, all needless bending of the body should be avoided. But one should likewise avoid tension, and the rigid repression of slight automatic movements of the body. Just as the head turns towards the various players as the conductor looks at them, so does the body slightly follow the gestures. But all this must be kept down to a minimum, and take place easily, unconstrainedly. It is only if a conductor is altogether free from constraint, and if his controlling energies are never cramped or distorted, that he is capable of carrying his orchestra to the utmost development of its power and getting the best from each player.

In any case let the student avoid the duplicating, simultaneous use of both arms, which never renders his motions clearer for the orchestra, more expressive, or more relevant. On the contrary, the practice robs a conductor of an important resource as regards expressive, representative conducting. When it remains independent of the right arm's motions (but still employing the unambiguous, basic metrical signs) the use of the left hand is a splendid method of articulating, intensifying, reinforcing, emphasizing, hushing, and refining. Hence, the proper and differentiated use of the left hand in conducting (during the use of the right) will have to be dealt with more thoroughly in the next section.

Clarity of conducting motions. By way of conclusion, I beg leave to repeat that all the prescriptions in this book refer to the cases in which conductor and orchestra meet without previous acquaintanceship with one another, or previous rehearsal for the purpose of mutual understanding. The object must remain perfect clarity of presentment—an unambiguity of gesture that will exclude all possibility of doubt. Even if the orchestral parts were devoid of indications the conductor's gestures should make easily and compellingly clear all points of dynamics, pace, quality, and degree of expression at every moment of the music.

The conductor must carry the whole of the work in his head, and thoroughly achieve the visible presentment of his conception. The ease and freedom with which he makes himself the carrier of the work communicate themselves to the players, who in turn are thus enabled to master without effort the matter they handle.

Conducting is a contact between human beings. The more simple, clear, and concentrated the contact is made, the more intelligible and telling its effect will be; and thus the players will be able, all the more joyously and enthusiastically, to allow the music to become a real work of art.

THE APPLIED TECHNIQUE, OR PRACTICE, OF CONDUCTING

When a student confronts an orchestra for the first time, he must have thoroughly mastered the practice of his craft. He must be not merely theoretically able to conduct an orchestra, but actually capable of dealing with the realities of the orchestra. It is not enough that he should be able to represent his ideal conceptions of works unambiguously and with infectious intensity: he must add to this capacity that of leading the orchestra so as, in the course of playing, forthwith to correct faults, to help through special difficulties, to adjust the balance in advance—in short, to establish a reciprocal relationship between conception and actual performance.

This is the part of conducting that proves most difficult to learn, the mastery of which is the only justification of the name of 'conductor.' The question is, how can practice be acquired without practice? How is the student to learn to overcome the technical problems of conducting without having an instrument upon which to practice? The only solution is for the teacher to represent this instrument; to play the part in turn of the intelligent and attentive player and the uninterested, reluctant player, varying in quality and in willingness, as actually occurs in orchestras. With his teacher, the student must experience all the cases that occur in practice; and in front of his mirror, he must find the way of studying and controlling his technique on his own. Before ever beginning to conduct, he must learn that if the orchestra goes wrong under his guidance, the fault lies with him. Therefore, his own contribution can never reach a high enough level; even when conductor and players cooperate with one another finely and sensitively, there is always room for an even clearer presentment and for an easier mastery of subject matter.

PAUL HINDEMITH

Conductors

There is one group of performers which in earlier periods of musical communication represented nothing but the simplest means of keeping several musicians, performing simultaneously, in line, but which has gained so much in importance that nowadays to most people its representatives alone are the figures that direct music, literally, socially, and spiritually. I am speaking of conductors. The earliest description of a conductor's duties, as we know them, can be found in the *Tractatus de musica* of Elias Salomon, a clerical writer on music in the late thirteenth century. Although his descrip-

PAUL HINDEMITH: Born in Germany in 1895; died in Switzerland in 1963. He was one of the foremost twentieth-century composers and conductors, as well as a fine viola player.

tion is not of great significance, it shows how the conducting of groups of musicians started, and therefore is worth reading. Elias' conductor had no orchestra to deal with, he was merely the director of a vocal quartet that sang the church services in the provincial town of Périgueux in France. It was the time when more-part music in the form of free organum had come to a certain perfection at the musical centers, that is, in northern France, Paris, and Limoges; and places like Périgueux with low-class performers and a conservative taste had just arrived at a style that in the centers was already outmoded: the old, improvised simple organum. It is the performance of this old-fashioned form of more-part singing which Elias describes. One of the group sings from the big chorale book in front of them, the three others singing in parallel octaves and fifths (or fourths) with him, occasionally modifying the strict parallelism with oblique or contrary motion of the voices, according to certain standard rules. This kind of shackled voice leading could be applied to slow-moving and simple-structured Gregorian pieces only, but even so, frequent opportunities were afforded for making mistakes, the singers being of minor quality and the rules of voice leading not unambiguous. Here the conductor's duties begin. He is one of the singers, and according to Elias "has to know everything about the music to be sung. He beats time with his hand on the book and gives the cues and rests to the singers. If one of them sings incorrectly, he whispers into his ear, 'You are too loud, too soft, your tones are wrong,' as the case may be, but so that the others don't hear it. Sometimes he must support them with his own voice, if he sees that they are lost."

Elias' conductor has essentially the same obligations our conductors have, the difference being that nowadays the practicing, correcting, and prompting are done at the rehearsals, while at St. Astère in Périgueux it was part of the performance. Unfamiliar to us is the complete lack of emphasis on the leader's work, the tendency to keep him the *primus inter pares*. Times have changed; no modern conductor would like to be hidden among his collaborators.

Of course, we all know that a group of musicians, especially one as large as our modern orchestras, could not play together without being directed—unless they spent sufficient time and money to satisfy their individualistic desire to live without a conductor. We further know how beautiful music can be if performed under inspiring leadership, and how a poor conductor turns even the best music into dullness. There was a time when leading an orchestra was the exclusive task of men with a universal musical wisdom, when outstanding musicianship and great musical and human idealism were the foremost requirements. Granted that today we have many conductors with these old-time qualities, we nevertheless cannot overlook the fact that with the many times greater number of orchestras and hence the multiproduction and consumption of conductors, their musical wisdom is frequently anything but universal, their musicianship doubtful, and their idealism replaced by an insatiable vanity and a deadly fight against any other being who happens also to wield a baton. That a great conductor, one of the first-mentioned class, has all the success he deserves according to his talents and efforts is understandable and praiseworthy, but that in general the caste of conductors plays a role in our musical setup that seems out of proportion when compared with that of other musicians, must have reasons that are not purely musical. Yet sentimental admiration, as accorded to players and singers, is hardly the source of this, since that admiration is an affection devoted to the immediate producer of the musical impression. We cannot recognize the conductor as such, since scores of musicians are needed to make the sounds he planned come true.

Certainly it is not the technical difficulty of the conductor's work that leaves people breathless. Even the most refined technique of beating time requires scarcely more skill than a good percussion player needs for his job, and considerably less than the ever-ready promptness of any first desk player. Frequently enough we see greatest conductorial success and a bad technique appearing together; likewise the combination of excellent beating dexterity and poorest musicianship is not infrequently found.

Musical proficiency as a general trait cannot be the reason for the estimation in which the conductor is held, since there are many solo players equal or superior to him, who with all their efforts will never impress the public as profoundly as he does. And it cannot be his overwhelming wisdom or human greatness, since everyone knows that just as among all other people we find among conductors every shade between dullards and wizards, quacks and cracks.

The extramusical reason for this somewhat disproportionate regard seems to be based on the following fact: In an era that leaves little opportunity in the individual's life for the application and the display of overt despotism, the demonstration of some refined and stylized form of oppression seems to be imperative. The listener in the audience who in his normal behavior has to suppress, thousands of times, his most natural human desire of governing, ordering, dictating to, and even torturing his fellow men, projects himself into the conductor's personality. Here he sees a man who with the consent of human society exercises a power which we would look upon as cruelty if we saw it applied to dogs or horses. Identifying himself with these activities the listener enjoys the perfect abreaction of his own suppressed feelings: he now swings the teacher's cane, the dignitary's mace, the general's sword, the king's scepter, the sorcerer's wand, and the slave driver's whip over his subjects, and quite contrary to the effects such dictatorial manners have in real life, the result seems to be pleasant to all concerned.

This is the reason why the conductor has to do his work in full visibility. Should he be hidden, it would be too much of a strain on the listener's imagination to identify himself with an authority whose directions can be felt but not seen. It is the reason why conductors who perform their work with musical perfection but neglect the showy part of inciting, soothing, spurring, urging, and whiplashing will lack the real conductor's success. It is the reason why we pay so much money for an almost tribal despotism which in this democratic world seems to be rather anachronistic.

And it is the reason why we have never heard of great conductors coming from countries in which political dictatorship is the form of government. One dictator can never permit another dictator to be his rival. Although the political dictator is the more powerful of the two, it is always dangerous for him if the people can choose their form of slavery, especially if one form is so much more agreeable. Under such conditions a great conductor would have to submit both politically and musically to his superior super-conductor—but a submissive conductor is an absurdity (except to the lady members of his orchestra's board of trustees). However, since the musical conductor is merely a symbol of dictatorship and not the real thing, we must be glad that he exercises so salutary an influence. Who knows whether the world would not see more delinquency and unhappiness if the beneficial habit of going to see a conductor at work did not cause so many people to get rid of their repressions. They enter the concert hall as unidentifiable members of the human crowd, filled with evil instincts and bad intentions against everyone and everything, and they leave as purified individuals, suave and with an appreciative understanding for the world's weaknesses.

Needless to say, these statements are not intended to minimize a conductor's work. On the contrary, they try to shed some light on acts which obviously cannot be explained on a purely musical basis, thus providing ground for a more profound understanding. I know that intelligent conductors are aware of their essentially nonmusical function. For them such knowledge is not disturbing but helps them in exerting their full power. A conductor who thinks that his successes are nothing but a just remuneration for his musical efforts short-sightedly underestimates his higher signification as a humane institution.

SIR JOHN BARBIROLLI

The Art of Conducting

The history of conducting can be traced back at least to the fifteenth century, by which time it seems it had become customary to beat time at the performances of the "Sistine Choir" in Rome with a roll of paper called a "Sol-Fa." In the next century, about 1516, we find writings describing performances of concerted vocal music at which these writings refer to "a certain motion made by the hand of the chief singer according to the nature of the marks, which motion directs a song according to measure." This rather tends to show that by the beginning of the sixteenth century the prac-

SIR JOHN BARBIROLLI: Born in England in 1899. He was the regular conductor of the New York Philharmonic Orchestra from 1937 to 1940. At present he is conductor of the Houston Symphony Orchestra.

tice was universal: as does also a passage from Galilei's *Dialogo* (1583), where he mentions that the ancient Greeks did not beat time "as is customary now."

However, with the decline of polyphonic music and its attendant rhythmic subtleties, the time-beater must have become less necessary, and as the idea of the conductor as an interpreter as well as a time-keeper was not yet born, the practice of directing music with the conducting-stick seems to have fallen into disuse.

How and when the change came about I am not certain, but by 1740 or so it was customary to direct opera performances sitting at the harpsichord, at least in Italy and Germany, and we have also, of course, descriptions of Bach to prove that he, in any case, was in the habit of directing the music while he himself played the organ. In France, though, the practice of using the stick seems to have continued, for someone writing in England in 1709 has rather an amusing account of the art as he saw it practiced in Paris and apparently copied with assiduous indiscrimination in London. I don't think I can do better than quote the passage as it stands:

"The Master of Musick in the Opera at Paris had an Elboe Chair and Desk placed on the Stage where, with the Score in one hand and a stick in the other, he beat time on a table put there for that purpose, so loud, that he made a greater Noise than the whole Band, on purpose to be heard by the Performer. By degrees they removed this Abuse [not the most polite way of referring to practitioners of my craft] from the Stage to the Musick Room [which must mean what we now term the orchestra pit], where the Composer beats the time in the same manner and as loud as ever, but since the Italian Masters [this must refer to the Italian Opera composers who enjoyed great popularity in the town at that time] have come among us, they have put a stop to that ridiculous custom, because the Eye was too much distracted, being obliged to mind the beating of the measure and the score at the same time: besides (and this will please some of my friends who sing in opera, if not my colleagues who conduct it), it kept the singer in too much subjection, and Fear of Errors."

To make some singers fear errors is something of an achievement; unless they happen to be singing the wrong opera, they seem blissfully unaware of them.

By the beginning of the nineteenth century, however, the practice of beating time seems to have become firmly established in Germany, though it was not until 1820 that conducting with a stick at orchestral concerts was tried and became an institution in London, where it was introduced by Spohr at a Royal Philharmonic Society concert. At the rehearsal this daring innovation (until then the orchestra was guided by the joint efforts of the principal violin or leader, and a gentleman at the harpsichord who came to the rescue with a few chords if things got a bit shaky) was received, as I suppose all innovations are fated to be, with the most profound distrust by the directors. But in Spohr's own words: "The triumph of the baton was complete."

Spohr's account of this historic occasion is very interesting: "I took my stand in front of the orchestra, drew my directing-baton from my coat pocket, and gave the signal to begin. Quite alarmed at such a novel proceeding, some of the directors protested against it, but the triumph of the baton as a time-giver was decisive, and no one was seen any more seated at the piano during the performance of Symphonies and Overtures."

The most famous practitioner of the art of conducting at this period was probably Mendelssohn, who presided over the

Gewandhaus Concerts in Leipzig from 1835 to 1843. As prime inspirer and founder of the modern school of conducting, I think we can safely point to Wagner, and a survey of his chief disciples, such as Bülow, Richter, Levi, and Mottl, quickly brings us to our own times.

Now I should like to say a little about the practical application of the conductor's art as a means of making orchestral or concerted music more easily intelligible by clarity and eloquence of presentation. This practical application of the art I divide into two sections: (1) the physical, with which I incorporate the psychological, and (2) the purely musical mathematics of the art. The possession of gifts of the former I regard as essential to the fulfilment of the other; for have we not often had the spectacle of a great musician unable to secure even a mediocre interpretation of a work of his own? Wagner laid it down that the two fundamental principles underlying the art were: (1) giving the true tempo to the orchestra; (2) finding the "melos," by which he means the unifying thread of line that gives a work its form and shape. Given these two qualities, of course, we have the conductor *in excelsis,* and most of our lives must be spent in trying to obtain these qualities, more especially the first. It is surprising how few conductors are capable of setting and maintaining a tempo for more than a few bars.

Having stressed the importance of tempo to this extent, I have sometimes advised students as a guiding principle that *no tempo should be so slow as to make it difficult for a melody to be recognizable, and no tempo so fast as to make a melody unrecognizable,* and that composers' metronome marks, though sometimes inaccurate, can be at any rate a guide which it would be dangerous to ignore. This is not to suggest that accuracy of this kind alone can make a perfect performance, for accuracy without imagination is useless, and some small, subtle, barely perceptible modifications of tempo will ever be necessary to a living rendering of any music. From the foregoing it will be realized that the possession and understanding of these fundamental principles laid down by Wagner can only be claimed by very sensitive musical minds endowed with the will, energy, and patience to probe them to the full in the interests of their art.

Now I would say a word on the physical-psychological aspect of conducting, which is so important because, however splendid a conductor's musical ideas may be, they will be nullified if these qualities are not present.

When I speak of the physical aspect I mean a natural gift of gesture which should be at once clear and eloquent, and in the term "gesture" is included the beat. I do not personally believe in any standardization in this respect, but I would always ask that every gesture should have a definite meaning, and only be inspired by the most complete sincerity towards the music, oneself, and the public.

By the psychological aspect I mean the early divination of the types of players with whom you have to deal and your power of making them do their 100 per cent best for you and the music.

This brings us to a very delicate and important problem—the latitude one can allow to players regarding expression in the rendering of their solos. No hard-and-fast rules can be laid down here, as some players need more guidance than others, and the conductor must be quick to realize these points. It is dangerous to worry a very sensitive player too much; on the contrary, during an important and difficult solo the conductor should provide him with a background of sympathy, trust, and help. I have sometimes been approached to explain various interpretations of the same piece due supposedly to "moods" of mine. But the explanation is not concerned with moods. This freedom, however, must not extend so as to permit any anachronisms in phrasing, and no "selfish" player, however good, should ever be tolerated in any first-class orchestra.

I think it could hardly be called a digression from my subject if I said something about the general duties and problems of conducting, which more or less bring us up to the immediate present. Few people seem to realise that conducting at the performance is the least important part of the business of conducting. I am not even referring to the continual rehearsals during the season, but to all the work of annotating parts, editing, the one hundred and one points of technical elucidation of scores which has to go on unceasingly.

Of course one of the most formidable tasks that faces the conductor of an organization such as the Hallé, for instance, is to make programs—programs that must have as a basis the great classical masterpieces, what we might call a representative selection of modern classics, and such contemporary music as might interest the public to hear—not forgetting the encouragement which it is our duty to extend to young and perhaps unknown composers. I myself have sometimes spent weeks reading scores, of which more than 90 per cent must finally be rejected, not because they are all unworthy of performance, but because I do not believe that the Hallé concerts should become merely an experimental forum. When the program material is all gathered together, I must try to obviate too many repetitions of items played during previous seasons, and, to ensure the retention of some degree of sanity to myself, must not attempt to please everybody. It is easy, by the way, to assemble four great pieces of music and produce a badly balanced program. Also, in a well-balanced program the substitution of one piece can completely ruin it. I can say without any exaggeration that it has taken me months to compile programs for one season, and obviously with the compilation of these programs there must be constant study. I personally find that after weeks spent in research and study the actual period of conducting comes as a kind of blessed release: musical thoughts that have been singing inside one's mind for months can be expressed at last.

Some questions which I am often asked, and which I might take the opportunity of dealing with here, concern the seating of the orchestra, the most suitable type of baton, accompaniment of soloists, and whether it is best to conduct with or without a score. These things are so personal that I can only state my own methods. First, the question of seating. The main bone of contention is that of the disposition of the strings. It has become usual of late years, both here and abroad, to mass the deeper-toned strings on the outside of the orchestra to the right of the conductor in the traditional place allotted the second violins. Sometimes the violas are placed immediately on the right of the conductor or sometimes even the 'cellos, and the first and second violins are massed together on the conductor's left. This perhaps creates an extra brilliancy of violin tone, while the proximity of the lower strings to the outside of the orchestra makes for a deep and dark sonority.

This method, however, has its drawbacks. The main one, I think, is that it tends to a preponderance of the bass parts. An even more vital one—especially in the performance of the older classical works where there is so often fugal and melodic interplay between the first and second violins—is that when they are massed together it is not so easy to distinguish between the two parts. It is difficult to deny the fact that this "visual" interplay which takes place aids the "aural" interplay when each section is placed on either side of the conductor. Obviously, as I have said, there can be no hard-and-fast rule laid down, and the conductor in the end seats his orchestra in the way in which he himself feels most comfortable and will satisfy his musical consciousness, which must always be his guide.

On the subject of batons, here again the choice is a personal one; but perhaps a much more important, sensitive, and delicate choice than is commonly imagined. It is a rather curious fact, which I have noted almost subconsciously, that some conductors change types of batons in different stages of their musical development. In my own case the batons that I find have suited me best have changed during what might be called the brilliant and showy period of my youth and the more sedate and sober period to which I am rapidly approaching. Apart from personal consideration, here as in everything, good taste and good sense should determine. It is as absurd to use a baton which resembles a diminutive lead pencil as it is to wave a weapon of exceeding length and frailty.

I have always taken pleasure in the compliments paid me by artists for my so-called accompaniments. I have used the word "so-called" advisedly, because with the majority of the great concertos, such as those of Mozart, Beethoven, Brahms, etc., to call the orchestra and conductor the "accompaniment" is about as accurate as referring to the piano parts of the Mozart, Beethoven, and Brahms Violin Sonatas as "accompaniments." Such success as may have attended my labors in this sphere is because I treat a concerto not as a virtuosic display by one individual, but as a collective musical accomplishment, and I spare no pains to that end. It must not be forgotten that the performance of the great concertos provided during a season is not merely a question of presenting soloists, but it is a part of a definite plan to put before the public as many of the symphonic masterpieces as possible. We must not forget that the great concertos should always be a considered part of the orchestral repertoire.

A still more controversial topic is the use or non-use of scores. I would immediately like to say that it is foolish to imagine that a man knows less about a work because he uses a score. On the other hand, it is just as foolish to accuse all those who dispose of them of being bluffers and charlatans. The prime duty of any conductor is to secure the best possible performance of any work with which he is entrusted, and to use such means as he conscientiously believes will ensure the best possible results. To some conductors a score may be an impediment, to others, even though they refer to it very seldom, it is a release from any anxiety which enables them to give a much freer vent to their imagination. At the outset of my career I did a considerable amount of conducting from memory, but I placed on myself the extremely arduous demand that what I conducted from memory I should also be able to write down from memory. As I could not continue to discharge faithfully this onerous conscientiousness, I reverted to scores. On the last occasion when I conducted *Die Meistersinger* some years ago in London, I amused myself by conducting the dress rehearsal without a score, but for the performance I decided it was more sensible and more respectful to the members of the company to have the music before me.

There is one last point I should like to make. I would venture the assumption, without any qualification whatever, that a conductor is born and not made. By this I am not referring to a musical quality, but rather to a purely technical capacity; and I also do not mean that a born conductor cannot find room for improvement. Some of the most involved technical problems are to be found in the opera house. I would advise any young man with the opportunity for doing so to graduate from the opera house, and it is an indisputable fact that some of the greatest conductors have come from there—Richter, Levi, Mottl, Weingartner, Nikisch, Toscanini, and Beecham. For there the conductor is faced with sudden and curious emergencies of all kinds. He cannot always proceed according to plan, not only because of the performances of singers, but also because of elements of an even more unnerving disposition. The number of little things that can happen for which the conductor is technically responsible are, I am sure, not realized by the audience. For instance, a character has to rush in and sing something and the door sticks—a little delay ensues, and yet all must be made to seem as if everything is proceeding smoothly. With choruses singing offstage, calculations of distance and sound are necessary that make the conductor's task more complicated, yet all must sound entirely unified in the front of the house. Experience of these things combines to equip an artist and make him a master of his craft.

Before I conclude, I would like to say to any young musician who contemplates this most arduous and responsible of careers make your watchwords "integrity and sincerity to yourself, and loyalty to the man whose music you are seeking to interpret." Never think, "What can I make of this piece?" but try to discover what the composer meant to say. We must bear in mind that the conductor has become, for good or ill, one of the most important and responsible personalities in the musical world, and by fine stylistic performances can do much towards a purification of musical perception amongst the general public. On the other hand, performances that are merely the vehicle for indulging the vanity of a personality, however gifted, can only tend to lead us farther from that which should be the goal of all true musicians: service to that great art which it is our privilege to practice.

EUGENE ORMANDY

Art of Conducting

The art of conducting, one of the most complex and demanding activities in the realm of music, comprises both the visual public performance and the constant application of technique. Although inseparable in performance they can be analyzed in the light of the unique problems which each presents. Similarly, the conductor himself functions on three levels, each dependent upon the other, all culminating in the performance itself.

EUGENE ORMANDY: Born in Hungary in 1899. He has been musical director of the Philadelphia Orchestra since 1936.

On the first level, his period of study, the conductor prepares himself both technically and artistically. On this level he must be musician, historian, stylist, orchestrator, and listener. He must study the score so that he "hears" it in his mind. As he does this he evaluates the music and makes a beginning toward balancing the many strands of musical line. He must understand the historical context in which a particular work is conceived, and bring to bear upon the growing interpretive edifice a thorough knowledge of the stylistic requirements inherent in the work. To study such a masterwork as Beethoven's *Eroïca* Symphony without some knowledge of the composer's response to the ideals of the French Revolution and Napoleon's unique political position in 1806 is to study music in a vacuum. Needless to say it was not created in a vacuum. Among the elements of stylistic validity are tempi and dynamics. A Mozart allegro differs by far from a Tchaikovsky allegro, Similarly, a *forte* in Haydn is an entirely different matter from a Wagner *forte.*

A thorough knowledge of the orchestral colors and timbres enables the studying conductor to "hear" the orchestral sound while he studies. When conducting older composers he must sometimes compensate for the technical inadequacies of the times by delicately rewriting certain passages in terms of today's more complete orchestras and more highly skilled players. Present-day performances of such works as the *Fifth Symphony* of Beethoven, the *Great C Major Symphony* of Schubert, the symphonies of Schumann, to mention but a few, are rarely given without many instrumental changes. Even so "pure" a conductor as Toscanini did not deny the composer the benefit of today's heightened instrumental resources.

Finally, while he studies, the conductor must "listen" objectively to the work, pacing its progress, spacing its climaxes, deriving a general aural concept of the musical architecture, and evaluating its merit as it will be heard by the public. He must recall Richard Strauss's dictum: "Remember that you are making music not for your own pleasure but for the joy of your listeners."

REHEARSAL

The second level upon which the conductor functions is the rehearsal, in which he prepares the orchestra both technically and artistically. It is on this level that he acts as a guide to the orchestra, building up in their minds a concept of the work parallel to his own, for the eventual public performance requires an enlightened and sensitive orchestra playing not "under" a conductor, but rather "with" him.

During the rehearsals he must clarify all problems of metrics and tempi, elucidating his own pacing of the work. He must temper all dynamic markings so that the instrumental "sound" is balanced in all its components. The older composers always wrote the same dynamics vertically (for each simultaneous part, straight down the page) in their scores. It was only composer-conductors, like Mahler or Wagner, who realized the pitfalls of dynamics incautiously marked.

As he rehearses, the conductor, surrounded by the physical sound of the work, checks his own concept of the music, comparing it with the actual music. In those particular instances where the two do not fit he must alter one or the other. It is essential that the two, the concept and the actuality, run amicably along. In addition, there are instances, such as the lengthy oboe solo in Strauss's *Don Juan,* where the prudent conductor who is fortunate enough to possess a highly sensitive oboe player, permits him to "have his head," acting almost as an accompanist rather than a leader.

PERFORMANCE

It is in performance that the conductor operates upon the highest and most demanding level. Here the work is finished technically; the orchestra is fully prepared for all of its demands; the conductor, his study and preparation behind him, now immerses himself in the music, identifying himself with it both emotionally and mentally. But it is at this crucial time that the most difficult function of the conductor comes into full play. He must, while identifying himself with the music, keep a constant watch upon the progress of the work, allowing a portion of his analytical mind to constantly evaluate the sound and pace of the performance. He must be prepared to make any adjustments instantaneously, large or small, in the actual performance required for the fullest realization of his inner concept. Many factors make this necessary: a different hall, a player's momentary inattention, the effect of several thousand persons upon the acoustics, even the understandable enthusiasm during a performance which might affect the tempo. At such a moment the conductor meets his greatest challenge, for the progress of the work must not suffer in the slightest; there must be no detectable "hitch." At such moments the experience of a conductor tells, for the young conductor, new to such emergencies, tends to do one thing at a time. Music does not permit this, for it flows in time and all adjustments must be superimposed upon the uninterrupted continuum.

In the extent to which he succeeds on any and all of these levels lies the measure of the conductor's merit, both as a musician and as an artist. In his study he can separate the art from the technique, but in performance he must strive fully and constantly for a total artistic experience. Otherwise he can never fulfill his high calling: recreating the reality of the work itself.

EUGEN JOCHUM

About the Phenomenology of Conducting

THOUGHTS ABOUT INTERPRETATION IN CONDUCTING

The statements which follow make no claim to completeness; nor do they present a theory or system of conducting. They are the observations of a recreative musician who thinks about his craft and who attempts to be aware of what actually happens when he works. The craft of conducting in the narrower sense (what is called baton technique) will not be included in this discussion.

Those arts which are realized in the course of time (literature, music, and dance) are associated with the inter-

EUGEN JOCHUM: Born in Bavaria, Germany, in 1902. He succeeded Karl Muck as musical director of the Hamburg State Opera and in 1949 became conductor of the Radio Orchestra in Munich.

preter. He was not there from the inception of the work.* At the start of the most primitive musical activities, "composer" and "interpreter" were one. The singing person, who expressed his feeling about life, joy, or pain in song, composed and interpreted himself. Very soon, however, a certain objectiveness appeared; feeling was transformed into the work of art, subjected itself to laws and rules, however simple (for example, the ones about contrast and repetition), and acquired form. Thus the form of the vocal or danced song originated. Still later, this song became the folksong: one person conceived and formed it in a happy hour as the expression of his response to life, and then all sang it. The interpreter came between the creative artist and the realization of the work. The more artistic the work to be realized the more important the interpreter became as the spokesman for someone else. The interpreter must be capable of submerging himself in another person's works and nature to the highest degree; one can even say that the strength of an interpretative talent is determined by the extent and depth of this capacity.

Among the interpreters the conductor was the last to appear. What distinguishes him is the following. Instrumentalist and singer are linked in the strongest way with their instrument (the singer with the living voice) and identify themselves to a great extent with it. The conductor does not have this link. Whereas with the former the spiritual coming to grips with the work of art goes largely hand in hand with the technical mastering of it, the conductor must, because of the peculiarity of his instrument—the orchestra—form an independent inner image of the work. His own inner analysis of the composition, the identification with the will of the composer, precedes his work with the orchestra. It would be too

*The cultic roots of music are deliberately not being considered here.

late to come to his conception of the piece when working with the orchestra, although certain aspects can still be perfected by actually hearing the work. This inner analysis—which can be a completely isolated process—is immediately followed by another process, the transfer of the inner conception to the orchestra, in the reality of sound, thereby achieving the second, physical reality.

This division of the conductor's labors shows why the composer is not always the best conductor of his work: to be sure, he naturally has, to a large extent, the inner image, the identification with the work. But this does not necessarily mean that he has the gift of transferring this image to the orchestra, or the insight into the quite special technique for this process. The transference presupposes a particular talent, the specifically interpretative one, which the composer does not always possess or cannot acquire. In so far as the rationally recognizable is concerned, however, there is no composer who does not exactly "know what he does." But isn't the work of art also a living thing, from which the creator detaches himself after creation like the mother from the child? And could it not happen that he thereby loses this vital relationship and is so "finished" with it that it no longer particularly interests him? And isn't it possible that he can only approach it again by working at it as an interpreter has to?

But now, back to the conductor's working procedure, which we have defined as two-fold. Let us first speak of what was described as "forming an inner image." How is this done? There are various ways by which the conductor possesses himself of the work to be interpreted. Personal experience has led me to select one of them as the most organic as well as the most appropriate to the entire process of reproduction. I shall try to describe it.

I take care first of all to have, so to speak, a passive attitude toward the work; that is, to establish a lack of bias, a receptiveness that will allow the work of art to best develop its own reality. First I abandon myself to the work, which I read through again and again. The ear (completely independent of the intervening piano thanks to absolute pitch) first registers the facts, without my thinking of particulars. What is this tempo? How does it relate to later tempi? What is the nature of the themes? How do they relate to one another? These questions are left for later.

In this manner the tempo focuses "by itself," the piece becomes so self-evident that it begins to live its own life, still practically completely withdrawn from my conscious will and shaping impulses. The condition described as passivity now reveals itself as having many layers; only the intellectual layers of consciousness are actually passive. The possessive, forming will is only excluded by the thinking mind. On the other hand, the deeper layers of consciousness are vibrantly awake, straining toward the work, so that an emotional field of tension is formed in which "the spark leaps over." This is the decisive point. When it is reached, conscious work of the greatest precision can and must begin. It is only important that the impulse of the will and conscious control do not take over too soon, and that one's own personality is not brought in at the wrong moment. It is thus a question of humble acceptance of a law, of listening to an inner meaning.[23]

The passivity returns, though naturally on a different plateau, at the performance. But then it is quite different, and the intervening phase of precise, conscious work without and with the orchestra is fused into it.

What we have called the conscious work of the conductor extends to the most exact analytical study of the work of art.

The work is examined: the structure of the individual themes, their changes and development in the course of the piece, their eventual relation to one another, the construction of the form and the resulting relationships of key, dynamics, orchestration, thematic differences in parallel places (as for instance in exposition and repetition), the reason for these differences (which can result from instruments in varying positions, but which can also be a means of intensification or expression), and so on. Naturally, recognition of tempi and their relation to each other take a most important place in these studies. We said before that the tempo focuses nearly by itself; henceforth this tempo must be examined critically. Primarily, the conductor must know clearly to what extent he can and must modify it in the course of the piece, and where. This *how* and *where* of the modification must never be accidental, but is decided by the structure of the piece and by the prevailing local function of the tempo. The tempo can be totally different in repetitions of the same theme and even when the course of the music is literally the same. The layman generally does not realize how great the variations can and must often be in a steady tempo within one movement in order to bring out the vitality of the musical flow. Yet the listener must always have the impression that the tempo does remain steady. A particularly interesting example of this is the first movement of the *Eroïca.* With its mighty proportions it cannot possibly be played through in the same unbending tempo, and can stand—even demands—extensive modifications. But these must have the right balance and not go to extremes: this is precisely the art of the interpreter, which presupposes a highly refined awareness of tempo.

Lastly, the memorizing of a piece also belongs to this conscious preparatory work of the conductor.

Even in this phase of the conductor's still private preliminary work, the all-important matter of actual work with the orchestra is always dominant. Obviously the conductor must know how he will transmit his knowledge to the sound body even during his own study of the work.

The orchestral instrument consists of living persons, each of whom has great artistic talent, insight and naturally also a will of his own.[24] It is important not to despotically choke off these manifold impulses of the will, these talents and temperaments, but to tie them into the whole, to fuse them and raise them to the peak of artistic achievement. The ideal is reached when the player is aware of the conductor's support and leadership, but retains the feeling that he himself is doing the shaping. The degree of vitality of an interpretation largely depends on this.

The conductor's task is always to manifest his intentions in a decisive way, while at the same time taking in, arranging, and inspiring the impulses of the will which come toward him. His function is thus not exhausted in the holding together of the many individual forces by giving the beat, fixing the tempo, and guaranteeing unimpeachable precision and dynamics. It means, in addition, infusing every detail of the melodic, rhythmic, and other elements with life, refining the sound so that the less important voices are in the background and the essentials are delicately put into relief; it means a blending of the sound in which, for instance, instruments that actually play the same part are shaded differently.

The molding of the tempo has already been discussed at length. It is not enough for the conductor to know the right tempi in private; the difficulty lies in transmitting his exact ideas. For this, he needs thorough training in baton technique. The player should be able to read a tendency toward slowing down or acceleration of a tempo from the connecting gesture (that is, the gesture executed between 1-,2-,3-,4 of the beat). Abrupt tempo changes, which also occur, are relatively easy to transmit to an orchestra. The completely unnoticeable, smooth, and gradual rising or abating of a tempo, however, demand a delicate physical sensibility from the conductor, as well as a thorough command of the physical means of expression. And the player must respond with alertness to the most subtle differentiations and have a highly developed receptiveness. The qualities of our foremost orchestras are primarily due to this receptiveness, and not only to beautiful sound or technical accomplishments.

Moreover, at this point a phenomenon becomes visible that most likely represents the particular core of conducting talent: a peculiar physical predisposition to receive a musical happening (with all of its accumulations, tensions, and resolutions, with all of its melodic, rhythmic, and other elements) and transmit it through conscious as well as involuntary gestures, so that the player responds with a physical perceptiveness, far below the threshold of rational understanding. The effect of the conductor's gestures extends, in a less refined form, to the listening and watching audience. This cannot be avoided; in fact, it can even lead to a heightened and more intensive participation in the work of art and is thus quite legitimate, if the gestures of the conductor are strictly limited to the clarification of the music.

In the conductor's work with the orchestra everything must naturally stay within the limits of the requirements of the score, and in fullest conformity to the composer's intentions. The handling of the many details, barely perceived by the listener and even by the participating players, determines what may be called the handwriting of the conductor. This process clearly extends from sharpest intellectual consciousness to actions which elude description. During rehearsals the control of artistic awareness, the pedagogic intention, the conscious work are dominant. At the performance the conductor's activity can in some ways be more passive; he can give himself more freely to the flow of the music. Thus the presentation acquires a new assurance, naturalness, and spontaneity.

IGOR MARKEVITCH

The Problems of the Education of Today's Conductors

The development of present-day musical life puts the orchestra leader face to face with entirely new problems which did not exist thirty years ago. They require us to look at the education of the conductor from an entirely new angle. Let us examine the principal elements of his education point by point.

The growth of the audience has increased the number of concerts. The permanent head of a symphony orchestra such as the Philadelphia, Boston, or Radio Turin must conduct more than one hundred and fifty concerts a year, a number

IGOR MARKEVITCH: Born in Kieff, Russia, in 1912. Though he started his career as a composer, he has devoted himself increasingly to conducting, and has been a guest conductor of many symphony orchestras throughout the world.

which would have been unthinkable at the start of the career of a Furtwängler. In addition, there are concurrent obligations, such as recordings, which a well-known conductor cannot evade.

One result is an ever-increasing expenditure of energy and need for stamina inconceivable to our predecessors. One need not even mention the steadily growing commercialization of musical activity, or the increasing speed of travel which enables a manager to place a conductor in New York, Paris, and possibly elsewhere within the span of one week.

A second matter to be considered is the repertoire. Because of the intensification of his activity the conductor must lead a greater number of concerts and a greater variety of pieces than in the past—a contradiction in itself, since the increased activity consumes the time needed for selecting and studying new works. This is one reason why, by and large, today's presentations are without the necessary depth, and why repertoires are so often limited.

In the third place, today's young conductor must be prepared to be confronted with an abundance of different styles. The steady expansion of programs has necessitated a constant search for obscure, forgotten music whose performance creates a great many stylistic problems. On the other hand, the constant enlargement of the orchestral body, provoked by Strauss, Debussy, Ravel, Stravinsky, Schoenberg, and their successors, demands a technique far more flexible and comprehensive than a Nikisch or Toscanini needed.

The repertoire not only imposes upon the conductor the knowledge of a variety of styles, but in addition makes it imperative to obtain quick results. We are no longer in the age of Mengelberg who took a month to prepare *Till Eulenspiegel*, or of Toscanini who insisted on twelve rehearsals for *La Mer*.

In the recent past orchestral musicians have undergone a training which Wagner could not dream of. The Philharmonia Orchestra of London will suffice as an example: I remember that it recorded *Le Sacre du Printemps* in 1949 with me in only two sessions, although it had never worked on the piece before. It is thus easy to see that the conductor's preparation is all-important to carry a well-trained orchestra over all difficulties.

While on the subject of recordings, we might say that this activity represents a skill of its own. It necessitates delving into the smallest detail; inaccuracies which often pass unnoticed at concerts come into prominence and are virtually unbearable on records. The conductor must also be in a position to consult with the technicians in order to get the sound he strives for, which is quite different from the sound heard in a concert hall; it can only be obtained by a particular seating arrangement in front of the microphone. To find one's way back to the living art in the midst of all these technical devices requires an ability which develops only after long, determined effort.

Finally, there is the problem of knowing the instruments, which have increased in number and potential. One need only mention the percussion section, which in the last century was limited to three or four instruments and has now grown to huge proportions. It has become so important that one sees concerts and compositions entirely devoted to it. Or electronic instruments, whose use in the orchestra is more and more frequent, which force the ear of the conductor to a new kind of control.

Several unavoidable conclusions must be drawn from the foregoing. If the conductor of the future is to have sufficient stamina, hearing, repertoire, and culture, his education must be adjusted. In my estimation, eight years represent the minimum for a talented young orchestra leader who wants to measure up to the demands of his career. Therefore I would recommend that actual study begin between the ages of twelve and fourteen. This allows for the training of the body (proper breathing, independence of arms and reflexes, and the agility which a conductor needs) as in the study of the violin and the piano, as well as certain sports.

Above all, the ear will receive the right preparation. It will become so familiar with the world of orchestral sound that it will later infallibly recognize errors, and know how to correct them. This is the first requirement for a conductor worthy of the name. Those who are strangers to orchestra routine (and among them are seasoned musicians) have no idea of how much experience it takes to hear the details of an orchestra. One violinist of the Berlin Philharmonic Orchestra confided to me that it had taken him more than six months at the beginning to "hear" himself; he saw his fingers play, but the noise of the trumpets, tympani, and other instruments prevented him from controlling his own actions. Obviously, for the conductor who must hear and control the entire orchestra, the problem is even greater.

Concerning repertoire, it is evident that a conductor has to know all classic symphonies, the most important operas, the best-known oratorios, and the standard concertos. Before starting his career he should also have led the most significant contemporary works, with particular attention to those which are already part of the standard repertoire, such as *Le Sacre du Printemps* or *L'Historie du Soldat,* by Stravinsky, Bartók's *Concerto for Orchestra,* or the *Variations Opus 31* by Schoenberg. To these I would add the *Turangalilla* symphony of Messiaen and Boulez' *Le Marteau sans Maître* in order to acquire a clear understanding of the fundamental ideas expressed in these works. It is obvious that the analysis, preparation, and rehearsal of this basic repertoire, which encompasses the entire musical literature, also provide considerable training for the memory.

Besides technical training, a physical preparedness and a strict comprehensive musical and cultural foundation are constantly becoming more necessary. It is not sufficient to place the works in their historical context; one must study the life and work of each composer. And, finally, I favor the study of several languages during these years of preparation; this will make it easier to have direct contact with orchestras of other countries.

One can see from this very sketchy outline that the education of an orchestra leader, as prescribed by contemporary musical life, must be as exact, as complete, and much more comprehensive than that of an instrumentalist. In conclusion, one can safely predict that the pedagogic problem involved in conducting, as I have tried to describe it here, will lead to the creation of an artistic species, extremely interesting and decidedly new.

LEONARD BERNSTEIN

The Art of Conducting

Mendelssohn fathered the "elegant" school, whereas Wagner inspired the "passionate" school of conducting. The ideal modern conductor is a synthesis of the two attitudes, and this synthesis is rarely achieved. In fact, it's practically impossible. Almost any musician can be a conductor, even a pretty good one; but only a rare musician can be a great one.

The qualities that distinguish *great* conductors lie far beyond and above . . . [technique]. We now begin to deal with the intangibles, the deep magical aspect of conducting. It is the

LEONARD BERNSTEIN: Born in Massachusetts in 1918. One of the most noted American conductors, he has been music director of the New York Philharmonic since 1958. He is also well known for his compositions and televised Young People's Concerts.

mystery of relationships—conductor and orchestra bound together by the tiny but powerful split second. How can I describe to you the magic of the moment of beginning a piece of music? There is only one possible fraction of a second that feels exactly right for starting. There is a wait while the orchestra readies itself and collects its powers; while the conductor concentrates his whole will and force toward the work in hand; while the audience quiets down, and the last cough has died away. There is no slight rustle of a program book; the instruments are poised and—bang! That's it. One second later, it is too late, and the magic has vanished.

This psychological timing is constantly in play throughout the performance of music. It means that a great conductor is one who has great sensitivity to the flow of time; who makes one note move to the next in exactly the right way and at the right instant. For music, as we said, exists in the medium of time. It is time itself that must be carved up, molded, and remolded until it becomes, like a statue, an existing shape and form. This is the hardest to do. For a symphony is not like a statue, which can be viewed all at once, or bit by bit at leisure, in one's own chosen time. With music we are trapped in time. Each note is gone as soon as it has sounded, and it never can be recontemplated or heard again at the particular instant of rightness. It is always too late for a second look.

So the conductor is a kind of sculptor whose element is time instead of marble; and in sculpting it, he must have a superior sense of proportion and relationship. He must judge the largest rhythms, the whole phraseology of a work. He must conquer the form of a piece not only in the sense of form as a mold, but form in its deepest sense, knowing and controlling where the music relaxes, where it begins to accumulate tension, where the greatest tension is reached, where it must ease up to gather strength for the next lap, where it unloads that strength.

These are the intangibles of conducting, the mysteries that no conductor can learn or acquire. If he has a natural faculty for deep perception it will increase and deepen as he matures. If he hasn't he will always remain a pretty good conductor. But even the pretty good conductor must have one more attribute in his personality, without which all the mechanics and knowledge and perception are useless; and that is the power to *communicate* all this to his orchestra—through his arms, face, eyes, fingers, and whatever vibrations may flow from him. If he uses a baton, the baton itself must be a living thing, charged with a kind of electricity, which makes it an instrument of meaning in its tiniest movement. If he does not use a baton, his hands must do the job with equal clarity. But baton or no baton, his gestures must be first and always meaningful in terms of the music.

The chief element in the conductor's technique of communication is the preparation. Everything must be shown to the orchestra *before* it happens. Once the player is playing the note, it is too late. So the conductor always has to be at least a beat or two ahead of the orchestra. And he must hear two things at the same time: what the players are doing at any moment, and what they are about to do a moment later. Therefore, the basic trick is in the preparatory upbeat. It is exactly like breathing: the preparation is like an inhalation, and the music sounds as an exhalation. We all have to inhale in order to speak, for example; all verbal expression is exhaled. So it is with music: we inhale on the upbeat and sing out a phrase of music, then inhale again and breathe out the next phrase. A conductor who breathes with the music has gone far in acquiring a technique.

But the conductor must not only make his orchestra play; he must make them want to play. He must exalt them, lift them, start their adrenalin pouring, either through cajoling or demanding or raging. But however he does it, he must make the orchestra love the music as he loves it. It is not so much imposing his will on them like a dictator; it is more like projecting his feelings around him so that they reach the last man in the second violin section. And when this happens—when one hundred men share his feelings, exactly, simultaneously, responding as one to each rise and fall of the music, to each point of arrival and departure, to each little inner pulse—then there is a human identity of feeling that has no equal elsewhere. It is the closest thing I know to love itself. On this current of love the conductor can communicate at the deepest levels with his players, and ultimately with his audience. He may shout and rant and curse and insult his players at rehearsal—as some of our greatest conductors are famous for doing—but if there is this love, the conductor and his orchestra will remain knit together through it all and function as one.

Well, there is our ideal conductor. And perhaps the chief requirement of all is that he be humble before the composer; that he never interpose himself between the music and the audience; that all his efforts, however strenuous or glamorous, be made in the service of the composer's meaning—the music itself, which, after all, is the whole reason for the conductor's existence.

MAX RUDOLF

Rehearsal Techniques

A frequently heard question is whether the conductor fulfills his most important function in rehearsal or in performance. No simple answer is possible. A wide scope of musical and psychological aspects exists in evaluating the work accomplished by a conductor and his team of players. People familiar with the inside workings smile at fanciful exaggerations such as the observation that a famous maestro "plays on his orchestra like on an instrument" and, by contrast, are amused when told that, with all the essential work completed in rehearsal, "the performance runs by it-

MAX RUDOLF: Born and trained in Germany. Came to the United States in 1940. He has conducted widely in the symphonic and operatic fields and has been music director of the Cincinnati Symphony Orchestra since 1958.

self." They are aware of numerous details whose proper rendition requires verbal clarification, or of passages where, without adequate rehearsals, the conductor will be wise to conform to the orchestra's established ways, lest he invite disaster. Also, they have seen a conductor harm a performance, no matter how well rehearsed, by an awkward gesture or, worse, when his spiritual forces fail him, lead a routine performance instead of an inspired one.

Similar to the conductor's baton technique, which may be defined as a highly individualized craft to evoke specific responses on the part of the players with the most effective gestures, his verbal communication in rehearsal must be equally specific, easily understandable, and congruous with his musical intentions. While rehearsal techniques vary according to each conductor's individuality, habits, and preferences, valid generalizations can be arrived at, and pertinent advice be given, supported by musical and psychological experience. The application of these techniques must fit changing rehearsal conditions and depends on the type of orchestra the conductor is to direct.

The following comments are offered with professional orchestras in mind, although only a limited number of communities in the United States can afford an orchestra that need not be augmented by students or amateur players. The conductor's handling of rehearsals would then have to take into account the different levels of musical skill and the divergencies in the players' general attitude, which cannot possibly be the same for those pursuing their training or avocation and professionals who come to earn their livelihood. Even when working with fully trained and experienced players, the conductor varies his rehearsal techniques according to the quality of the group and the kind of program which is to be prepared within a certain number of rehearsal hours. Familiarity with the program, the technical capacity of an orchestra, and acoustical contingencies all affect the planning of rehearsals. Unfortunately, not all orchestras enjoy the use of their concert halls for preliminary work.

It has been said that the music director, if nothing else, is a "timesaver." Orchestras performing without a leader must rehearse more hours and, incidentally, they usually rely for advice on the concertmaster or another knowledgeable musician who attends rehearsals with critical ears.

Since, as a rule, rehearsal time is restricted and costly, the conductor must put available hours to the best possible use. This entails detailed planning by day, week, and month as part of his preparatory work. It includes seeing to it that properly marked parts in good condition be ready for distribution to the players prior to the first reading.

In planning his schedule, the conductor makes certain that within the total number of rehearsal hours each composition receives its fair share of preparation. Technically intricate works and difficult contemporary music, whose reading is sometimes aggravated by poorly printed parts, require extra rehearsal time. Therefore, in devising his programs, the conductor will do well not to overload them with such scores. Also, he will attempt to commence readings of unfamiliar works several weeks prior to performance, possibly in sectional sessions which allow string and wind players to rehearse at different times. When the conductor decides exactly what to practice at each meeting he is led by considerations too diversified to be enumerated, but knowing the capacity of his players, he can frequently foretell to the minute how much work will be accomplished. Obviously a guest director finds himself in a situation unlike that of the permanent leader and may have to arrange his schedule from day to day. But even the regular head of an orchestra must be flexible, to meet situations such as a musician's sudden illness or the late arrival of solo artists. The threat of emergencies has caused some organizations to insist that all musicians be present for the duration of every rehearsal. However, keeping musicians sitting around in idleness for long periods is hardly desirable. A well-planned schedule permits excusing those players who are not needed during the initial or concluding portions of a session.

Before starting a rehearsal the conductor greets the orchestra briefly, assures himself that all the musicians for whom the score calls are present, and makes certain that the tuning of the instruments has been completed. Generally, conductors should be cautioned against making speeches, giving detailed instructions prior to actual playing, or attempting to enlighten the orchestra by musical analyses. Professional musicians tend to be critical and suspicious of words until convinced in terms of music. The suggestion that the conductor quickly ascertain whether everybody is ready to rehearse is justified, and also useful at concert time. It would be embarrassing for the director (and this has actually happened) to be forced to stop a performance because a musician, mistaken about the order of program, remained in the musicians' lounge instead of being on stage.

Careful tuning must not only precede a rehearsal but be repeated during its progress whenever the intonation is out of line. Problems of intonation, partly due to the nature of the instruments and different for strings, winds, and percussion, arise from various sources and cannot all be solved by tuning. Instruments must be in perfect shape, each player's technical ability must be matched by a keen ear and, last but not least, all musicians must make a constant effort to maintain a unified pitch by listening to their colleagues' playing. Keyboard instruments and harps add special complications, because in spite of the best efforts, the orchestra's pitch is apt to rise in the course of several hours' playing. Still, initial tuning is the first step toward achieving true pitch. The concertmaster usually supervises tuning, which should be completed before the rehearsal begins, and must never be permitted to degenerate to a perfunctory routine. The manner in which the tuning is handled is most important. Sounding the *A* for two or three seconds and letting the entire orchestra plunge immediately into the all-too-familiar chaos of "tuning up" cannot produce good results. Stringed instruments, woodwinds, and brasses must check the *A* separately while the others maintain silence.

With the rehearsal under way, it is for the conductor to decide when to interrupt for corrections or discussions. Experience alone teaches him up to what point his gestures and facial expressions will suffice to communicate his intentions to the players, and which details make verbal clarification imperative. In the first instance he will rely on his skill with the baton, and will refrain from repeating a passage if he is sure that he can straighten out imperfections without explanation when the same music is played later on. However, he will not waste time repeating a page over and over, if problems at this particular place call for discussion. Some conductors first go through an extended portion of a piece without interrupting. There may be a virtue in this procedure if a composition is new to both conductor and orchestra; some kind of perspective can then be gained as a guide for further rehearsal work. Otherwise its value is doubtful, and letting errors pass just for the purpose of "playing through" is usually a waste of time. This is not to advocate stopping the music for every mishap. A musician frequently notices his error at least as quickly as the conductor and would rightly resent it if a fuss were made over every wrong note, an oversight of change of key or clef, or a misunderstanding perhaps caused by blurred print. In such cases an exchange of glances settles the matter. But the conductor must not hesitate to act when technical or stylistic details render explication necessary, or when the general quality of playing is not satisfactory. It is the conductor's responsibility to establish the highest possible level of performance from the very beginning of a rehearsal. Indeed, the first five minutes are often decisive for the results of a working session.

Four principal objectives must be kept in mind in preparing an orchestra for performance: familiarity with the music for flawless reading; apprehension of the tempi and their modifications; coordination of dynamics, rhythm, articulation, and phrasing; and a conception of style and spirit germane to the composition. It should be added that the success of a rehearsal depends to a large extent on the orchestra's general training in ensemble playing and the conductor's discernment in applying rehearsal techniques without losing sight of his final target: a performance which combines precision with expressiveness, balanced sound with animation. He will gain time for essential practice if the players are accustomed to watching him to the best of their ability. A well-trained, attentive orchestra need not be instructed about tempo, about slowing down or speeding up, about holds, breaks, and other elementary details, because skilled musicians are able and willing to follow a clear beat and to be guided by telling gestures. They also expect authority and efficiency from their leader when he finds it necessary to repeat passages whose rendition did not satisfy him. This aspect of the conductor's craft is important enough to justify a number of practical suggestions.

1. Before interrupting be sure of what you are going to say.

2. Educate your orchestra so that everyone stops right at your signal and then observes silence.

3. Begin your comments without hesitation and whenever possible formulate them in terms of clearly defined technical advice. (Paul Hindemith, when a young concertmaster, once reported in exasperation: "Now we have rehearsed Brahms' *First* under three conductors within a few weeks and each time we arrived at the horn solo in the finale, the conductor started talking about the sunrise.")

4. Never say "Once more" after interrupting without giving a good reason, unless things have gone wrong to such an extent that the necessity for repeating is obvious.

5. Frequently remarks are addressed not to all musicians but to sections or individual players. In this case, first identify the instruments concerned, then the passage in question, then explain why you are not satisfied. Discussions of extended solo passages ought to take place in private, which is preferable to lengthy explanations in the presence of the orchestra.

6. Do not discuss musical details without being sure that the players have turned to the right page and know exactly what you are talking about.

7. Once you have begun working on a passage you must persist until improvement is noticeable, unless a player is not capable of coping with a particular problem because of technical limitations. (Even a taskmaster such as Toscanini, in

rehearsing Debussy's *Fêtes* with a renowned European orchestra, went on without fussing when he noticed that some bars were beyond the capacity of a certain player.)

8. Announce distinctly and unmistakably the place where the music is to be resumed. "We begin *three bars before* letter X" cannot be misunderstood, but it is safer to say "*the third bar after* letter Y." To find the place some players may have to count many measures of rest, so allow sufficient time and perhaps repeat the announcement. Materials should be marked abundantly with rehearsal numbers and letters. When singers participate, do not forget to give them word cue and pitch.

9. After proper announcement, resume the music as soon as practicable, and without lingering.

10. Spoken comments while the musicians are playing should be used sparingly by the conductor.

11. Do not spend so much time on the first movement of a work, or the first act of an opera, that the remaining portions will be under-rehearsed.

12. Do not rehearse every piece each time in its entirety. To play in rehearsal, other than the final one, long stretches of music without problems is a waste of time. Use rehearsals for passages that need work.

This list of suggestions, by no means complete, can be augmented by helpful advice of various kinds found in the writings of practised and resourceful musicians, including the amusing set of rules which Richard Strauss once proposed to young conductors.

Some supplementary words seem to be in order to affirm the superiority of technical advice as compared to more or less general criticism. With regard to dynamics, we know that disapproval indicated by saying "too loud" or "too soft" rarely remedies the fault if the material is not marked properly. Wisely calculated dynamic markings in the parts, not necessarily identical for all instruments, must indicate a sound level for each player which in turn produces a well-balanced sonority for the orchestra.

Methods other than markings can improve dynamics. String players may have to be instructed to include more notes in one bow for greater softness, or to change the bow frequently to develop more strength. Pressing the bow on the strings, or moving it slightly, obviously affects the dynamics, as well as the bow's traveling speed. Again, the best sonority may be achieved by playing a passage in another position, that is on a different string. Conductors knowing the nature of each instrument are familiar with these and many other tricks of the trade and get results quickly with a minimum of verbal explanation. For delicate effects they will let some string stands pause so that a passage is performed by a smaller group, or for better definition of a slurred passage they will make a few strings play detached notes. These and other devices often require some experimentation in rehearsal. "*Probieren ist selbstverständlich, aufs Ausprobieren kommt es an,*" is a phrase of Otto Klemperer—rehearsing is taken for granted; what matters is experimenting.

With wind instruments, dynamics is closely connected with breath technique. An extended *pianissimo* requires a long breath, while for powerful passages the conductor will ask the players to breathe more frequently, sometimes even for each note. However, there are instances where lung power alone does not suffice, but doubling instruments, woodwinds in particular, is the only means of achieving a satisfactory balance. This method, incidentally, has been in use since the eighteenth century. The decision when to double often depends on experimentation in rehearsal, with the conductor listening from the rear of the hall. As a rule, though, familiarity with stage and auditorium enables him to judge the over-all effect from the podium in spite of the greatly distorted sound picture which, unavoidably, the conductor must endure. In most halls the sound level of trumpets and trombones is just right if the conductor barely hears them. The same is true for horns in *piano* passages, while they often must be encouraged to bring out a *forte marcato.* Woodwind solo lines should hit the conductor's ears quite strongly to make sure that their sound carries into the auditorium. This, of course, must not be accomplished by forcing the tone, which would hurt the solo instrument's sound quality and intonation. The solution lies in having the accompanying instruments play more softly, but no amount of entreaty will help unless the musicians listen to the solo passage, so that they themselves can hear it clearly. In general, whenever essential details of the orchestral texture are covered by heavy accompaniment, it is useful to let players demonstrate an obscured passage to the rest of the orchestra by performing it alone. In this and similar situations the seating arrangement is of considerable importance. Appropriate seating helps the players to hear one another better, and thus facilitates rehearsing. Music written for chamber orchestra and other unusual combinations may make special seating desirable to achieve a better blending of sound or to bring out solo lines with more distinction.

For articulation in wind instruments the conductor may have to discuss different ways of tonguing; for coordinated phrasing short breaks, with or without taking a breath, must be marked in the parts. Unified articulation in strings requires a clear understanding of the various bowing styles, both for "off-string" and "on-string" playing, while for molding of phrases the players must know when to lift the bow for a moment, or which portion of the bow to use for a group of notes. Nor must one forget the rule that every note is to be held for its full value, not longer and not shorter; and furthermore, that one is not to drop the end of a phrase by making an uncalled-for *diminuendo*. The discussion of such basic elements of good music-making points vividly to the twofold function of rehearsing. Rehearsals, while serving to prepare a program, must also be aimed toward the long-range purpose of training a team of musicians by creating understanding between the orchestra and its leader as well as cooperation between the players themselves. Good playing habits must become second nature. The rendition of works from the wide scope of music literature benefits from accumulated knowledge shared by all members of the group. This includes numerous questions of style such as embellishments, whose execution often calls for comment. Once aware of such problems, players will not begin every trill (to mention only one of the most frequently occurring ornaments) on the main note as a matter of routine but be anxious to have the question discussed in rehearsal.

Versatility is indicative of a professional orchestra. To do justice to music from many periods and of diverse national backgrounds, the conductor must establish a conception of musical styles so that his musicians are ready to change their approach from one composition to another. After having rehearsed a Tchaikovsky symphony for an hour, the orchestra may sound heavy in a Mozart work which follows next, but when asked to recall the orchestral texture required for Mozart skilled players will adjust their performance without hesitation. In establishing high standards in the performance of a large repertoire the members of an orchestra acquire both technical virtuosity and musical insight. Versatility and skill are linked together. After a subtle reading of a Haydn symphony, a Debussy work will receive a more delicate treatment; painstaking delivery of intricate rhythms in contemporary pieces can sharpen rhythmic awareness in classical music. This is not meant to imply that rehearsal techniques are the same in all these instances. The conductor's methods vary according to the character and technical aspects of music. Selecting a sequence of measures typical of a composition's style and using it for extended practicing sets a valuable pattern for the entire rehearsal. Tricky passages often call for special attention. For a correct reading of certain rapid runs or for securing good intonation in spite of troublesome intervals, each string section or small wind groups may have to play alone to "clean up" their lines before the *tutti* is "put together." Another useful device is to single out instruments from various sections which happen to play a difficult passage in unison or are faced with the same intricate rhythm, for the purpose of repeating those bars for perfect coordination. This method of "dissecting" is very helpful in rehearsing polyrhythmic patterns in contemporary music, because it serves to throw light on episodes whose musical context might otherwise remain obscured. In so-called pointillistic music there is an added problem for the players who, unlike the conductor, are not aided by the full score and find themselves in need of orientation. To learn in rehearsal how their entries relate to other instruments can be a tedious and time-consuming process; it could be facilitated by including in each player's part a condensed score of complementary voices, showing how brief cues, frequently only one or two notes falling on an off beat, fit into the whole.

So far, the technical aspect of rehearsing has received preference although, directly or by innuendo, questions connected with psychology have come into view. It has been pointed out that the conductor must try to formulate his ideas so that whatever he intends to communicate to his players finds attentive and willing ears. In rehearsing a professional orchestra, the director's position cannot be explained simply in conventional terms referring to leader-group relationship but, for a number of reasons, deserves special consideration in terms of group psychology. First of all, the director deals with a heterogeneous group of individualists, a circumstance which is not only unavoidable but desirable. It is not skill alone which makes a first-rate orchestra player; he must be an artist in his own right, with the temperament and qualities characteristic of a performer. Secondly, by virtue of their talent, ability, and experience, musicians are likely to be critical, sometimes even resentful, of their leader. Many of them consider themselves, not always without reason, at least his equal when it comes to interpreting and rehearsing music. Thirdly, excellence in performance cannot be expected from musicians merely obeying orders, but only if they are motivated by an impulse derived directly from the music to which they devote their skills, hearts, and minds. If education is the art of opening people's minds, then the conductor's function in rehearsal must be called educational, not in the sense of formal teaching but of bringing to the fore all the best qualities latent in his musicians. To accomplish this he must be regarded by his group as *primus inter pares.*

To exercise authority in rehearsal is a challenge not easily met by a young conductor who has to give directions to musicians older and more experienced than he. He is not supported by a set of incontestable regulations like a young lieutenant commanding his platoon. In fact, he may feel almost like having to "fake" an authority which is made difficult by the many critical eyes focused on him. However, thorough knowledge of the score, a clear beat, and enthusiasm for the music help to overcome the mental resistance toward a conductor of limited experience. Psychologists have noted that adults as members of a group develop juvenile traits, unfairness or even rudeness, which they would never permit themselves when acting as individuals. Thus the conduct of usually well-controlled and reasonable people can turn into mischievous classroom behavior if the leader of the group lacks authority. This problem does not exist for a conductor who knows how to maintain discipline without forgetting his sense of humor, who combines firmness with diplomacy, and, still more important, who keeps interest alive throughout the rehearsal by impressing on each player that his cooperation is essential. When the conductor notices lack of attention he should first ask himself if perhaps his leadership has been deficient. It must be added, though, that it is difficult for a young conductor to judge who is to blame for unsatisfactory results, he or the orchestra. Nowadays it seems almost superfluous to warn against falling victim to what could be called an occupational disease among conductors a generation ago, namely the loss of a sense of proportion caused by an egocentric "power complex" which made them act unfairly and rudely toward the orchestra. Conductors are liable to err as much as players, and it would be unwise to try to hide an error. As Pierre Monteux once told his students: "When you make a mistake you must admit it, but of course"—he added with a twinkle—"you must not make mistakes too often."

Much has been written to unveil for the general public

the secret world of orchestra rehearsals. The stories and anecdotes found in books and other publications are legion. They tell, not always accurately, about the legendary abilities, or eccentricities, of famous musicians. Tales of this sort are a boon to hero worshipers, but of limited interest to professionals. They rarely hit a musically significant point, and sometimes even support mediocrity, as in the often repeated story of the orchestra player who, after having listened impatiently to the famous maestro's explanations, retorted brusquely: "Just tell us whether you want this passage played *forte* or *piano.*" If the story is true, this man was either a disagreeable person or a semi-educated musician unable to realize that the sweat and toil the creators of great music put into their work obliges us to make every possible effort in bringing their compositions to life. It cannot be done in terms of mechanical measurements alone. There are many gradations of *piano* and *forte*, numerous ways of playing *staccato*, and many other means of musical expression which evade definition. Likewise there are limits to the conductor's efforts to translate his intentions into technical language. The intrinsic meaning of music, the subtleness of a phrase, or the dramatic impact of an emotional outburst may not be felt by all the players unless the conductor possesses the suggestive power of revealing what is "behind the notes." How to do this cannot be taught. Each conductor must find his own way to project his feelings, by virtue of his personality, by singing a phrase with the appropriate expression, or by hitting on the illuminating word.

A flair for what to say, and what not to say, is part of a conductor's psychological perception and calls for presence of mind. To know how to word criticisms, to feel when to give encouragement, to sense when a tense moment is best relieved by a joking remark, all this affects the relationship between the leader and his group. Still, the reason why one conductor wins the cooperation of an orchestra while another fails is difficult to explain. It would be wrong to assume that there is a certain type of personality or a particular trend in musicianship which appeals to players, but it is safe to state that there is one attitude which they resent, the "chummy" approach of pseudo-camaraderie. Basically, it is not a question of liking or disliking their leader, but of feeling respect for him. Unless musicians respect the conductor, they will not "play for him," as the saying goes. This feeling, of course, must be mutual and evident in the way the conductor comports himself in working with his orchestra.

Rehearsals with guest soloists can be irksome due to limited time and differences in musical taste. The first circumstance usually proves to be less serious, because with the help of an expeditious rehearsal an attentive orchestra led by a conductor who has mastered the art of accompaniment has little, if any, trouble as far as coordination is concerned. It is the general style and details of interpretation which can cause embarrassment. It is therefore essential that conductor and soloist meet prior to the rehearsal to discuss important points and try to establish a general understanding. It is comforting to know, though, that most artists of real stature are eager to co-operate with the orchestra. In any event, the conductor need not fear loss of prestige by trying to adjust the accompaniment to suit the soloist, as long as this can be done without jeopardizing the orchestra's playing. His main concern is to achieve the best possible performance and it would be unreasonable to expect the soloist to alter substantially, within the span of a brief rehearsal, a rendition which has become part of himself. Once the conductor has consented to the choice of solo artist, it is his duty to show courtesy to a guest in spite of disagreement and disappointment; he would be ill-advised to demonstrate his feelings to the orchestra or, worse, to the public.

The survey of psychological factors which make their influence felt in the conductor's work would be incomplete without giving some thought to a problem he shares with performers in general. It stems from the dualistic nature of artistic activities and must be solved by balancing emotional impulses with rational control, a complicated process and not necessarily the same in rehearsal and actual performance. Bruno Walter once remarked that in rehearsal, while working with full mental intensity, he was careful not to be carried away emotionally, not just for the sake of saving physical strength but in the interest of undivided concentration on the orchestra's delivery of the music. Other performers have spoken about the "control mechanism" whose functioning they consider to be of fundamental importance, and they have warned against being "a hundred per cent absorbed." Without listening with an alert mind and adjusting gestures to whatever the moment demands the conductor would cease functioning as a leader. Conducting students, due to nervousness and involvement in their preconceived ideas, often do not hear what is actually going on in the orchestra and must first learn the art of unbiased listening. The simplest and most effective method for self-education is to stop beating and let the orchestra play by itself. As a rule, the student is surprised to find how much momentum is provided by the players without his efforts and that he had been wasting gestures on details which needed no directions. He also notices that he perceives the sound of the orchestra with greater clarity and objectivity, to the benefit of his over-all judgment.

Another point which sometimes escapes attention is closely related, namely the invaluable opportunity for the conductor to utilize rehearsals for testing his rendition of a work, particularly a composition he leads for the first time. Even conductors endowed with exceptional musical minds are known to have changed their readings considerably in the course of several performances, and more so from one rehearsal to the next. No parallel can be drawn between a solo artist practicing for himself and a conductor's private studying, which can never substitute for the results attained by teamwork. Musicians called to go over a familiar piece have been heard to remark that they could have played as well without rehearsal, which was needed only by the conductor. While such a statement should be taken with a grain of salt, it is certainly true that the conductor "needs" rehearsals; they are no less essential for him than for his players. The primary consideration is not *who needs* a rehearsal but *what use* is being made of it. Indeed, the fact that the conductor, while working with the orchestra, still has to decide on details of interpretation which are of vital importance to the performance, should contribute to making a rehearsal an exciting experience. It is the happy combination of objectivity and initiative, rationalization and feeling, discernment and intuition that, in addition to technical ability, is the decisive factor in leading a successful rehearsal.

GUNTHER SCHULLER

Conducting Revisited

The problems relating to the conducting of contemporary music are, as might be expected, as varied and unpredictable as contemporary music itself. An unprecedented plethora of compositional schools, techniques, conceptions, and philosophies dominate the current scene, and it is, therefore, very difficult to generalize either about the compositional problems themselves or the performance and conductorial problems raised by them. The art of conducting is presently being subjected to some rather fundamental re-evaluations, and in a few instances new compositional approaches have

GUNTHER SCHULLER: One of America's best-known and most important composers. At present he is associate professor of Composition at Yale University, and has recently been increasingly active as a conductor, particularly of contemporary works.

radically changed conducting techniques or indeed eliminated them altogether.

However, leaving aside these extremes for the moment, if we compare conducting problems relating to contemporary music—which now, in 1964, ought no longer to include works composed in the first decades of our century—with those relating to eighteenth- and nineteenth-century music, we discover that there are certain crucial differences in conductorial requirements. These are in some respects differences in *kind*, but more frequently differences in *degree.*

By that I mean that the conductor of a contemporary piece is trying to do essentially the same thing as the conductor of a nineteenth century work: to express the music with clarity, to shape it into that form which the composer indicates in the score, and to capture the essence of that composer's expression and style. Certain specific compositional techniques or styles will, of course, require rather specifically different conducting techniques, not to speak of a different musical orientation. But at the most fundamental level the conductor's job is still to provide a rhythmic frame of reference (through his beat) and a visual representation of the music's content (through the expression *in* his beat). On a purely technical level this would apply, for example, whether a given work made use of serial techniques or neo-Classic or freely atonal principles of organization.

But what has changed in the performance of contemporary music is the *degree* of involvement and participation—I am tempted to say physical participation—required of the conductor.

In order to substantiate this point, we must first be very clear about certain fundamental differences between most twentieth-century music and the music of previous eras. A great deal has been said and written about the alleged increase of dissonance in contemporary music and the increased complexity of its rhythms, as if these were the only and primary problems for the listener and performer. But what really has complicated the performer's and listener's task are the radical changes in the *continuity* of most new music, i.e., its higher degree of variability and contrast. Not only does contemporary music involve a greater range of technical possibilities (instrumental registers, dynamic levels, timbral variety, rhythmic complexity, textural density, etc.), but the new forms of continuity involve a much greater *rate of change and contrast* in these respects. Whereas in earlier music it was highly unlikely that contrasts—other than in dynamic levels—would disrupt the even flow of a given phrase or theme (or indeed sometimes an entire movement), today one can almost expect the opposite. A single measure or a single musical idea may in itself involve a maximum degree of contrast in some or all of the above characteristics. And, of course, the progression from measure to measure or from one musical idea to another may also be marked by constant contrast and change. In a Mozart, Beethoven, or Brahms symphony we can reasonably expect a phrase to end more or less with the same instruments, the same number of instruments, more or less within the same range, and in the same meter and rhythm as it started.

In the music of our own time obviously no such guarantees can be made. Any one of a number of factors—singly or jointly—may serve to disrupt the continuity: changes of meter, of tempo, fragmentation of texture, use of extreme registers, of large intervals, of contrasting sonorities, and so on.

This new kind of continuity obviously requires a much

higher degree of involvement on the part of the conductor. Purely statistically, there is more to control, more to shape, and at a greater rate of change. This does not yet take into account the fact that new music is, of necessity, less familiar to the performers, in terms of both specific compositions and general stylistic conceptions. Therefore on that account too, a contemporary work will require much more conductorial guidance.

It would appear that the points I have thus far raised should be self-evident. But unfortunately the majority of performances of new music offer no such evidence. Whether from a lack of knowledge of the specific composition involved or from a failure to understand these basic conducting requisites, too many conductors still conduct our new music as if it were shaped in eight-bar phrases and easy symmetrical patterns.

In this connection, it is time that several myths were disposed of once and for all. These center around the notion that the best conductor is one who uses a minimum of motion and physical energy. Any number of theories and half-truths are constantly invoked to perpetuate this idea; and conductors are fond of quoting stories associated, for example, with Richard Strauss, who by all accounts had an absolute phobia of sweating while on the podium, and who prided himself on the dryness of his armpits after a performance.

My point is not to question the quality of Strauss' conducting, which was indeed great, and altogether exceptional. Nor do I wish to imply that this approach is totally invalid. I am simply saying that in most instances it is not applicable in contemporary music.

It is not only entirely possible but highly desirable to conduct a Mozart symphony, for example, with a minimum of physical motion. Such a work to a large extent plays itself, and the conductor—once he has rehearsed any unsatisfactory details—merely guides and shapes the performance in its over-all form and expression. This is possible, obviously, because both the work and the style are familiar.

But if we move to a "contemporary" work by, let us say, Webern or Schoenberg or Babbitt or Nono, we are facing a totally different set of compositional and performance criteria. Performances of such works by conductors of the "no-sweat" school are with few exceptions disastrous. At worst they suffer from a complete lack of control over structural details, and at best from lack of emotional involvement with the work. And in many cases this approach may simply be a suave camouflage for an inadequate knowledge of the score. I have also seen conductors, who pride themselves on their clean technique and a beat which is near the point of invisibility, resort of necessity to a large vigorous baton technique when faced with a contemporary piece. But at least these gentlemen allowed their innermost instincts—instincts of musical self-preservation, one might say—to supersede baton mannerisms and a bogus visual elegance.

It is, of course, not a question of either large or small beats, which is primarily a matter of conductors' personal styles. And I am certainly not advocating various forms of over-conducting (excessively large baton motions, incessant subdivision of the beat, etc.). I am simply suggesting that baton techniques must be related to the music they serve, and that contemporary music is apt to make entirely different demands in this regard.

It seems to me that the primary areas in which a greater conductorial control is required are those of "cues" and "dynamics." In music where continuity is characterized by fragmentation and multilinear polyphony each individual orchestral part consists by definition of short phrase fragments, sometimes—as in certain *Klangfarben* structures—even of single notes. Beyond that, orchestral writing of the twentieth century in general is characterized by a greater independence of each instrumental part, a chamber music conception first initiated in the works of Mahler and Schoenberg. All this, coupled with the player's unfamiliarity with new music, necessitates a much greater cueing ability and knowledge of the score on the conductor's part.

Similarly, highly contrasting dynamics—sometimes several in one measure, or indeed several dynamics simultaneously—must be clearly delineated by the conductor. In such music the average "common-denominator" beat, usable in earlier music, no longer can do the job. The scale of reference has simply been narrowed down. Whereas the conductor in earlier music might have had to change course in baton movements only at the beginning of a phrase of a thematic unit, he now—in extreme cases—may have to do so every beat.

In respect both to cues and dynamics, one might assume that, if a piece is sufficiently rehearsed—this is in itself usually a big if—the players might on their own initiative deliver all entrances and proper dynamics. In practice, however, even the most experienced orchestral players will play with more conviction and expressivity if their cues and dynamic levels are confirmed by the conductor's beat. The conductor, after all, is presumably the one performer who, by virtue of knowing the score, understands the multiple relationships of all the parts to each other, something the individual player usually does not. Nor can the player be expected to know this in unfamiliar music. Actually, orchestral musicians are trained to give what the conductor demands. But if the conductor demands nothing, the player—with very few exceptions—will take the path of least resistance, and give nothing beyond the most matter-of-fact rendition of the notes on the page.

There are types of music which, once they are carefully rehearsed, can be left more or less to perform themselves. But even the most painstaking rehearsal procedures in contemporary music offer no guarantees for subsequent concert performances. Aside from the complexity of the musical relationships the sheer energy and concentration required of the player in negotiating all the extremes of contrast and technical problems need constant substantiation on the part of the conductor. Anything less will result in the blandness and inaccuracies we usually get in performances of new music.

Another area in which conducting conceptions and techniques need to be focused more precisely is style. Again the great proliferation of techniques and styles in our century is at the root of the problem. For I doubt if such stylistic opposites as Brahms and Wagner or Mozart and Beethoven require different conceptions of baton technique. But Schoenberg and middle-period Stravinsky do; and so does Webern and, beyond that, such distinctive composers as Boulez and Babbitt and Xenakis.

It is always difficult to divorce technique from conception, but the specific compositional techniques involved in the works of the three last-named composers and the conducting conceptions required to realize them are so different as to constitute differences in technique. Certain kinds of texture, continuity, and expressive content determine the specifics of these styles, and in turn require variegated conducting styles. This does not even take into account the radically different techniques required in the works of the aleatory and "indeterminacy" schools. Common to these is a beat which is no longer a *sine qua non* of conducting, either because the beat as an integrating unit has been supplanted by larger time sequences (such as intervals of fifteen seconds, for example, which are visualized by the "conductor" in the manner of the hands of a clock), or because conducting is assumed to mean the delineation not of beats or metric units, but solely of actual sonic events (such as indicating only the initial attack of a sustained musical event and not the beats following it). This latter technique, which would seem to have far-reaching consequences since the conductor no longer conducts the rhythmic scaffold underlying a work, but instead the actual impulses that characterize the musical continuity—in other words, not the beat but the actual music—such a technique obviously places a much greater responsibility on the conductor. And it involves once again the reflexive capacities of conductor and performer, thus restoring a vital sense of spontaneity and urgency which, as a basic ingredient, is sorely lacking in much concert music.

To be sure, one aspect of conducting has *not* changed: the role played by the ear. The ear is still the final controlling arbiter, and in contemporary music, perhaps more than any other, no amount of baton dexterity can make up for deficiencies in either the ear or the mind. This is not to imply that one needs to know a Schoenberg score better than one by Mozart. It is simply to say that the Schoenberg score is apt to be more complex than the one by Mozart, and there is thus, purely statistically, more to learn and more detail to control. There is probably also a great deal of unfamiliar territory to explore, and—in turn—to transmit lucidly to the player. This cannot be done without an awareness of the compositional techniques involved, a thorough knowledge of the structural outlines which define the work, and a total immersion in the expressive essentials of that work's style.

It will be noted that this is in essence no more and no less than what was always required, and these qualities still mark the highest achievements in the art of conducting. But the demands made by the music have multiplied; and the conductor's art, if it is to continue to serve the music, must reflect these increased demands.

WILLIAM STEINBERG

Conducting—Overestimated or Underestimated?

These lines are addressed to the young ones. They are written by one who, despite his decades of experience with the orchestras of the world, did not find out what it was all about until his fiftieth year. I have not written any books, and certainly do not intend to participate in the contemporary fad of autobiography. I also do not want to raise my finger in admonition lest I evoke the impression of doubting, attacking, or degrading the "personality" of young men—which is certainly not my intention. I merely want to jot down a few thoughts, remembering Verdi's words to the effect that he was

WILLIAM STEINBERG: Born in Cologne in 1899. In the United States he has been conductor of the Buffalo Philharmonic Orchestra, and is now music director of the Pittsburgh Symphony Orchestra.

not an erudite litterateur, but simply someone who had a great deal of practical experience.

I don't believe that nowadays any profession in the realm of the performing arts is as misunderstood as the orchestra conductor's, which is the reason for the unbelievable degree of either its over- or underestimation by the public. This gross misapprehension starts with the word "profession." "Call" and "profession" are not at all the same. A call is a summons which can come from anywhere—talent, natural vocation, heredity—from a thousand sources. You might be destined by nature for your profession; however, it is usually something determined by factual reasoning, practical considerations, opportunities, favorable circumstances. Call or vocation, however, is a compulsion from which there is no escape, which one has to follow unresistingly in order to avoid a collision of natural forces. The irrationality of the vocation of conducting is obvious simply because one does not do things by oneself, but makes other people do them—which means the motive of one's own responsibility is entirely eliminated—and yet the conductor is held responsible for the doings of others. This peculiar contradiction imposes upon the conductor a false position as regards both the music and the audience. Is there any solution for this dilemma? I do not think so. This, then, is the starting place from which to clarify the basic misapprehension, and to explain the simultaneous over- and underestimation of the role of the conductor.

The dichotomy lies first of all within the conductor himself. My exposition, of course, does not take into consideration any, young or old, whose actual call or vocation is dubious. I am thinking solely of those whose character and integrity are beyond argument and who follow up the compulsion of their call only because they are destined for it by higher forces. How does one become a conductor? Certainly not by chance. It seems to me that, putting aside the mere musical ability which can manifest itself in the most variegated forms, the human character has to decide the issue. One is, so to speak, born to be a leader. One who wants to lead other humans must, however, understand the responsibilities of leadership. The awareness of God-given leadership and its utterances do, as we know, reach from the sublime to the ridiculous. Both extremes have brought the conductor into a position of absolute power, frequently evoking in the spectator's mind a godlike aura, especially with recognized master conductors. Hero worship can make of both professional critics and amateur listeners blind worshipers and imbue them with a lack of judgment which exalts infallibility and uniqueness above the objective value of a work of art. Strangely enough, this overestimation exists also in the minds of many actual creators and is justified only if the conductor is able to achieve an elucidation of hidden depths or discovery of new perspectives hitherto concealed even to the composer. Overestimation and presumption are correlative—the first does imply the second.

I mean neither to moralize nor to advocate underrating the conducting role. Both overconducting and underconducting are equally bad and can be cured solely by experience. Both evils do have a reflection in the mind of the listener, who usually wonders why he is compelled to listen to his cherished masterworks in either a distorted or a sluggish representation. Both types of deficiency result from a misunderstanding of the conducting function and necessarily lead to another bad judgment, a very practical one.

What is called nowadays "baton technique" is a myth the very existence of which I have rejected my entire life. Let me illustrate this controversial point. I do not deny that there are certain basic rules which have to be studied and perfected. Every kind of technique—if this is the label given manual dexterity—has its origins in the brain. Vocal or instrumental technique can be achieved in solitary training—not so conducting. One cannot conduct for oneself alone, and the whole enterprise of conducting is rather a means to an end. I don't favor conducting, to the accompaniment of gramophone records, in front of empty chairs or even (as is supposedly done quite frequently) a mirror—because one does not lead, but follows. One learns conducting only from conducting. In order to train and foster manual dexterity one needs the live instrument, the orchestra, which aggravates the situation from the first, since one cannot produce an orchestra at any given time. However, in order to establish such a situation there do exist today quite a number of courses, schools, and workshops, which do in fact substitute for the many theaters in Europe which usually served as training grounds. This can take care of the practical part of the problem. The psychological difficulties arise when the young man is confronted with the professional orchestra, the mentality of which is very different from his training groups. Here, it will become evident whether his manual abilities, which were fostered to a certain point, are really sufficient so that he can make himself understood.

I know that by my scepticism concerning technique I strongly contradict some of my colleagues who have written fine books about the subject and who swear by the so-called diagram without which—so they say—no orchestra would be able to react properly. Both from my own experience and from the observations of others I learned that an orchestra simply does not care what kind of a diagram is beaten before their noses. Since all orchestras in the whole world want to play well (I never encountered an orchestra which wanted to play badly) the player simply expects a method which enables him to play well. The clumsiest conductors, those who do not know a thing about diagrams, get marvelous results with whatever means are at their disposal, some of which they are completely unaware of. I am thinking here also of conducting composers who sometimes have had very limited conducting experience. But from the so-called methodical conductors I have heard the most boring performances imaginable.

What does all this prove? I think mainly that every man develops his own method with which he expresses himself after his own nature and that the only factor that counts is the power of his personality. Personality, however, is something which cannot be forced into a system, and for which no textbook has ever set forth any standards or regulations. I certainly do not want to speak in favor of a personality which reproduces or re-creates a work of art in an arbitrary fashion subject to some highly personalized concept. But how would it be possible to eliminate personal concept from the operational field of the conducting profession? And how can one draw border lines on the hotly disputed battlefield of "personal interpretation"? Solely, I think, through the knowledge and consciousness of style.

Each masterwork has its own style, conditioned by time, period, temperament, performance technique, etc. It is expected that a conductor will know all this. One can learn a lot from studying history—or textbooks—about the different periods of creation and prevailing performing techniques. But all this does not help much if it is not filtered through the sieve of intuition. Knowledge and intuition do seem to me the basic requirements for the sense of style. I think no one exists today who could not distinguish between the variety of styles. But the conductor must be able to create them with only those means put at his disposal by nature. There are many conductors—mainly of the younger generation—who in conducting are solely occupied with conducting, which means that they are so much involved with technicalities that they lose every sense for the organic structure and style of the work in question. I do not mean to say that structure and style are hidden to them—those things one can learn from studying. These men have simply been conditioned to overrate all technical functions and consequently underrate the absolute necessity of structure and style. There were orchestras—and I recount this as a practical illustration of the above—which did away with conductors entirely, and in this way underrated the importance of the role. Their performances, which, as a matter of course, could be brought about only with an excessive number of rehearsals, had great technical perfection; all notes were played beautifully and cleanly. What was missing was the functioning of the governing mind which should have woven together the threads of structure, style, melos, physiognomy in order to materialize the spiritual image of the music.

We thus return again to the overriding danger of subjugating all these characteristics to the yoke of personal interpretation—something that is, unfortunately, too often carried out at the expense of the intentions made manifest by the composer. It is part of the uncontested duties of the conductor to perform a work of art literally, which means after the letter, but not as a mere demonstration of how it was written. It is clear that the written letter does not necessarily indicate the final meaning of a work. Mozart's famous saying that the most important part of music is not contained in the notes becomes a more and more debatable point with the ever-growing diversity of opinions. We are constantly besieged by the questions "What does it signify? What does it mean?" Who today has sufficient perception and authority of judgment to answer these questions? I think it is only he who is capable of making the work speak entirely for itself, who, besides integrity, possesses all implied spiritual traits and virtues of character which he polishes in the furnace of intuition and inspiration, and he who can muster enough modesty to hide himself from the eyes of a crowd craving to be entertained or provoked.

COMMENTS ON CONDUCTING

ARTURO TOSCANINI

Any asino can conduct—but to make music . . . eh? Is difficile!

La routine—the death of music! The routine! The curse of music! Study your part—I always look to my score no matter how many times I play! What is routine but the last bad performance!

To a musician: What means "forte"? Is a thousand fortes —all kinds of fortes. Sometimes forte is pia-a-a-no, piano is forte! You play here in *this* orchestra? In a village café house you belong! You don't listen to what others play. Your nose in the music—szshrump! You hear nothing! You cover up the oboe solo! One poor oboe—one!—and you szshrump! Szshrump! Where are your ears? Look at me!

In Verdi—never too soft the piano—but naturale! Never too soft the piano in Italian music—is different from German music.

What good is to play "piano" if nobody hear the notes? Play mezzo forte. Must be clear.

The correct tempi—that is the important thing—the right tempi! Oh, how difficult! But the sonority, too . . . molto importante! The tempo must change—weaving in and out, but always close and always returning. Yes, in music, just to have the correct tempo without all that goes with it means nothing.

Don't look at the stupid stick in my hand! I don't know myself what it does. But feel—feel what I want. Try to understand!

About conductors: Who do they think they are, those musical assassins, changing, distorting? They think they are greater than God!

How I suffer when I conduct. I am never happy with myself—never. I am always so nervous when I have to step before the orchestra—even after all these years—it is as though the first time I conduct!

[*These quotes are from Samuel Antek's intimate memoir,* This Was Toscanini. *The late Mr. Antek played under Toscanini for the entire seventeen years of the NBC Orchestra's existence, was a conductor himself, and so was in a unique position to know the Maestro and his work.*]

To Fritz Busch: The performance may have been good—but I shall be *satisfied* only when every musician in the orchestra feels exactly what I feel. . . . Isn't it sad—I've been conducting for more than a generation, and only now begin to understand how it should be done.

GIUSEPPE VERDI

As to conductors' inspiration . . . and to "creative activity in every performance." . . . That is a principle which inevitably leads to the baroque and untrue. It is precisely the path that led music to the baroque and untrue at the end of the last century and in the first years of this, when singers made bold to "create" (as the French still say) their parts, and in consequence made a complete hash and contradiction of sense out of them. No: I want only one single creator, and I shall be quite satisfied if they perform simply and exactly what he has written. The trouble is that they do not confine themselves to what he has written. I often read in the papers about effects that the composer never could have thought of; but for my part, I have never found such a thing. I understand everything you say about Mariani; we are all agreed on his merit. But it is not a question of a single person, were he ever so eminent, it is a question of art itself. I deny that either singers or conductors can "create," or work creatively—this, as I have always said, is a conception that leads to the abyss. . . . Shall I give you an example? You spoke to me recently in praise of an effect that Mariani achieved in the Overture to *La Forza del Destino* by having the brass enter fortissimo on *G*. Now then, I disapprove of this effect. These brasses, intended to be *mezza voce*, could not express anything but the Friar's song. Mariani's fortissimo completely changes the character of the passage, and turns it into a warlike fanfare. It has nothing to do with the subject of the drama, in which all warlike matters are mere episodes. And there we are again on the path to the baroque and untrue.

A mediocre Aïda! A soprano singing Amneris! And on top of all that, a conductor who dares to change the tempi!!! . . . . I hardly think we need to have conductors and singers discover new effects; and for my part I vow that no one has ever, ever, ever even succeeded in bringing out all the effects that I intended. . . . No one!! Never, never. . . . Neither singers nor conductors!!

. . . . But now it is the style to applaud conductors too, and I deplore it not only in the interest of the few whom I admire, but still more because I see that the bad habits of one theater spread to others, without ever stopping. Once we had to bear the tyranny of the prima donnas; now comes that of the conductors as well!

FRITZ BUSCH

Part of the talent of a born conductor is the ability to utilize this talent, and the strength to carry it through.

The great opera houses make it a point of pride to have as large a repertoire as possible. For many reasons, but especially because a many-sided repertoire is thought to bring greater financial rewards, more stress is laid on quantity than on quality.

One feels a difference from the very first chord when a real conductor lifts his baton. The secret lies in the bearing, the superior will, which are part of the born conductor's endowment. It is as impossible to learn as musical talent itself, and yet is the conductor's most precious possession: personality.

ARTHUR NIKISCH

I do not pursue technical goals at all. If one of my colleagues were to ask me, after a concert, how I achieved this or that particular effect I would be incapable of answering him. One has questioned me about the way in which I convey my feelings to my musicians; I simply do it without knowing how. When I conduct a work it is the stirring power of the music which draws me along. I never follow definite, strict rules of interpretation, never sit down and think out in advance how I will want every note to sound. Therefore the details of my interpretation change at nearly every concert, in accord with the emotions that are especially aroused in me. But I emphasize that this is only in details. To experience a Beethoven symphony in a particular way today, and in an entirely different style tomorrow—that would be ridiculous as well as illogical. It would be nothing but a charlatan's trick, and would have nothing to do with art.

GUSTAV MAHLER

Of course the works of Beethoven need some editing. He counted on artists, not craftsmen, in conducting as well as execution. He did not put down everything as precisely as Wagner did later; nor was he so experienced in orchestra technique that he might not be mistaken about written notes and their corresponding sound, especially after his deafness made direct control impossible. In order to bring out everything which the sense of the music makes self-evident, one has to put in dynamic markings, so that the main themes stand out and the accompaniments are subdued; one must also see to it that bowings and manner of execution are such that the composer's intentions are achieved.

There are frightful habits, or rather inadequacies, which I have encountered in every orchestra; they cannot read the score markings and thus sin against the holy laws of dynamics and of the hidden inner rhythm of a work. When they see a crescendo they immediately play forte and speed up; at a diminuendo they become piano and retard the tempo. One looks in vain for gradations, for the mezzo-forte, forte, fortissimo, or the piano, pianissimo, pianississimo. And the sforzandos, fortepianos, shortening or extending of notes, are even less in evidence. And should one ask them to play something that is not written down—as is necessary a hundred times when one accompanies singers in opera—then one is lost with every orchestra.

ARNOLD SCHOENBERG

The more exactly a musician knows what he wants to achieve the more fault he will find with what orchestra and singers give him, and the more rehearsals he will be capable of having, in order to bring the performance closer to his conception. Whoever has few rehearsals either has no conception or only a moderately clear one; or he is incapable of noticing the differences between his conception and reality, to point them out and correct them. In my opinion, it is no great feat to manage with few rehearsals, as that only makes the work suffer. But it is a feat to have material for many rehearsals. [*From letter of July 29, 1922 to the conductor Paul Scheinplug, Duisberg.*]

In the realization of the musical ideas which I put down in notes, I cannot allow the acceptance of a will other than my own. [*From letter of August 16, 1922 to the singer Marya Freund.*]

It is my experience that only the best musicians know how to prepare themselves; all instrumentalists, no matter how good, only learn at rehearsals.

Notes

1 This is not to be taken as a statement that there is no contrast or dramatic intent in pre-Classical music. One need only think of the opening chorus of Bach's *Passion According to St. Matthew,* in which mankind expresses its misery in E Minor, while the angelic chorus hovers above it in joyous G Major, reflecting the idea of space, of heaven and earth. This was conceived three-dimensionally, but is not the sort of tonal drama which develops in time.

2 A method of indicating an accompanying part by the bass notes only, together with figures designating the chords and chief intervals to be played above the bass notes, rather than writing out the entire chord.

3 Louis Spohr, a violinist, composer, and one of the early conductors, describes a concert in a graphic and moving manner: "I and my orchestra were, of course, among [the audience] and I had my first experience of Beethoven's conducting. Although I had heard a good deal about it, the actuality still came as a shock. Beethoven had adopted the habit of communicating his expressive desires to the orchestra by all sorts of odd movements of the body. For a sforzando he would throw apart his arms, hitherto held crossed on his heart. For a piano he would bend down, the more piano, the lower. Then at a crescendo he would rise up gradually, and at the onset of the forte, literally spring into the air. He often shouted, too, in order to contribute to the forte, although probably unconsciously." (From *The Musical Journeys of Louis Spohr,* trans. and ed. by Henry Pleasants, University of Oklahoma Press, Norman, 1961, p. 103).

4 *A Short History of Music,* 4th American ed., revised, A. A. Knopf, Inc., New York, 1954, p. 171.

5 His idea of the characteristic physiognomy of a sequence of tones.

6 These problems are illustrated by the reply of an eminent conductor to a contemporary composer's poetic suggestions for the interpretation of a rhythmically complicated passage in one of his works: "This would be very helpful if I didn't have to concentrate on counting."

7 An opera by Gasparo Spontini

8 Printed in Pohl's pamphlet "The Carlsruhe Musical Festival in October, 1853" (by Hoplit). Leipzig, Hinze, 1853.—The addressee, a writer on music (born 1826), one of the oldest and most faithful adherents of Liszt and Wagner, lived in Weimar after 1854, his wife Jeanne (*née* Eyth) having a post there as a harp virtuosa: after Liszt's departure he was occupied as editor in Baden-Baden.

9 "Bericht ueber eine in München zu errichtende deutsche Musikschule" (1865).

10 Wagner, however, subsequently admitted that the passage was rendered to his satisfaction at the memorable performance of the *Ninth Symphony,* given May 22nd, 1872, to celebrate the laying of the foundation stone of the theatre at Bayreuth.

11 Concert of the Philharmonic Society, 26th March, 1855.

12 *Symphony No. 3* ("Eroïca").

13 *Symphony in C Major* ("Jupiter").

14 A sentimental song by Proch.

15 "Ûber das Dirigieren." ("About Conducting"). Selections appear on page 70 of this volume.

16 The "continuo" or "basso continuo" is the equivalent of the English thorough bass.

17 See Wagner's article on "The Rendering of Beethoven's *Ninth Symphony.*"

18 Wagner's "Report to His Majesty King Ludwig II of Bavaria upon a German Music-School to be founded in Munich" . . . .

19 See Mr. Ellis's translation of "About Conducting," in Wagner's *Prose Works,* Vol. IV.

20 See Mr. Ellis's translation of "About Conducting," in Wagner's *Prose Works,* Vol. IV. pp. 295, 296, 306–308. Wagner says Mendelssohn himself informed him that "a too slow tempo was the devil, and for choice he would rather things were taken too fast," because "things might be glossed over" by "covering the ground at a stiff pace." [Tr.]

21 From Wagner's *Siegfried,* Act II: 'I hold what I have—let me sleep!'

22 'Herrlich wie am ersten Tag': quotation from Goethe's *Faust,* Prologue in Heaven.

23 Obviously these processes will occasionally overlap. But it is important to give an exact analytic presentation. That is why the chronology, which of course essentially remains, receives such emphasis. This holds true for the further course of this presentation.

24 Here the conductor's work is very close to the stage director's, insofar as psychological facts and rehearsals are concerned. The basic difference, however, is that the conductor is involved and decisively influences the last step in the realization of the work, the performance, whereas the stage director normally withdraws completely at that point.

Index

ABOUT THE EDITOR

Carl Bamberger was born and trained in Vienna. He conducts extensively throughout Europe, and has concertized in Russia, South America, and Canada. His activities in the United States include appearances with the New York Philharmonic Orchestra at Lewisohn Stadium, the NBC and CBS Operas, Rudolf Serkin's Marlboro Festival, the Columbia, South Carolina, Spring Festival, and the New York City Center Opera, as well as the resident conductorship at the Mannes College of Music in New York. He has made numerous recordings for Concert Hall, Columbia, and Urania. Mr. Bamberger now lives in New York.

ABOUT THE ILLUSTRATOR

B. F. Dolbin is Viennese by birth and a resident of New York since 1935. His work has appeared in such publications as *Musical America, Fortune, The New York Times Book Review, Theatre Arts Monthly*, and the *Aufbau.* He has exhibited at the Brooklyn Museum and a number of galleries and has illustrated many books.